PRESTEL GUIDE

Berlin

by
Joachim Fait

Prestel

This guide contains 186 full-color and 23 black-and-white illustrations,
3 double-page color maps, 20 district locator maps, and a transit system map.

Front cover: Schloss Charlottenburg, central tract
Photographer: Ralf Freyer, Freiburg im Breisgau

Inside front cover: Artists on Breitscheidplatz, Charlottenburg
Photographer: Fritz Mader, Hamburg-Barsbüttel

Back cover: Frederick the Great Monument on Unter den Linden
in front of Humboldt-Universität. Neue Wache, Zeughaus, Dom, and Fernsehturm
in background.
Photographer: Fritz Mader, Hamburg-Barsbüttel

Originally published as *Prestel Führer Berlin,* © 1992 Prestel,
using parts of Michael Stone, *Prestel Städte-Führer Berlin,* © 1989 Prestel.

Introduction by Bernhard Schulz
Practical Tips on pp. 159-85 compiled by Helma Hörath

Edited by Barbara Jürgensen
Translated from the German by John William Gabriel,
with Holly Richardson-Streese and Wendy Wegener

© 1992 by Prestel, Munich.

Prestel-Verlag, Mandlstrasse 26, D-8000 Munich 40, Germany
Tel. (89) 381 7090; Fax (89) 38170935

Copyright of illustrations: see photograph credits, p. 191

Distributed in continental Europe by Prestel-Verlag
Verlegerdienst München GmbH & Co KG
Gutenbergstrasse 1, D-8031 Gilching, Germany
Tel. (8105) 21 10; Fax (8105) 5520

Distributed in the USA and Canada by te Neues Publishing Company,
15 East 76th Street, New York, NY 10021, USA
Tel. (212) 288-0265; Fax (212) 570-2373

Distributed in Japan by YOHAN-Western Publications Distribution Agency,
14-9 Okubo 3-chome, Shinjuku-ku, J-Tokyo 169
Tel. (3) 208 0181; Fax (3) 209 0288

Distributed in the United Kingdom, Ireland, and all remaining countries by
Thames & Hudson Limited, 30-34 Bloomsbury Street, London WC1B 3 QP, England
Tel. (71) 6365488; Fax (71) 6361695

Design: Norbert Dinkel, Munich

Color separations: Karl Dörfel Repro GmbH, Munich
Maps: Franz Huber, Munich
Typesetting, printing, and binding: Passavia Druckerei GmbH Passau
Printed in Germany

ISBN 3-7913-1183-2 (English edition)
ISBN 3-7913-1202-2 (German edition)

Contents

Contents

All around the Center   *map on pages 8-9*   79

Outer Districts   *map on pages 10-11*   125

Practical Tips 159

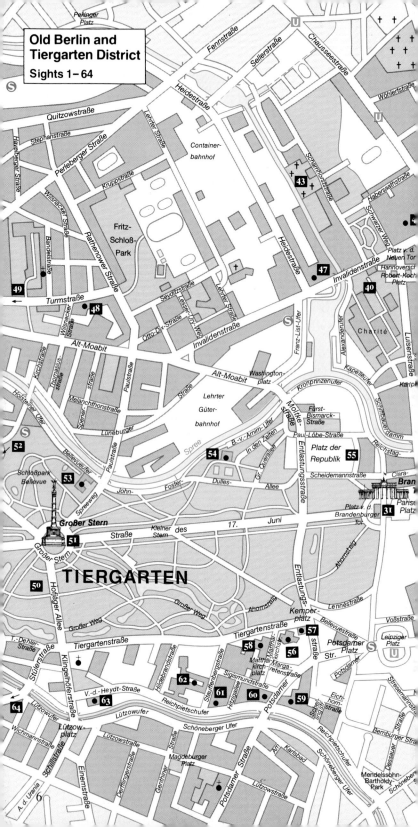

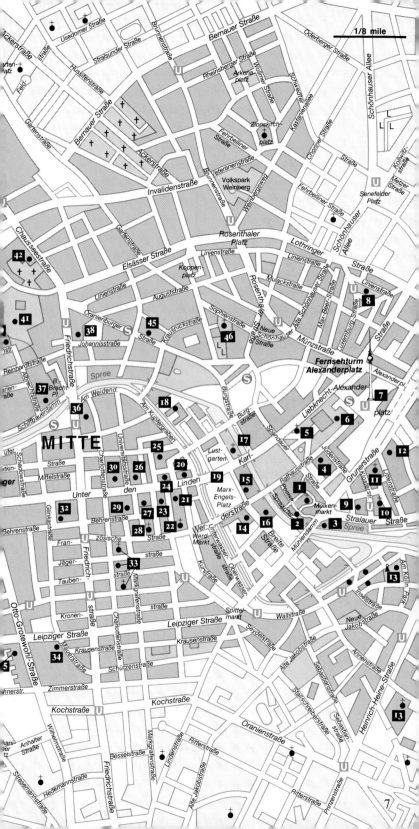

Berlin
Center Districts
Sights 65–124

Berlin-Tegel
Otto-Lilienthal

WEDDING

Volkspark
Rehberge

86

87

85

81

CHARLOTTENBURG

80

83

82

84

79

78

95

93

94

92

88

90–91

89

WILMERSDORF

TIE GART

74

75

76

74

77

73

65

72

71

67

69

70

106

102

103

104

105

I25-I70
map, pp. 10–11

1 mile

8

Berlin, a City of Contrasts

An Introduction

A grand capital with round-the-clock action, world-class museums, traces of an imperial past, a "Little Istanbul," elegant boulevards, galleries, a lively "alternative" scene—Berlin today is perhaps Europe's most exciting city. But not all grandeur and glamour, Berlin is also a wound just beginning to heal on the border of East and West, a vibrant metropolis marked like no other by recent world history. Perhaps this explains why it is the most liberal and cosmopolitan city in Germany, as well as the country's largest. The Berliner is a special breed: tolerant and open-minded but sporting a gruff exterior, he is famous for his caustic wit and quick good humor.

From the end of World War II until quite recently a traveller who wanted to visit Berlin had a choice of destinations: there were two cities that bore the name. In the aftermath of the war the German capital, residence of Prussian rulers since the fifteenth century and later capital of the German Empire as well as of Hitler's Third Reich, was divided down the center and kept separate by a fiercely guarded concrete barrier complete with death strip. The Berlin Wall (map on p. 26), built in 1961, was the most horrifying manifestation of the "iron curtain," a symbol familiar to millions throughout the world. The city lay deep in the Soviet sector of conquered Germany, and its eastern half became the capital of the German Democratic Republic, the state founded in that sector. The western half became an island in Communist-ruled Eastern Europe. When

The Wall in front of Brandenburger Tor, November 1989
Top: *Unter den Linden, Monument to Frederick the Great*

Mitte: Schlossbrücke, Zeughaus, and Unter den Linden

the Federal Republic, the western, democratically governed part of Germany, set up its government in far-off Bonn, West Berlin became a city on the periphery. It was shaken periodically by crises, initially kept alive by an airlift of supplies, and then, when times grew calmer, by West German subsidies.

The events of the fall of 1989—tens of thousands of East Germans escaping from their country across the borders of Hungary and Czechoslovakia, weekly demonstrations, then the first stunned East Berliners crossing the Wall in the early hours of November 9, later hundreds of joyous revellers dancing on the Wall—these events shook the world. Since then, change in Berlin has progressed at a frenzied pace. East and West Germany were reunified in 1990, the Wall has been torn down almost everywhere (although its scar

will be visible for years to come), the government of the Federal Republic plans to move back, neighborhoods divided for decades are growing together again, museums are arranging the reunification of their collections. More mundanely, forty years of separately developed infrastructure, including telephones and transportation systems, are being integrated. The task facing the national and local administration, not to mention the people of Berlin themselves, is a staggering one.

The visitor will still recognize the two cities of Berlin: the center of one is the historic core in Mitte district which belonged to the East during the years of division. The center of the other is the glitzy hub of capitalist West Berlin around Bahnhof Zoo [No. 65].

To get to know Berlin and to begin to understand it, the best place to begin a

Facing page: *Museumsinsel, in front of
Altes Museum (top), a reflection of the Dom
in the Palast der Republik (bottom)*

Right: *Street scene in Mitte*
Below: *Mitte, Karl Friedrich Schinkel's
Schlossbrücke*

tour is in the geographic and historical center, Mitte district. Here, on the grand avenue Unter den Linden, a bronze Frederick the Great gazes east toward a parking lot, Marx-Engels-Platz [No. 15], the site of his official residence, the Berlin City Palace [photo, pp. 22-23]. The palace was the political center of the city and of Germany, and it, like most of Berlin, was badly damaged in World War II. Unlike many other historic buildings, however, it was demolished after the war. Part of the site is today taken up by the Palast der Republik, now a politically functionless structure, and yet something of a focal point of national identity of the former GDR and its citizens, who once came here as the highpoint of a trip to their capital to promenade and visit one of the cafés.

The earliest settlements, the towns of Cölln and Berlin founded in the thirteenth century, were southeast of the palace on both sides of a shallow spot in the Spree River. Little remains of old Cölln, but parts of old Berlin have been reconstructed in the Nikolaiviertel [No. 1]. North of Marx-Engels-Platz, beyond the Lustgarten, is the Museumsinsel [No. 18], laid out by Karl Friedrich Schinkel, Berlin's master architect in the early nineteenth century. His Altes Museum faces Lustgarten and was intended as a bold counterpart to the Palace: the intellectual opposite the political world. Schinkel, for a quarter century chief architect to

the rulers of the former state of Prussia, of which Berlin was the capital, determined the appearance of the city more than any architect before or since. He designed numerous buildings in the center of imperial Berlin, and many of the uncomfortable gaps in the streetscape of Berlin Mitte today were created by the destruction of his work during World War II and its aftermath. Even the Museumsinsel is no longer as Schinkel intended it. On the right it is now flanked by the Dom [No. 17], built under Kaiser Wilhelm II to replace a far more modest, Schinkel-redesigned structure—a move typical of a time when pomp and sheer size were preferred to the elegantly proportioned neoclassicism of the Schinkel school. The postwar reconstruction of the Dom simplified the ornament and has rendered the building even less attractive.

Right: *Charlottenburg, café on Kurfürsten-damm with a view of the Kaiser-Wilhelm-Gedächtniskirche*
Below: *Wilmersdorf, the Schaubühne, Berlin's leading theater company*

A few blocks to the east is the urban center of Communist Berlin: Alexander-platz [No. 7] with the Fernsehturm [No. 6] and the boxy high-rise Hotel Stadt Berlin.

A stroll to the west of Marx-Engels-Platz along Unter den Linden gives a taste of old Prussia, leading past palaces built for the Hohenzollern family who ruled Berlin from 1415 to 1918, past stately libraries, the Opera, and the University [Nos. 19-30]. The westernmost blocks of Unter den Linden are lined by dull office buildings before the avenue culminates in the splendid Brandenburger Tor [No. 31]. Imposing as it is, the gate was never meant to be so isolated. It was built as part of a twenty-foot-high city wall and until World War II was flanked by buildings.

Passing through the Brandenburger Tor, one enters the Tiergarten [No. 50], Berlin's "Central Park." To the left and right of the gate is the strip of land that was most noticeably marked by the course of the Wall. It is also the area that will see the most change in coming years. The Reichstag [No. 55], the gray colossus to the right, will once again become the seat of the German parliament. At a distance to the left, past the desolate urban wasteland that was once the government district (and included Hitler's bunker) and past Potsdamer Platz, is the Kulturforum, West Berlin's answer to the loss of virtually all museums and cultural institutions when the city was divided. They have since become world-class institutions in their own right. The Philharmonie, home of the Berlin Philharmonic Orchestra, and Mies van der Rohe's Neue Nationalgalerie, housing a superb collection of twentieth-century art, are among those situated there.

Before leaving Mitte district, visit the Museumsinsel collections [No. 18]. To see them all, even at a hurried pace, requires at least half a day, despite the fact that many of their treasures will not return from their postwar homes in West Berlin for several years. If there is time to visit only one museum, it should probably be the Pergamon [No. 18e] to see its world-famous altar, the magnificent Gate of Ishtar, and the Market Gate of Miletus.

A visit to the other, western, center of Berlin best begins at Kaiser-Wilhelm-Gedächtniskirche [No. 64]. This symbolic union of war ruin and new, uncompromisingly modern construction stands where Tauentzienstrasse, one of Berlin's busiest shopping streets, meets Kurfürstendamm. The "Ku'damm," as Berliners and visitors alike call this boulevard, is Berlin's glamour mile. Once the city's best residential address, today it is the main street of the most fashionable business and enter-

Left: *Lichtenberg, in Schloss Friedrichsfelde park*
Below left: *Charlottenburg, Paris Bar on Kantstrasse*
Center: Lilienthal Revue *at Friedrichstadtpalast*

tainment district: restaurants, cinemas, fancy shops and boutiques, as well as hundreds of prestigious offices line Ku'damm and its side streets.

For a taste of the old imperial residence, visit Schloss Charlottenburg [No. 80-81]. It is the only Hohenzollern city palace that remains standing in Berlin. Its lovely park is a fine example of the synthesis of architecture, landscaping, and nature that distinguishes the Hohenzollern palaces. In and near Schloss Charlottenburg are several noteworthy museums.

Art enthusiasts should not miss the museums in Dahlem [No. 137], which include a collection of old master paintings that boasts over twenty works by Rembrandt and are well worth the detour.

For those with a little more time, Berlin offers many other attractions. For one, the city often described as a sea of stone and cement is actually nestled in green woodlands. An excursion to the Havel River and the Pfaueninsel [No. 148] reveals the sandy soil and waterways typical of the area. This is the other side of the urban metropolis—lush parks whose transformation of nature into cultured landscape is barely perceptible, a style that had its heyday during the Romantic period, the era of Schinkel and landscape architect Peter

Joseph Lenné. An excursion by boat to Potsdam and a visit to the park of Schloss Sanssouci there will give the visitor a glimpse of a Prussian Arcadia.

The architecture buff will find much of great interest: "Onkel Tom's Hütte" [No. 143] in Zehlendorf, an exemplary 1920s housing development; the Hansa Viertel [No. 52] on the edge of the Tiergarten, a veritable inventory of 1950s housing design with contributions by most leading architects of the day; the buildings of the 1984/87 IBA International Building Exhibition, erected throughout West Berlin but concentrated in Kreuzberg and the southern part of Tiergarten; and, not least, the public housing projects in the former East—the 1950s "workers' palaces" along

Karl-Marx-Allee and the later, prefabricated slab-style developments housing over 400,000 people on the eastern edge of the city in Marzahn, Hohenschönhausen, and Hellersdorf, a utopian vision that seems to have failed.

And there are neighborhoods to explore: Kreuzberg district, home of the counterculture scene as well as of a majority of the 125,000 Turkish immigrants in Berlin; Prenzlauer Berg, sanctuary of artists, writers, and dissidents in former East Berlin; to name but a few. A visit to one of Ku'damm's world-famous cafés is a must. And after dark there is Europe's best nightlife to be sampled: bars that never close, opera, theater, cabarets, jazz, film—the possibilities are nearly endless.

This guide features all of the important sights and gives many practical tips for your visit. But Berlin is far more than an agglomeration of sights; it is a city to be experienced, discovered, and explored.

An Outline Chronology

Circa 700 B.C.   Early Germanic settlement.

6th-7th century A.D.   Slavic settlement.

8th century   Fortified castle built south of Spandau.

9th century   Earliest Slavic fortifications at Köpenick.

1134-70   Reign of Albert I, the Bear, first Margrave of Brandenburg, founder of the House of Ascania and leader of German colonization of Eastern Europe.

1197   First mention of Spandau in written records.

Circa 1210   Members of the Templar order settle in the area and found the villages of Tempelhof, Mariendorf, and Marienfelde, today all part of Tempelhof district.

1237   Town of Cölln first mentioned in written records.

1244   First recorded reference to Berlin.

1249   Earliest reference to the Franciscan Monastery [see No. II].

1251   Town of Wedding first mentioned in documents. Right of free trade granted to Berlin.

1264   Schöneberg first mentioned in written records.

1297   Establishment of Dominican Monastery in Cölln.

1307   Unification of Cölln and Berlin. Common town hall erected at today's Rathausbrücke.

Earliest city seals
Berlin, 1253   *Cölln, 1334*

1308-19   Margrave Waldemar the Great.

1320   End of the rule of the Brandenburg Ascanians.

1323-47   Louis I, the Elder. He receives Brandenburg as an imperial fief from his father, Emperor Louis IV, the Bavarian, of the Wittelsbach dynasty.

Bird's-eye view of Baroque Berlin in 1688, from a colored engraving of about 1700. Fortifications built between 1658 and 1683 surround the double city: Berlin is to the north of the Spree,

1338 First use of a Berlin bear as the signet on a council document.

1348 Great fire.

1359 Berlin becomes a member of the Hanseatic League.

1373-78 Reign of Emperor Charles IV of Luxembourg.

1376, 1380 Great fires.

1415-40 Frederick IV of Hohenzollern, Burgrave of Nuremberg, is given Brandenburg in fief and raised to the rank of Prince Elector Frederick I, ending Luxembourg rule.

1432 Berlin and Cölln confirm union to emphasize their independence from Frederick I.

1440-70 Frederick II, the Iron Monarch. He revokes the common administration of Cölln-Berlin, and his troops occupy the town hall.

1448 Revolt of Berlin and Cölln patricians against the prince elector. Victory of the feudal lords over municipal self-administration.

1484 Great fire.

1486-99 Berlin becomes the permanent residence of the prince elector.

1539 Joachim II converts to Protestantism.

Frederick William, the Great Prince Elector (1640-88), as depicted in Schlüter's equestrian monument [see No. 80]

1576, 1598, 1611 Plague epidemics: chronicle of the Cölln town scribes registers 4,000 deaths by plague for the year 1576, 3,000 for the year 1598, and 2,000 for the year 1611. By about 1600, Berlin's population is reduced to approximately 10,000 from a high of about 14,000.

1618-48 Thirty Years' War. Impoverishment of the city, as trade diminishes and the region is pillaged several times by Swedish and imperial troops. Plague victims number 3,000 in 1630-31. By the end of the war, Berlin has only about 6,000 inhabitants.

and Cölln, with the suburbs of Neucölln and Friedrichswerder, to the south. On the left are Unter den Linden (laid out in 1647) and the Dorotheenstadt district (begun in 1663)

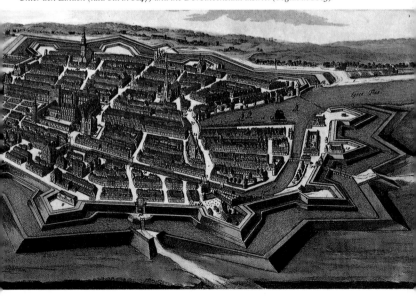

Frederick William I, the Soldier King (1713-40)

Berlin coat of arms of 1710, combining the red eagle of Brandenburg and the black eagle of Prussia with the Berlin bear

1640-88 Frederick William, named Great Prince Elector after his victory over the Swedes at Fehrbellin (1675), lays the foundations for the rise of Brandenburg-Prussia.

1647 The first tree is planted on an avenue leading from Berlin Palace to Tiergarten hunting preserve, to create the renowned "Unter den Linden."

1658 Fortifications are built around the city. The wall with thirteen bastions encloses land on which the suburbs of Friedrichswerder and Dorotheenstadt are built in the following years.

1662-69 Building of the Frederick William Canal between Spree and Oder rivers, which establishes a direct connection between Breslau (Wroclaw) and Hamburg, with Berlin serving as port of transshipment.

1685 Edict of Potsdam: Huguenots driven from France are taken in by Prussia and in many cases receive key posts in government, administration, and military. Berlin's population rises to 18,000.

1688-1713 Reign of Frederick III. After crowning himself King of Prussia in Königsberg in 1701, he assumes the name Frederick I.

1688 The suburb of Friedrichstadt is laid out.

1696 Founding of the Akademie der Künste, the Berlin Academy of Arts.

1700 Establishment of the Akademie der Wissenschaften (Academy of Sciences) by Gottfried Wilhelm Leibniz, who becomes its first president.

1709 The five districts of Berlin, Cölln, Friedrichswerder, Dorotheenstadt, and Friedrichstadt are united as the Royal City of Berlin. The magistracy convenes in the new town hall of Cölln.

1710 Berlin numbers 61,000 inhabitants, including 6,000 French and 500 Swiss nationals.

1713-40 Reign of Frederick William I, the Soldier King.

1717 Introduction of compulsory education for all five- to twelve-year-olds.

1727 Charité Hospital founded.

1734-36 New, twenty-foot-high city wall built, as customs barrier and to prevent army desertion.

King Frederick II, the Great (1740-86)

1740-86 Frederick II, the Great, transforms Berlin into a capital of European rank. In 1740, population numbers 91,000.

1740 Abolishment of torture.

1753-60 Seven Years' War: Austrian and Russian troops occupy Berlin.

1786-97 Friedrich Wilhelm II. Spread of Enlightenment and early Romantic nationalism.

1788 Johann Gottfried Schadow is nominated court sculptor. Literary salons flourish.

1797-1840 Friedrich Wilhelm III.

1806-08 French occupation of Berlin.

1809 Election of a City Council based on government reforms introduced by Baron Karl vom und zum Stein. Wilhelm von Humboldt establishes Friedrich-Wilhelm-Universität.

1810 Heinrich von Kleist edits the new evening newspaper *Berliner Abendblätter*.

1812 French armies reoccupy Berlin.

1816 After liberation from the French occupation, the architects Karl Friedrich Schinkel, Christian Daniel Rauch, and the landscape designer Peter Joseph Lenné begin designs for a new capital. The first steam-driven ship built in Germany is launched on the Spree. Industrial Revolution begins.

1819 Berlin numbers 200,000 inhabitants.

1821 Peter C. W. Beuth founds the Trade Institute, which in 1879 advances to the rank of technical university.

1826 The first gasworks, built by English engineers, brings gaslights to Unter den Linden.

1834 The German Zollverein (customs union) is established.

1838 Prussia's first railroad takes up service between Berlin and Potsdam.

1839 Berlin's first horse-drawn omnibus begins service.

1840-61 Friedrich Wilhelm IV. Economic upswing makes Berlin into a leading European industrial center.

1847 The first Prussian parliament (Landtag) convenes in Berlin.

1848 March 18: outbreak of the March Revolution.
Berlin's population has reached 400,000.

Wilhelm von Humboldt (1767-1835), founder of the University, in his study in Schloss Tegel [No. 154]

1861-88 Reign of Wilhelm I.

1861 Incorporation of the suburbs Wedding, Moabit, Tempelhof, and Schöneberg nearly doubles the area of Berlin to 22¾ square miles.

1862-90 Prince Otto von Bismarck serves as minister-president of Prussia and from 1871 as chancellor of the new German Empire.

1866 Berlin becomes capital of the North German Confederation.

1868 The city wall of 1735 and seventeen of its eighteen gates are torn down. Only the Brandenburger Tor remains.

The night of March 18, 1848: fighting on the barricades rings in the revolution

Berlin in 1903: Panorama photograph of the heart of the city. From left, Schlossbrücke [No. 19], behind it the Lustgarten and the Altes Museum [No. 18a], the Dom [No. 17], Marienkirche

1871 King Wilhelm I is proclaimed German Emperor (Kaiser) in Versailles; with a population of 823,000, Berlin becomes capital of the German Reich. *Gründerzeit* era (1871-73), a period of economic expansion, brings building activity to a peak.

1877 Berlin's population reaches the million mark.

1878 Law banning activities of Socialist and Communist groups is passed.

1879 The Siemens Company demonstrates the world's first electric railroad at the Berlin Trade Exhibition.

1881 Telephone service introduced, with 45 subscribers. World's first electric tramline goes into operation in Lichterfelde, today part of Steglitz district.

1882 First S-Bahn train line, from Charlottenburg to Schlesischer Bahnhof (today Hauptbahnhof), begins operation.

1888-1918 Kaiser Wilhelm II. He succeeded his father, Kaiser Friedrich III, who had ruled for only 99 days.

1890 Bismarck dismissed from his post as chancellor. Law of 1878 banning Socialist groups is repealed.

Chancellor Prince Otto von Bismarck (1815-98)

Wilhelm I, king of Prussia from 1861 to 1888, and German Kaiser from 1871 to 1888

(in the background; No. 5), the Berlin City Palace (demolished in 1950-51), and the national monument to Kaiser Wilhelm (demolished)

1900 Berlin's population reaches the 1.9 million mark.

1902 First elevated and underground railroads begin operation.

1905 Motor omnibus service introduced. Max Reinhardt becomes director of the Deutsches Theater.

1912 The bust of Queen Nefertiti is excavated in Egypt and acquired by the Ägyptisches Museum.

1914-18 World War I.

1918 November 9: Philipp Scheidemann proclaims the Republic from a window of

Industrial Berlin: the AEG motor factory in about 1900

the Reichstag building. Hours later, Karl Liebknecht proclaims the "Free Socialist Republic" from a portal of the Berlin City Palace. The Kaiser abdicates. Political turmoil follows.

1919 The Spartakus group, led by Karl Liebknecht and Rosa Luxemburg, founds the German Communist Party and instigates an uprising against the Social Democratic government.
January 15: Liebknecht and Luxemburg are arrested and murdered.

1920 Incorporation of eight towns, fifty-nine rural communities, and twenty-seven estate domains into Greater Berlin, bringing the total population to 3,858,000.

Kaiser Wilhelm II, 1888-1918

1924 First broadcasting exhibition.

1929 The Great Depression puts 600,000 Berliners out of work.

1930 First rocket launching in Tegel.

1933 January 30: Hitler comes to power. Beginning of the "Third Reich."
February 27/28: Reichstag Fire.
April 1: First boycott of Jewish-owned businesses.
May 10: Some 20,000 books are burned by the Nazis on Opernplatz.

1936 XI Summer Olympic Games held in Berlin.

1937 Berlin's 700-year jubilee. Albert Speer is named municipal architect and put in charge of redesigning the imperial capital.

1938 November 9/10: Reichskristallnacht. Pogrom in the course of which nearly eighty Berlin synagogues are damaged or destroyed.

1939 At the outbreak of World War II, Berlin's population numbers 4,300,000.

1942 January 20: Wannsee Conference, at which "the final solution to the Jewish question" is agreed upon.

1943 Hitler's propaganda minister Joseph Goebbels demands "total war."
March 1: First heavy Allied bombing raid on Berlin.

1944 July 20: Abortive attempt on Hitler's life.

1945 April 30: Hitler commits suicide.
May 2: Red Army takes Berlin.

Potsdam Conference, 1945: Churchill, Truman, and Stalin

May 8: Capitulation of the German Wehrmacht signed in Berlin-Karlshorst.
At war's end, Berlin's population is decimated, now only 2.8 million; its Jewish population, which numbered 170,000 in 1933, is about 6,500. Thirty-two percent of its housing lies in ruins. The rubble has an estimated volume of 2.7 billion cubic feet. The Allies divide the city into four sectors.

1946 August 13: The Allies draft a provisional constitution and prepare elections for Berlin, which becomes a city-state.

1947 State of Prussia abolished by decree of the Allied Control Council.

1948 Currency reform in the three western sectors of Berlin.
June 26: Beginning of blockade of West Berlin and the Airlift.

The Berlin Wall, 1961-89: a double row of concrete barriers with watch towers, here seen at Potsdamer Platz. Martin-Gropius-Bau [No. 113] at rear left

December 7: Ernst Reuter is elected first mayor of West Berlin.

1949 May 12: End of the blockade.
October 7: German Democratic Republic proclaimed in East Berlin.

1950 October 1: New West Berlin constitution comes into force. Marshall Plan aids reconstruction.

1951 Opening of the first International Film Festival Berlin (Berlinale).

1953 June 17: Popular uprising in East Berlin and other East German cities.

1958 Outbreak of Berlin Crisis when the Allies reject Soviet Premier Khrushchev's demand that they leave Berlin and that West Berlin be declared a "free city."

1961 August 13: Building of the Berlin Wall begins. When finished, it had a total length of one hundred miles, of which twenty-eight miles bisected the city. Some 60,000 East Berliners are cut off from their jobs in the West.
August 16: Over half a million people demonstrate outside Schöneberg City Hall against the isolation of West Berlin.

1963 President John F. Kennedy visits Berlin.
December 17: Permit agreement enables West Berliners to visit their relatives in East Berlin for the first time in two years.

1967-68 Campus revolt in West Berlin.

1971 Resumption of telephone service between West and East Berlin, which had been interrupted since 1952.
Opening of the first International Radio and Television Exhibition.

John F. Kennedy, 1963: "Ich bin ein Berliner."

September 3: Signing of Four Power Agreement on Berlin, which brought about free transit between West Germany and West Berlin.

1975 Opening of new airport in Tegel.

1979 Opening of the International Congress Centrum (ICC).

1987 Berlin's 750-year jubilee.

1989 Peaceful demonstrations in East Berlin lead to the November 9 opening of the Wall, ending the division of Berlin and Germany.

1990 October 3: German Democratic Republic dissolved. East Germany becomes part of the Federal Republic.
December 2: Election of new government of City and State of Berlin.

1991 June 20: Berlin again becomes the capital of Germany.

Brandenburger Tor: from 1961 to 1989 it was inaccessible, wedged between the inner and outer wall. Since November 9, 1989, a favorite tourist sight

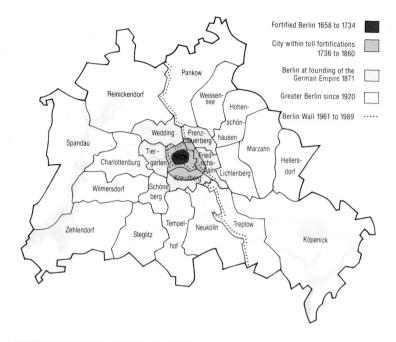

Fortified Berlin 1658 to 1734
City within toll fortifications 1736 to 1860
Berlin at founding of the German Empire 1871
Greater Berlin since 1920
Berlin Wall 1961 to 1989

Statistics, etc.

Importance: Berlin is the capital of Germany and the country's largest city. Until 1945 it was the capital of the German Empire. The post-World War II division of the city in 1948 and, even more so, the construction of the Wall in 1961 bound Berlin's fate to the Cold War division of Europe. The two halves of the city, reunified in 1990, will become the seat of the German government over the course of this decade. Reunification has made Berlin Germany's largest and most important university center once more, and its many cultural treasures, particularly the museums and theaters, make it a metropolis of world rank.

Position: Latitude 52°31′12″ N, Longitude 13°24′36″ E. Average height above mean sea level: 111½ feet. Highest points: Teufelsberg and Müggelberge, both 377 feet.

Area of the city: 343¼ square miles.

Length of the city boundary: 142 miles.

Local time: 6 minutes and 22 seconds behind Central European Time, which is the official time.

Population (on May 31, 1991): 3,436,843.

Transportation infrastructure: 3,035 miles of streets, of which 34 miles are *Autobahns*.

Public transportation system annual ridership: 571 million on buses, 453 million on U-Bahns, 226 million on S-Bahns, and 207 million on trams.

Housing: 1,727,900 units, 511 per thousand residents. Average size of apartments: 716 square feet.

Economy: Estimated 1992 city budget: expenditures DM 41.876 billion. Federal subsidies: DM 13.182 billion. Total number of people employed: 1,619,000.

Administration: A city council with a minimum of 200 members, currently 241. A senate is presided over by a governing mayor who has one deputy mayor. Seat of the city government is the Berliner Rathaus in Mitte district. The city is made up of 23 districts.

Coat of arms: A black bear walking on silver ground; above the escutcheon, a five-pointed gold crown.

Sister cities: Brussels (1992), Budapest (1991), Istanbul (1989), Los Angeles (1967), Madrid (1988), Moscow (1991), Paris (1987), and Warsaw (1991).

Postal code: until mid-1993, Berlin-West: 1000, Berlin-East: O- plus the old four-digit code. From 1993, 1000 for all of Berlin.

Telephone area code: 030.

Brandenburger Tor ▷

Old Berlin and Tiergarten District

Mitte district is the historic center of the city. It includes the oldest parts of Berlin, the areas where the cities of Berlin and Cölln were founded at the beginning of the thirteenth century. The medieval double city, united in 1307, was located on both sides of the Spree River, Cölln to the west, on the island formed by branches of the Spree, and Berlin to the east. Parts of medieval Berlin, the Nikolaiviertel [No. 1], have been reconstructed, but most architectural evidence of Cölln's early development is lost. With the 1443 to 1451 construction on Cölln Island of the Berlin City Palace, heart of the city and the district for five hundred years, the city became the residence of the prince electors of Brandenburg, and in 1709 it was elevated to the status of royal residence. A new fortification was built from 1732 to 1737 around an area about six times larger than the older walled city and encompassing much of the area of the present-day Mitte district. The fortification and all but one of its eighteen gates are gone, although some of their names live on as U-Bahn stations.

Today, Mitte district is an area of some four square miles, or 1.2 percent of the total area of Greater Berlin. In 1939 the population of the district was 264,000, but World War II had a particularly devastating effect on the district. Two-thirds of its buildings were destroyed. After the war the district became part of East Berlin, and the government of the German Democratic Republic had its seat here. Some of the district's historic buildings were repaired or reconstructed, others remained ruins or were replaced by large-scale building projects that turned parts of the district into a showcase of socialist architecture. The badly damaged Berlin City Palace was razed in 1950-51.

The reunification of the city is affecting this district perhaps more than any other: it is once again the center of all Berlin; buildings are undergoing renovation; construction sites are everywhere; museums and government offices are being reorganized. The present population of Berlin Mitte is 80,000, and increasing.

I Nikolaiviertel and Nikolaikirche

Nicholas Quarter and St. Nicholas Church

Between the banks of the Spree, Mühlendamm, and Spandauer Strasse

Berlin's picturesque oldest core, recreated around the Nikolaikirche, the oldest architectural monument of the city.

The reconstruction of the old **Nikolaiviertel** was completed in 1987 in time for the 750-year jubilee of the city. The unity and the winding, narrow character of the old center was recreated by relocating historical monuments from other parts of the city and by adding new period-style houses to fill the gaps between surviving buildings.

Standing in the center of the quarter is the **Nikolaikirche**, Berlin's oldest parish church: it was here that the Reformation was introduced in Berlin and the Mark Brandenburg, in 1539. Begun around 1230 as a three-naved, cruciform basilica in fieldstone, it was restyled from about 1260 to 1270 as a Gothic hall church. Work on the choir commenced before 1379, and a new nave was constructed about 1470. A pair of neo-Gothic towers replaced the original single tower on the late Romanesque west front during an 1876 to 1878 restoration. In 1944-45 the church was bombed flat, and it was not rebuilt until 1980 to 1983. Today it serves as a concert hall and conference facility, and it houses the exhibition "Berlin from 1237 to 1648" as a branch of the Märkisches Museum [No. 13]. It also displays sacred objects

and sculpture of the late Middle Ages from the Mark Brandenburg region, as well as the remnants of its once richly appointed interior, for example, the Krauth burial chapel (1725) by Johann Georg Glume and the *Todespforte* (Death Gate, 1700) by Andreas Schlüter. On the north side of Nikolaikirchplatz stands a copy of the old Berlin tavern Zum Nussbaum, formerly located on Fischerinsel, where Heinrich Zille, famous caricaturist of the "Berlin Scene" at the turn of the century, was a regular guest.

The monumental bronze **equestrian statue** of St. George and the Dragon, designed in 1849 by August Kiss and today standing on the banks of the Spree, was unveiled in 1865 in the first courtyard of the Berlin City Palace, a gift of the artist to Kaiser Wilhelm I.

Bird's-eye view of Nikolaiviertel as seen from above Mühlendamm and the Spree River. Nikolaikirche is at center, the Rathaus [No. 4] and Fernsehturm [No. 6] are behind it. The tall building at a distance on the right is the Hotel Stadt Berlin at Alexanderplatz

The elegant facade of the Ephraim Palais

2 Ephraim Palais and Knoblauchhaus

Ephraim Mansion and Knoblauch House

Poststrasse 16 and 23

A jewel of Rococo architecture and one of Berlin's most beautiful street corners.

The **Palais** was constructed from 1761 to 1764 to designs by Friedrich Wilhelm Diterichs for Frederick the Great's banker, court jeweler, and mint master, Veitel Heine Ephraim. It was torn down in 1935-36 for the sake of traffic flow and was rebuilt, set back some forty feet from Poststrasse, from 1985 to 1987, using original parts of the facade. The building contains an exhibition of Berlin cityscapes from the Baroque to the Biedermeier era, and a period room with a reconstructed stucco ceiling designed by Andreas Schlüter in 1704.

Diagonally across Poststrasse is the **Knoblauchhaus** of 1759-60; the early neoclassical vine-scroll ornament on the facade is from around 1800. The former residence houses a permanent exhibition—part of the collection of the Märkisches Museum [No. 13]—about Berlin's history in the nineteenth century and about the Knoblauchs, the family who owned the building until 1928.

3 Former Palais Schwerin and former Münze

Former Schwerin Mansion and former Mint

Molkenmarkt 1-3

Baroque mansion with a multifaceted past, including use as a private retirement home, a criminal court and police headquarters, and the seat of a government ministry.

The Palais was built by Jean de Bodt in about 1704 for the Minister of State Otto von Schwerin, incorporating an older residence. To the west it is attached to the former Münze, whose rebuilding in 1935 necessitated recessing the facade of the Palais Schwerin from the street. Above the windows of the main floor are lunettes with reliefs of putti.

The facade of the Münze displays a copy of the relief frieze from the mint at Werderscher Markt, demolished in 1886: a multifigured composition representing the history of forging and minting techniques that was designed by Friedrich Gilly and executed by Johann Gottfried Schadow around 1800 in imitation of models from classical antiquity. The original sandstone frieze, one of the outstanding neoclassical works in Berlin, now adorns a house in Charlottenburg, at Spandauer Damm 42-44.

4 Berliner Rathaus ("Rotes Rathaus")

Berlin City Hall

Rathausstrasse/Spandauer Strasse

A broadly laid out, imposing nineteenth-century building in the historical revival style, which, inspired by a synthesis of the original design proposals, unites elements of monumental architecture from fifteenth- and sixteenth-century models in Italy, Flanders, and Old Prussia. Seat of the Senate of the reunited Berlin since October 1991.

Its medieval predecessor, enlarged in the seventeenth century, was replaced in 1869 by the present red-brick structure (hence its nickname "Red City Hall") designed by Hermann Friedrich Waesemann. The building occupies an area of 325 by 290 feet, has three interior courtyards, and an imposing, 243-foot-high tower. The whole is encircled at the main floor level, below the windows, by a relief frieze in red terracotta (1876-79), the "Stone Chronicle" of Berlin, by Ludwig Brodwolf, Rudolf Schweinitz, Alexander Calandrelli, and Otto Geyer. Extensive war damage was repaired between 1950 and 1958.

Berliner Rathaus, called "Rotes (Red) Rathaus" for its red brick exterior

The two over life-size bronze figures by Fritz Cremer in front of the main entrance of the Rathaus, both of 1958, are reminders of the difficult reconstruction work of the immediate postwar years.

Reinhold Begas's 1891 **Neptunbrunnen** (Neptune Fountain, between the Rathaus and the Marienkirche) is one of the biggest fountains in the world, and obviously was inspired by Bernini's Triton, and Four Rivers fountains in Rome. It originally stood in the south court of the Berlin City Palace. The sculpture, in a naturalistic, markedly picturesque neo-Baroque style, consists of Neptune with four female figures reclining on the rim of the basin—personifications of the Elbe, Weichsel, Oder, and Rhine rivers.

Marienkirche, interior with the baptismal font of 1437

5 Marienkirche

Saint Mary's Church
Neuer Markt

Berlin's second-oldest parish church, furnished with important treasures of religious art from Berlin and Brandenburg.

Begun around 1270 and first mentioned in documents in 1294, the three-naved hall church was damaged in the city fire of 1380 and rebuilt. The western tower over the narthex was begun in 1418, completed in 1466-67 by Steffen Boxthude, and given its present neo-Gothic top in 1789-90 by Carl Gotthard Langhans. Among the many superior-quality furnishings to be found in the spacious **interior** are: a bronze baptismal font of 1437; a Baroque marble pulpit (1703) by Andreas Schlüter, which—a masterly technical achievement for the period—replaced the lower portion of a Gothic pillar; an organ (1720-21) by Joachim Wagner; and a fresco, most likely painted after a plague epidemic around 1484, with a representation of the Dance of Death, the most important wall painting

of this subject to have survived in northern Germany. The Cross of Atonement next to the main portal recalls the murder of the provost Nicholaus von Bernau in 1325.

West of the Marienkirche is the broad expanse of the **Marx-Engels-Forum**, a green laid out in 1985-86, with a monument to the two "fathers" of Communism.

North of Karl-Liebknecht-Strasse, just behind the Palast Hotel on Spandauer Strasse, was the site of the **Heiliggeist** (Holy Spirit) **Hospital**, which had stood at the very edge of the city in the Middle Ages. All but the chapel was torn down in 1825. The hospital is first recorded in 1272, its chapel in 1313; the deconsecrated interior of the chapel, today used as a dining hall, is still topped by a Late Gothic star-ribbed vault of 1476.

6 Fernsehturm

Television Tower
Neuer Markt

At 1,200 feet, the tallest structure in Berlin.

The **tower** was built from 1965 to 1969 to plans by Fritz Dieter and Günter Franke, based on a concept by Hermann Henselmann. In its spherical head it contains an observation deck at a height of 666 feet and a revolving café at 679 feet which completes one revolution per hour. Both provide a magnificent panorama of the city. Pavilions for travelling exhibitions are found at the foot of the tower. A stairway with illuminated fountains continues the hexagonal geometry of the pavilions and ties them into the design of the open area, at the center of which is the Neptunbrunnen [see No. 4].

Southeast of the open area, along Rathausstrasse, is the **Rathaus-Passage**, designed by Heinz Graffunder and the Lothar Köhler Collective and built from 1968 to 1972. A slab construction with clinker facing, it consists of a mall of shops and inner courtyards.

7 Alexanderplatz

Once narrow and teeming with life, from 1945 to 1989 the dead square of Berlin: vast, and with the exception of mandatory public gatherings, desolate. Gradually coming back to life with the help of Eastern European flair.

The **"Alex"** took its name from a visit by Czar Alexander I to Berlin in 1805. Originally a marketplace and parade ground, the square was transformed in the nineteenth century into the largest

Alexanderplatz, the global time clock

public transport interchange in the east of Berlin. In its center stood, from 1885 on, the *Berolina* statue by Emil Hundrieser, the emblem of the city, which was

Nikolaiviertel, street musicians

later melted down. The **Scheunenviertel** (barn quarter), once an impoverished district with appalling living conditions inhabited mainly by Eastern European Jewish immigrants, lay to the northwest of the square. It is no coincidence that Alfred Döblin chose the title *Berlin Alexanderplatz* for his critical novel about the Berlin of the Twenties. A mass of rubble after World War II, the "Alex" was rebuilt in the Sixties by Joachim Näther and Peter Schweizer to embody a completely new urban planning concept: the square itself became a pedestrian zone, with traffic flowing around or under it.

Two office buildings put up from 1928 to 1931 remain standing on the south side of the square: the Berolina Haus and the Alexander Haus, now a store; both are reinforced concrete structures designed by Peter Behrens. The thirty-three-foot-tall steel, aluminum, and enamel global time clock by Erich John has stood in front of the Alexander Haus since 1969. The north side of Alexanderplatz is dominated by the thirty-nine-story Hotel Stadt Berlin (1967-70), the west side by a department store built at the same time. The brightly colored *Brunnen der Völkerfreundschaft* (Fountain of Friendship among Peoples, 1969) by Walter Womacka stands in front of both.

33

8 Volksbühne

People's Theater
Rosa-Luxemburg-Platz

Berlin's first modern theater.

The Volksbühne was built in 1913-14 with funding from the savings of a private theatrical group, the "Freie Volksbühne," founded in 1890. Its first director (1915-18) was the famous Max Reinhardt. The **building**, designed by Oskar Kaufmann, has an imposingly clear and simple main facade that is bowed in the center. Gutted by a fire on November 20, 1943, it was rebuilt in simplified form from 1952 to 1954.

The **residential buildings** around Rosa-Luxemburg-Platz were designed by Hans Poelzig in 1928-29; the **cinema** that is part of the complex, Kino Babylon, is a protected landmark.

The Altes Stadthaus, today the home of government offices

9 Altes Stadthaus

Old State House, formerly House of the Council of Ministers
Klosterstrasse 47

Imposing turn-of-the-century administration building in the historical revival style.

Soon after its completion, the Rotes Rathaus [No. 4] proved too small. To house additional administrative offices and to accommodate ceremonial functions as well, this massive structure was erected from 1902 to 1911, after the old quarter on the site had been torn down. Until 1990 it housed the Council of Ministers of the German Democratic Republic. The plans, by the city's master architect, Ludwig Hoffmann, are based on a roughly trapezoidal foundation with four interior courts. Three elements dominate the richly ornamented **exterior**: the tall, strongly sculptural rusticated base of gray shell-limestone; the colossal orders of the columns, emphasized by recessions and projections and increasing mass toward the central protruding bay; and the tower atop the west wing. At 330 feet, the tower dominates the eastern part of Berlin. Its design was clearly derived from Gontard's towers of the two cathedrals on Gendarmenmarkt [No. 33]. The sculpture on the facade is by Ignaz Taschner, Georg Wrba, Wilhelm Widemann, Josef Rauch, and Franz Naager; some is currently undergoing restoration.

10 Parochialkirche

Klosterstrasse/Parochialstrasse

First major ecclesiastical building of the Baroque period in Berlin.

A central-plan **structure** based on the Dutch four-conch model, the Parochialkirche was begun in 1695 by Johann Arnold Nering and continued in modified form by Martin Grünberg, who also built the narthex in 1705. The **tower** was built in 1713-14 by Philipp Gerlach, incorporating bells intended for Schlüter's ill-fated Mint Tower (commissioned by Frederick I for a site next to the City Palace, it was built in 1706 on unsuitable ground and collapsed). The church burned out in 1944, and the roof was replaced in 1950-51. In the congregation hall there is a charming model of the tower contemporary with its construction, the only eighteenth-century model of its kind to have survived in Berlin.

To the left of the Parochialkirche, at Klosterstrasse 68, is the former **Palais Podewils**, now the Haus der jungen Talente (House of Young Talents), a Baroque mansion built between 1701 and 1704 to plans by Jean de Bodt. Heavily damaged in World War II, it was rebuilt in 1952 but burned down in 1966. By 1970 it had been restored to its original form. East of it, on Waisenstrasse (named after an orphanage [Waisenhaus] that once stood here), stands a short row of reconstructed eighteenth-century **houses**, including the tavern Zur letzten Instanz (Final Appeal), whose name alludes to the nearby municipal court but is possibly also a wry reference to the nearby cemetery. The houses are supported by remnants of the **city wall**, approximately thirteen feet high, dating from the thirteenth and fourteenth centuries.

Parochialkirche, the Palais Podewils at left

II Former Franziskaner-Klosterkirche
Former Franciscan Monastery Church
Klosterstrasse

An outstanding example of brick Gothic architecture of the Mark Brandenburg region.

Its location—at the time of its construction it was on the periphery of the city as is typical of churches of the mendicant orders—conveys an idea of the size of medieval Berlin, when considered together with the Nikolaikirche [No. 1] and the

Former Franziskaner-Klosterkirche, sculpture exhibition

Marienkirche [No. 5] as well as the former Heiliggeist-Kapelle [see No. 5]. After its destruction in World War II, the **church** was preserved as a ruin, an admonitory monument against war.

Franciscan monks had settled here by 1249, but the extant building, a basilica with low arcades and squat Romanesque pillars, was not built until around 1300. The polygonal choir with beautiful window tracery, inspired by the Cistercian monastery church in Chorin, near Eberswalde, east of Berlin, is particularly impressive. The monastery buildings on the north side —likewise damaged in World War II— were demolished in 1968. In the surrounding grounds are two column capitals from the former Berlin City Palace.

I2 Stadtgericht Mitte
Mitte District Municipal Courthouse
Littenstrasse 13-17

A palace of justice par excellence. Model for other Berlin court buildings.

The **Stadtgericht Mitte**, like the courthouses in Moabit, Schöneberg, Lichtenberg, and Pankow, was designed by Paul Thoemer and Rudolf Mönnich. It was constructed between 1896 and 1905 by Otto Schmalz, but with extensive alterations to the original design. Behind the facade, originally 720 feet long, are five interior courts. The north wing with its imposing stairway was demolished in 1968-69 to accommodate the widening of Grunerstrasse. Today, the **entrance hall** on Litten-

Stadtgericht Mitte

strasse is the highlight of the interior—a unique synthesis of the clear structure of the Gothic, the interlocking spaces of the Baroque, and the elongated curves of Art Nouveau.

13 Am Köllnischen Park

Historically part of "Neukölln am Wasser," a city quarter laid out around 1680 between a branch of the Spree and the bastions of the seventeenth-century fortifications.

The most important building bordering on the park is the **Märkisches Museum** complex, built by Ludwig Hoffmann between 1901 and 1907, a picturesque group of buildings meant to recall the brick Gothic and Renaissance architecture of the Mark Brandenburg region: the tower resembles the Bischofsburg in Wittstock, while its gables are reminiscent of the Katharinenkirche in the city of Brandenburg. The wing facing the park has picturesque, ivy-covered Renaissance-style gables and bay windows. Idyllic, too, is the ground-level Lapidarium, where stone sculpture is displayed.

The museum contains **collections** devoted to the pre- and early history of the Berlin region, the history of the city from 1648 to 1815, art and decorative arts from Berlin of the seventeenth to the twentieth century (including more than 1,000 works by Berlin's popular folk artist and caricaturist Heinrich Zille), and the his-

tory of Berlin theater from the eighteenth to the twentieth century.

On the southeast corner of the park stands the **Wusterhausener Bär**, a small, round tower that was part of the city fortifications of 1718; it was moved to this site in 1893. Next to it is a popular bear cage and playground, and, closer to the riverbank, a bronze **monument** (1965) to Heinrich Zille by Heinrich Drake. To the east of the square is an insurance company building constructed in 1903-4 by Alfred Messel, and to the south a clinker structure with an Expressionist facade, built from 1931 to 1933 by Albert Gottheiner. On the corner of Wall- and Inselstrasse is one of Berlin's earliest reinforced concrete buildings in the style of the *Neue Sachlichkeit* (New Objectivity), built in 1922-23 by Max Taut and Franz Hoffmann.

Among the houses along this branch of the Spree, stacked together like those lining a Dutch canal, are two that house the **Otto-Nagel-Haus** museum, at Märkisches Ufer 16 and 18. Otto Nagel (1894-1967) was a painter of socio-critical leanings, influenced by the *Neue Sachlichkeit* style.

The **Ermeler-Haus**, at Märkisches Ufer 10, was already well known before World War II for its unique interior decorations. Today it is entirely a creation of historical conservationists: moved to this address in 1968-69 from Breite Strasse 11, the patrician mansion, built from 1760 to 1762, was given a new basement level and large front steps at the time of its relocation. The

Märkisches Museum

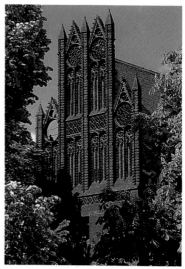

View across the Spree Canal of the former Staatsratsgebäude. The former Berlin City Palace portal is brightly lit at the center of the building. At right is the former Foreign Ministry of the GDR

neoclassical stucco of the **facade** with its vine and palmetto ornamentation dates from 1805. In the interior only two rooms, the banquet hall and the bedroom, still contain elements of the graceful Rococo decor by Carl Friedrich Fechhelm and Johann Christoph Frisch. Today, it houses a tavern.

A few blocks to the southeast, at the edge of Mitte district, is the **Michaelkirche** on Michaelkirchplatz. It is a focal point of the Luisenstadt neighborhood. Despite its severely dilapidated state, which since 1945 has permitted only partial use, it is an impressive structure, particularly its **south facade** and the **tower** over the crossing in the post-Schinkel historical revival style, here influenced by Lombardian Renaissance tradition. Built between 1851 and 1856 by August Soller, St. Michael's is the second-oldest Roman Catholic church in Berlin, after St. Hedwig's [No. 28].

14 Former Staatsratsgebäude

Former Council of State Building
Marx-Engels-Platz/Breite Strasse

As a reminder of the Berlin City Palace, which originally occupied this site, a replica of its portal was integrated into the stone-clad facade of the steel-skeleton construction.

Erected from 1962 to 1964 by Roland Korn and Hans-Erich Bogatzky for the Council of State of the German Democratic Republic, the main **facade** integrates a re-creation of the former portal IV from the north wing of the demolished City Palace that once stood here. The original portal of around 1710, with atlantes by the Dresden sculptor Balthasar Permoser, was by Johann Friedrich Eosander von Göthe. Karl Liebknecht proclaimed the "Free Socialist Republic" from the balcony of the portal on November 9, 1918. The **interior** is not open to the public.

Across from the Chancellery wing, at Breite Strasse 36-37, is the **Alter Marstall** (Old Royal Stables), the only surviving early Baroque structure in Berlin, built between 1666 and 1670 by Michael Matthias Smids; next to it, at No. 35, is the **Ribbeck-Haus** of 1624, the oldest Renaissance house in Berlin. Its portal, replaced in 1960 by a copy, is in the so-called gnarled style of the early seventeenth century. Behind the modern glass facade next door, at No. 34, is the **Berliner Stadtbibliothek** (Municipal Library, founded in 1901), designed by Heinz Mehlan and built from 1964 to 1966. Its wrought-iron portal by Fritz Kühn consists of 117 variations on the letter A.

On Brüderstrasse, which runs parallel to Breite Strasse, are two Baroque dwellings of interest: No. 10, the **Galgenhaus** (Gallows House), from the late seventeenth century with neoclassical alterations carried out in 1805, and No. 13, the **Nicolaihaus**, named after its owner Friedrich Nicolai, who set up a famous bookshop here in 1787. It was renovated by Karl Friedrich Zelter, an influential composer, director of the Singakademie [No. 25], and a friend of Goethe. On the facade are plaques recording the exceptional historical importance of the house and listing its occupants and guests. The Baroque stairs of the front building are original, while the stairs, in Schinkel's style of around 1830, in the rear house were moved here from another building in 1977.

A branch of the Spree flows past nearby, separating the old town of Cölln from Friedrichswerder to the west. Two bridges connect the two districts: the **Jungfernbrücke** of 1798, its original drawbridge construction having survived unaltered, and the **Gertraudenbrücke** with the 1896 bronze monument by Rudolf Siemering depicting St. Gertraud offering a drink to a traveller—a reminder of the Gertraudenhospital, torn down in 1881.

15 Marx-Engels-Platz

A place of particular historical significance ever since the Hohenzollerns took power in 1415.

On this spot, Prince Elector Frederick II, the Iron Monarch, had a fortress erected between 1443 and 1451 against the double city of Berlin-Cölln, whose show of independence reminded him all too strongly of the behavior of an imperial free city. From 1538 onward the fortress was enlarged to form the center of the Renaissance **Berlin City Palace**. This, in turn, was remodelled between 1698 and 1716 by Andreas Schlüter and Johann Friedrich Eosander von Göthe as a Baroque palace of unified monumental aspect; it survived in this form until 1945. The palace covered an area of approximately 650 by 384 feet, had a height of nearly 100 feet and a dome on the west wing that was almost 230 feet high (photo on p. 23).

Severely damaged in 1945, it was blown up in 1950-51. The **Palast der Republik** with its large parade ground now stands on the site, along the Spree, on the palace's east wing. Also part of the original palace complex were the old and new royal stables [No. 16]. Facing the south side of the square is the building of the former Council of State of the German Democratic Republic [No. 14].

Until 1935 the **Lustgarten** (Pleasure Garden), set up in 1645 by Frederick William, the Great Prince Elector, with a park, a botanical garden, and a kitchen garden, closed off the north side. The remnants of the 1832 park, which was designed by Peter Joseph Lenné, were leveled and paved in 1935. After World War II the Lustgarten, Schlossplatz, and Schlossfreiheit together were made into Marx-Engels-Platz. The northern part is now once again called Lustgarten. The northeast corner of the square is dominated by the Cathedral [No. 17].

16 Neuer Marstall

New Royal Stables
Marx-Engels-Platz

A sumptuous complex—functionally but an appendix of the demolished City Palace—giving an intimation of the grand scale of the lost building.

The main facade of the Neuer Marstall originally faced the south wing of the City Palace; now it faces the Palast der Republik. Built to plans by Ernst von Ihne from 1898 to 1900, the building displays the characteristically severe forms of the Berlin Baroque style around 1700. The sculptural decoration by Otto Lessing is preserved on the middle projecting bay of the facade facing the Spree River. The Neuer Marstall now houses exhibitions of modern art as well as the Stadtbibliothek (Municipal Library).

Andreas Schlüter's famous equestrian monument to Frederick William, the Great Prince Elector, formerly stood on a projection, now removed, on the nearby bridge, the Rathausbrücke, leading over the Spree. Removed during World War II, the monument was installed in the courtyard of Schloss Charlottenburg [No. 80] in 1952, where it still stands today.

17 Berliner Dom

Berlin Cathedral
Lustgarten

The burial church of the Hohenzollerns: a flamboyant example of the historical revival style under Wilhelm II.

The predecessor of this cathedral, a simple domed structure with two wings built under Frederick the Great by Johann Boumann the Elder and remodelled in a similar spirit by Karl Friedrich Schinkel from 1820 to 1822, had to give way to the present building in 1893, because Wilhelm II desired a more grandiose "flagship

*Berliner Dom, view from the Altes Museum.
In the foreground are the bronze Battling
Amazon by August Kiss and Gottlieb Christian Cantian's granite basin [see No. 18a]*

church of Prussian Protestantism in Berlin." The imposing structure, laden with domes and towers deriving from Italian High Renaissance models, was constructed between 1894 and 1905 to a controversial design by Julius Raschdorff. Its **crypt**—currently not accessible—holds ninety-five sarcophagi of the Hohenzollerns, among them the bronze tomb of Prince Elector Johann Cicero (1530) by Peter Vischer of Nuremberg, the ornate sarcophagus of Frederick I (1713) and the tomb of Queen Sophie Charlotte (1705), both by Andreas Schlüter, as well as works by Christian Daniel Rauch and Christian Friedrich Tieck. The Cathedral was damaged severely in World War II; the exterior renovation was completed in 1982, but the restoration of the interior is still in progress. It is scheduled to be finished for the Cathedral's centenary in 1994. The **Taufkirche** (Baptistery) on the south side, however, is in use and open to visitors, as is the **Kaisertreppe** (Imperial Stairway) at the southwest corner.

18 Museumsinsel

Museum Island
Am Kupfergraben

*A unique ensemble of five major museums,
erected to Karl Friedrich Schinkel's master
plan on the lines of an antique temple precinct—a kind of "Acropolis of the Spirit."*

Berlin's art collections, many of which were split or relocated during World War II and remained separated during the years the city was divided, are in the process of reorganization. Before the war, most of Berlin's national collections were housed on the Museumsinsel. The collections were stored outside of the city during the war, and after 1945 the objects were returned either to East or to West Berlin depending on the location of their wartime storage. The Museumsinsel then housed East Berlin's collections, and West Berlin built new museums to house theirs. This makes for some duplication at present: a Nationalgalerie both in the east and the west, two Egyptian museums, and so on. In 1992 the administration of all Berlin's national collections was reunited as the Staatliche Museen zu Berlin – Preussischer Kulturbesitz. Schinkel's Museumsinsel will eventually house all of the city's archeology and antiquities collections.

18a Altes Museum
Old Museum
Entrance on Lustgarten

Home of a collection of drawings, a superb print collection, and a gallery of twentieth-century art.

The Altes Museum building, a major work of the "Romantic" neoclassical style, designed by Karl Friedrich Schinkel and built between 1825 and 1830, is the third oldest museum building in Germany, preceded by only the Fredericianum in Kassel and the Glyptothek in Munich. Its central stairway, leading into a foyer behind a colonnade of eighteen Ionic columns, is flanked by two bronze sculptures, a Battling Amazon (1842) by August Kiss to the right and a Lion Fighter (1858) by Albert Wolff to the left. The sculptures atop the entrance rotunda's domed roof are by Christian Friedrich Tieck (front, 1827-28) and by Hugo Hagen and Hermann Schievelbein (rear, 1861). The building was damaged severely by a fire in World War II. Rebuilt between 1958 and 1966, it houses several departments of the Berlin collections today: the **Collection of Drawings of the Nationalgalerie**, with works by Adolph von Menzel, Schinkel, and Carl Blechen, among others; the **Kupferstichkabinett**, one of the most important collec-

Bode Museum, Münzkabinett: Tetradrachma, Athens, 2nd half of the 5th century B.C., silver

tions in Europe of prints from the fifteenth century to the present (will move to Kulturforum in Tiergarten district in 1993); and part of the **Department of Twentieth-Century Art of the Nationalgalerie**, opened in 1964 as the **Neue Berliner Galerie**, with works from the postwar period up to the most recent creations.

The **granite basin** (22½ feet in diameter) in front of the entrance was carved from a boulder in 1830 by Gottlieb Christian Cantian; originally intended for the rotunda, it was a much-admired curiosity at the time of its installation in 1834.

◁ *Bird's-eye view of Museumsinsel. At bottom, the Bode Museum [No. 18d], behind it the Pergamon Museum [No. 18e], then the Nationalgalerie [No. 18c] (left) and the ruins of the Neues Museum [No. 18b] (right), and behind that the Altes Museum [No. 18a], facing Lustgarten, Dom [No. 17], and the modern Palast der Republik. At a distance, the Marx-Engels-Forum, Berliner Rathaus, and Nikolaiviertel.*

Below: Altes Museum, a neoclassical masterpiece by Karl Friedrich Schinkel

18b Neues Museum

New Museum

Once rebuilt, home of the Egyptian and the Pre- and Early History Museums.

Of the five museums on the Museumsinsel, the Neues Museum building (1843-47) was hit hardest by the bombing raids of World War II. It is the work of Schinkel pupil Friedrich August Stüler. Once reconstruction is completed, the Ägyptisches Museum and the Museum für Vor- und Frühgeschichte will return here from the Bode Museum and from Charlottenburg.

Above: Nationalgalerie, on the banks of the Spree. At left, part of Neues Museum, at right, rear of Pergamon Museum and the domed Bode Museum

Below: Nationalgalerie: Adolph Menzel, Eisenwalzwerk (Iron Works), 1875

Facing page: Pergamon Museum, Museum für Islamische Kunst: The Emperor's Siesta, *Indian miniature (left)*

Bode Museum, Ägyptisches Museum: Mummy portrait of a young man, c. 130 A. D. (right)

18c Nationalgalerie

Entrance on Bodestrasse

A museum of nineteenth- and twentieth-century art.

Friedrich August Stüler provided the designs for this building, a Corinthian temple on a high socle with a double stairway, built between 1866 and 1876 by Johann Heinrich Strack. The equestrian monument (1886) to Friedrich Wilhelm IV above the entrance was cast by Alexander Calandrelli from a design by Gustav Bläser.

A large part of the original collection of the Nationalgalerie is now housed in the Neue Nationalgalerie on Potsdamer Strasse [No. 60]. The core of the Museumsinsel collection is the section devoted to nineteenth-century art, including the largest collection anywhere of works by Johann Gottfried Schadow, and to twentieth-century art, with works of Expressionist, Bauhaus, and *Neue Sachlichkeit* artists. The collection "Art from the German Democratic Republic," comprising 110 works, is also housed here.

The Bode Museum at the northern tip of Museumsinsel

Bode Museum, Gemäldegalerie: Lucas Cranach the Elder, Portrait of Katharina von Bora

18d Bode Museum
Am Kupfergraben

Seven collections under one roof.

The neo-Baroque building (1897-1904) by Ernst von Ihne, with a triangular ground plan designed to fit the point of the island, is an imposing urban landmark. It is named after its founder and first director, Wilhelm von Bode. An 1896 bronze cast of Schlüter's equestrian monument to the Great Prince Elector (the original is in front of Schloss Charlottenburg [No. 80]) stands in the domed entrance hall. At the present time, the Bode museum houses the **Ägyptisches Museum** (Egyptian Museum; some important pieces, including the famous Queen Nefertiti, are in Charlottenburg [No. 82]), the **Papyrus Collection**—one of the largest of its kind—the **Museum für Spätantike und Byzantinische Kunst** (Late Antique and Byzantine Art), the **Museum für Vor- und Frühgeschichte** (Pre- and Early History; see also No. 80), the **Gemäldegalerie** (paintings) with European art of the fifteenth to the eighteenth century, the **Münzkabinett** (Numismatic Cabinet), and the **Skulpturensammlung** (sculpture; see also No. 137).

◁ *Pergamon Museum, Vorderasiatisches Museum: Procession Street of Babylon (detail), from the reign of Nebuchadnezzar II, 6th century B.C.*

Pergamon Museum, Antikensammlung: Pergamon Altar, 2nd century B. C. One of Berlin's most prized possessions

18e Pergamon Museum
Am Kupfergraben

A world-renowned museum.

The massive three-wing complex in a neo-classical Greek temple style, designed by Alfred Messel and Ludwig Hoffmann, was built between 1912 and 1930 as one of the first architecture museums in the world. The most famous attraction and core of the **Antikensammlung** (antiquities) is the

Pergamon Altar from the second century B.C., excavated in Asia Minor between 1878 and 1886. Incorporated in the museum are a number of other collections: the eastern branches of the **Vorderasiatisches Museum** (Near Eastern art), the **Museum für Islamische Kunst** (Islamic art), and the **Museum für Ostasiatische Kunst** (East Asian art) as well as the **Museum für Volkskunde** (folklore). [See also Nos. 83, 137, 138.]

Pergamon Altar: detail of the north wing

45

View across Schlossbrücke toward Unter den Linden. Palais Unter den Linden (Kronprinzenpalais) at left, the former Zeughaus housing the Museum of German History at right

19 Schlossbrücke and Unter den Linden

Palace Bridge and Unter den Linden Boulevard

Magnificent parade street linked by an imposing bridge with the Spree island, the heart of Old Berlin.

The stone **bridge**, erected between 1821 and 1824 to designs by Karl Friedrich Schinkel, rests on eight pilings. Dolphins, hippocampi, and tritons adorn the panels of the cast-iron railings. The eight marble **statues** depicting warriors and victory goddesses were created to Schinkel's designs between 1842 and 1857.

Unter den Linden, a grand boulevard leading from Schlossbrücke to the Brandenburger Tor [No. 31], once constituted the cultural center of Berlin. It had its origins in a 1573 royal bridle path running between the palace and the Tiergarten; in 1647 it was planted with six rows of linden trees. The stately appearance of the street, which is three quarters of a mile long and two hundred feet wide, was not completed, however, until the reigns of Frederick I and Frederick the Great. The equestrian monument to Frederick the Great by Christian Daniel Rauch stands in the center of Unter den Linden in front of the Altes Palais [No. 29].

With the construction of the **Forum Fridericianum**, a master plan for the area around Bebelplatz designed by Georg Wenzeslaus von Knobelsdorff, Frederick the Great designated Unter den Linden the central axis of the city. Linden-Forum is the name of this ensemble of buildings today. Not all of Knobelsdorff's plan was carried out. New buildings erected—the Zeughaus [No. 20] was already there—were the Opera [No. 27], the Humboldt-Universität [No. 26], erected as a palace for Frederick the Great's brother along the north side of Bebelplatz, and, on the south side, the Alte Bibliothek [No. 29] and the Roman Catholic St.-Hedwigs-Kathedrale [No. 28].

The eastern terminus of Unter den Linden, between the chestnut grove and the Schlossbrücke, was completed at the beginning of the nineteenth century to plans by Schinkel. The area suffered extensive damage in World War II, and today the western part of the street, between Friedrichstrasse and Pariser Platz, consists mainly of new construction, including various embassy buildings (the Russian embassy, built from 1950 to 1953, among others), and the renowned Komische Oper [No. 32]. Along the eastern part of the street, though, past the new Hotel "Unter den Linden," the historical buildings have been reconstructed.

20 Former Zeughaus – Deutsches Historisches Museum

Former Arsenal – Museum of German History

Unter den Linden 2

Leading museum of German history and the most beautiful Baroque building in Berlin, with important sculptures by Andreas Schlüter.

The **building**, with its 300-foot-long facade rising from a square foundation, was begun by Johann Arnold Nering in 1695 and completed in 1706 under Martin Grünberg, Andreas Schlüter, and Jean de Bodt. It served as a munitions arsenal from 1730 to 1875, then as a military museum, the largest collection of historical weapons in Europe at the time. Rebuilt after World War II, the building housed the Museum of History of the German Democratic Republic from 1952 until 1990. Today, it is a museum of all German history.

Beside the main portal are allegories, on the left, of the art of engineering and geometry, and on the right, of arithmetic and pyrotechnics, all by Wilhelm Hulot; the originals were replaced with copies in 1969. The bronze medallion portrait of the building's patron, King Frederick I, over the portal is also by Hulot.

A key work of European Baroque sculpture, the twenty-two masks of dying war-riors by Andreas Schlüter, is displayed in the courtyard.

Plaster casts of Schlüter's *Slaves*, which were once part of the furnishings of the Elisabeth Hall in the demolished City Palace, are exhibited in the restaurant of the Spree wing.

21 Palais Unter den Linden

Unter den Linden Palace

Unter den Linden 3

Former residence of Crown Prince Frederick II. Today a government guest house and possible future seat of the German presidents.

In 1732 Frederick William I commissioned Philipp Gerlach to remodel the original palace—built in 1663 by Johann Arnold Nering—in the Baroque style as the residence for the Crown Prince. In 1810 a connection with the Princesses' Palace [No. 23] was built. The structure was enlarged in 1857-58 by Johann Heinrich Strack for the future Kaiser Friedrich III: a side wing attic story and a projecting central bay with a portico over the entrance were added. Left a ruin by World War II, it was torn down in 1961. In 1968-69 Strack's enlarged version was reconstructed.

A **pavilion** to the rear of the grounds, on Werdersche Rosenstrasse, incorporates the left portal (with terra-cotta reliefs and door casements by Christian Friedrich

Friedrichswersche Kirche, today Schinkel Museum

22 Friedrichswersche Kirche
Friedrichswerder Church
Am Werderschen Markt

The first neo-Gothic brick building in Berlin, an attempt to meld the German neoclassical style with Gothic elements. The only Karl Friedrich Schinkel building in Berlin that has been reconstructed inside and out using his original plans.

Built between 1824 and 1830 and restored from war damage by 1987, the two-towered hall construction with its star-ribbed vault serves today as the **Schinkel Museum**. Exhibited here are nineteenth-century Berlin sculptures by Schinkel as well as works by Johann Gottfried Schadow and Christian Daniel Rauch and their followers. On the green of Werderscher Markt is the **Bärenbrunnen** (Fountain of the Bears, 1928) by Hugo Lederer, featuring Berlin's heraldic animal.

23 Operncafé
Opera Café
Unter den Linden 5

Reconstruction of the former Princesses' Palace.

Friedrich Wilhelm Diterichs connected two existing residential buildings by means of a new central tract to build this elongated Baroque palace with mansard roof for the Prussian Minister of Finance in 1733. It was later sold to the royal family, and in 1810 it became the residence of the Prussian princesses. Completely destroyed in World War II, the Palace was rebuilt in

Tieck and August Kiss) of Karl Friedrich Schinkel's Architecture Academy, which burned down in World War II and was razed in 1961. On the site of the former Architecture Academy, between Niederlagstrasse and the Spree canal, rises the former German Democratic Republic Foreign Ministry, built between 1964 and 1967 by Josef Kaiser. The city is considering rebuilding the Architecture Academy here. At the eastern end of Unter den Linden stands the monument to Baron vom und zum Stein (1875) by Hermann Schievelbein and Hugo Hagen.

Operncafé. The former residence of Prussian princesses today welcomes hungry guests: a restaurant, café, and bar in a lovely setting

Neue Wache, Karl Friedrich Schinkel's first neoclassical building

1962-63. Today it houses restaurants with a garden terrace and a bar.

On the green between the Staatsoper [No. 27] and the Operncafé are **monuments** to the generals of the Napoleonic Wars: bronzes of Gneisenau (1855), Blücher (1828), and Count Yorck von Wartenburg (1855), and a marble statue of Scharnhorst (1819-22), which faces Unter den Linden; all are by Christian Daniel Rauch.

24 Neue Wache
New Guardhouse
Unter den Linden

Schinkel's first neoclassical-style building.

Constructed from 1816 to 1818 to Karl Friedrich Schinkel's plans, the building has a neoclassical portico featuring Doric columns. The ten Victories on the frieze are by Johann Gottfried Schadow, the pediment relief (1842) by August Kiss. The interior was converted in 1931 into a War Memorial, and in 1960 into an admonitory Monument to the Victims of Fascism and Militarism.

25 Maxim Gorki Theater (former Singakademie)
Am Festungsgraben

As a concert hall, a center of Berlin cultural life in the nineteenth century. Today it is a playhouse.

The **concert hall** was built for the Singakademie between 1824 and 1827 by Schinkel's student Carl Theodor Ottmer.

The Singakademie was founded in 1792 by Karl Friedrich Fasch and its director at the time the concert hall was built was Carl Friedrich Zelter, a composer and friend of Goethe. The auditorium, once world-renowned for its acoustics, was remodelled after World War II to form a theater.

East of it is a mansion, today called **Palais am Festungsgraben**, built between 1751 and 1753 by Christian Friedrich Feldmann. It became the official residence of the Prussian finance ministers in 1787. Its late neoclassical exterior dates from 1863, when the building was enlarged to house the finance ministry. Between 1950 and 1990 it served as the Center for German-Soviet Friendship. Today it houses an international auction house, several smaller theaters and galleries, as well as restaurants.

Maxim Gorki Theater

Central tract of Humboldt-Universität

1809. The complex, extended between 1913 and 1920 by the north wing, designed by Ludwig Hoffmann, was severely damaged in World War II and restored from 1949 to 1967; the remaining original attic statues were augmented by some from the demolished Potsdam City Palace. The portal is flanked by **monuments** to the Humboldt brothers (1833) by Martin Paul Otto and Reinhold Begas. The University, renamed in 1949 after its founder, Wilhelm von Humboldt, owes its renown to its many famous scholars: Fichte, Hegel, Schleiermacher, the brothers Grimm, Mommsen, Einstein, Planck, Helmholtz, and Virchow, among others.

26 Humboldt-Universität

Unter den Linden

Successor of the Friedrich-Wilhelm-Universität with its fine intellectual tradition.

Constructed between 1748 and 1753 to plans by Johann Boumann the Elder as a residence for Prince Henry, brother of Frederick the Great, the **building** was, thanks to the efforts of Wilhelm von Humboldt, turned over to the Friedrich-Wilhelm-Universität at its foundation in

27 Deutsche Staatsoper

German State Opera

Unter den Linden 7

World-renowned opera company and the first theater in Germany not to be incorporated in a palace complex; its main facade is considered the earliest example of the Palladian style in Berlin.

The former court opera was built from 1741 to 1743 to plans by Georg Wenzeslaus von Knobelsdorff. He designed a Corinthian temple-style structure in the north German late Rococo style. It burned down in 1843 and was rebuilt the following year by Carl Ferdinand Langhans. After

Deutsche Staatsoper, a masterpiece by Georg Wenzeslaus von Knobelsdorff

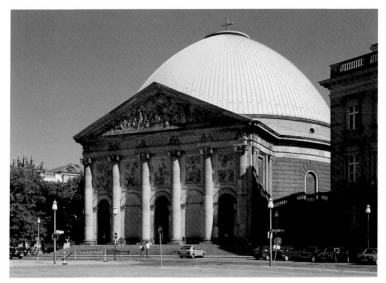

The Roman Catholic St.-Hedwigs-Kathedrale

World War II it was rebuilt once again. Work was completed in 1955, and a thorough modernization followed in 1986.

The "**Lindenoper**," as it was called until 1955, was the site of the world premieres of Weber's *Der Freischütz* (1821) and Berg's *Wozzeck* (1925). Its former conductors include composers Giacomo Meyerbeer (1842-1845) and Richard Strauss (1898-1919), and virtually every German and foreign singer of note performed here in earlier times.

28 St.-Hedwigs-Kathedrale
Bebelplatz

Dedicated to the patron saint of Silesia and, aside from the original Berlin Cathedral [No. 17], the only ecclesiastical building sponsored by Frederick the Great. It is a sign of the king's religious tolerance and shrewd political mind, but also of his architectural dilettantism: he had a Roman pantheon built for the Roman Catholic church.

The main church of the diocese of Berlin, St. Hedwig's, was built between 1747 and 1773 by Johann Boumann the Elder to sketches by Frederick the Great and plans by Jean Legeay. It fell victim to the bombing raids of 1943, and in the course of the 1952 to 1963 reconstruction, the interior was given a modern appearance. The most recent alterations to the interior were carried out from 1976 to 1978.

29 Alte Bibliothek
Old Library
Bebelplatz

Viennese imperial Baroque architecture for the Prussian capital: an animated, southern European counterpoint to the severe neoclassicism of the other buildings around Bebelplatz.

The library was built between 1775 and 1780 to plans by Georg Christian Unger and Georg Friedrich Boumann, the last **building** of the Forum Fridericianum, Knobelsdorff's master plan for the area, to be completed. It is an imitation of Joseph Emanuel Fischer von Erlach's Michaeler Wing of the Viennese Hofburg. Paradoxically, the copy was completed before the Vienna original, which, although begun in 1723, was not completed until 1893. Burned out in 1945, the Alte Bibliothek, nicknamed "Kommode" for its boldly curved main facade reminiscent of a chest of drawers, was rebuilt from 1967 to 1969. Since 1914 it has housed several University institutes.

To the right of the Alte Bibliothek is the **Altes Palais** (Old Palace), built by Carl Ferdinand Langhans the Younger from 1834 to 1836 in the taut, clear forms of neoclassicism. It was the residence of the future Kaiser Wilhelm I, who lived there until his death in 1888. Severely damaged in World War II, the palace has been used by Humboldt Universität since its reconstruction in 1963-64.

51

In the middle of Unter den Linden stands Rauch's **equestrian monument to Frederick the Great**, his most important as well as most popular work. It equals the height of the buildings in the Forum with its forty-six-foot rise. Although spared by the war, in 1962 it was relocated to the hippodrome in far-off Potsdam, near Schloss Charlottenhof; it was restored to the "Linden," only a few feet from its original site, in 1980. Prussia, which had been erased from official consciousness in East Germany, was thereby rehabilitated—a sensation at the time.

Alte Bibliothek, Viennese Baroque architecture in Berlin

30 Staatsbibliothek zu Berlin – Preussischer Kulturbesitz (I)

State Library of Berlin
Unter den Linden 8

One of the largest academic libraries in Germany.

Founded as the Prince Elector's Library by the Great Prince Elector Frederick William in 1661 and once housed in the Apothecary Wing of the Berlin City Palace, the **former Prussian State Library** moved in 1780 to the Alte Bibliothek [No. 29], built under Frederick the Great. Some 134 years later it received a new, larger home in this magnificent neo-Baroque building, erected between 1903 and 1914 by Ernst von Ihne. Part of the three-million-volume holdings was lost in World War II; a larger part was stored in the

Johann Gottfried Schadow's Quadriga *atop the Brandenburger Tor*

West, from where it was transferred to the West Berlin Staatsbibliothek [No. 59] after 1945. In 1991 the two were united as one institution with two buildings. The combined holdings at present include more than eight million volumes; twelve reading rooms are available to users. The rear part of the building (entrance at Clara-Zetkin-Strasse 27) houses the main library of the Academy of Sciences of Berlin and the **University Library**, with holdings of four million volumes and a collection of one million dissertations.

3I Brandenburger Tor

Brandenburg Gate
Pariser Platz

One of the earliest city gates in the neoclassical style. Western termination of, and scenic landmark on, Unter den Linden boulevard. A symbol of the divided city from 1961 until 1989. Since the fall of the Wall on November 9, 1989, the Tor has become a symbol of the re-unified country.

Berlin's eighteenth-century city wall had eighteen gates. The Brandenburger Tor is the only one still standing. Designed by Carl Gotthard Langhans and built between 1788 and 1791, it was modelled on the Propylaeum of the Acropolis in Athens. The structure was given its crowning element in 1793 with Johann Gottfried Schadow's *Quadriga*, depicting the goddess of victory in her chariot. The *Quadriga* was removed to Paris in 1806 on Napoleon's orders after he defeated Prussia, and it was not returned until 1814. After the demolition of the city wall in 1867-68, the structures to the right and left of the gate that had connected it to the wall were remodelled by Johann Heinrich Strack. The gate was severely damaged in World War II and rebuilt in 1956-57. The Prussian eagle and the iron cross on the victory goddess's staff, which were removed at that time, were restored in 1990-91.

At Schadowstrasse 10-11, a northern side street of Unter den Linden, is the former **residence** (completed in 1805 and renovated in 1959) of the sculptor Johann Gottfried **Schadow**, with facade reliefs and plaster casts by Schadow, Hermann Schievelbein, and Christian Friedrich Tieck. The 1837 mural on the upper floor, *Fountain of Life*, is by Schadow's son-in-law Eduard Bendemann.

32 Komische Oper

Unter den Linden 41
Entrance at Behrenstrasse 55-57

Behind the modern facade, a nineteenth-century theater with a rich tradition. Under Walter Felsenstein, director from 1947 to 1976, and his successors, Joachim Herz and Harry Kupfer, one of the pioneering companies of modern musical theater.

The Theater Unter den Linden (called Metropol-Theater from 1898 to 1945), built by Ferdinand Fellner and Hermann Gottfried Helmer in 1891-92, once stood on this site, and it still forms the core of the present building. The front part of the theater was destroyed in World War II, but in 1966 it was remodelled and modernized, preserving the Viennese-style neo-Baroque **auditorium** in its original form. The wrought-iron ornamentation on the exterior is by Fritz Kühn.

33 Gendarmenmarkt Square and the former Schauspielhaus Theater

Most beautiful square in Berlin. Dominated by Schinkel's magnificent theater, one of the major works of "Romantic" neoclassicism.

Karl Friedrich Schinkel's **Schauspielhaus**, adorned with pediment figures by Christian Friedrich Tieck, was built between 1818 and 1821. It reopened in 1984 as a concert hall. It is the focal point of **Gendarmenmarkt** square, considered one of the most important neoclassical architectural ensembles in Germany. To the north it is flanked by the **Französischer Dom** (French Cathedral) of the former Huguenot community, a masterwork of late Baroque classicism built between 1701 and 1705 by Jean Louis Cayart and Abraham Quesnay. During the remodelling of the Gendarmenmarkt under Frederick the Great, the cathedral and its pendant across the way, the **Deutscher Dom** (currently in restoration), built between 1701 and 1708 by Martin Grünberg, were given prominent domed towers designed by Carl von Gontard. The tower of the Französischer Dom houses the Hugenottenmuseum, and it has an observation deck and a Carillon, which plays daily at 12:15 and 7 p.m.

In the center of the square is Reinhold Begas's **Schiller Monument**, an early work by the artist. Unveiled in 1871, it is twenty feet tall and of Carrara marble. At the corners of the socle are allegorical figures of lyric and dramatic poetry, history writing, and philosophy.

On the east side of the square is the **Akademie der Wissenschaften** (Academy of Sciences), which gave the square its name from 1950 to 1990. Endowed in 1700 by Prince Elector Frederick III on the initiative of the philosopher Gottfried Wilhelm Leibniz, it has had such famous

Karl Friedrich Schinkel's former Schauspielhaus. In front, the monument to Friedrich von Schiller by Reinhold Begas

Gendarmenmarkt, the Französischer Dom (in foreground) and Deutscher Dom (rear) flank the Schauspielhaus, shown opposite, to form one of Germany's most important neoclassical architectural ensembles

members as Euler, Einstein, the brothers Grimm, Planck, and Virchow. The surviving neo-Baroque structure was built from 1901 to 1903, and added to in 1926 and 1936.

The scholarly society has been renamed Berlin-Brandenburg Akademie der Wissenschaften. Its valuable **archive** contains the papers of more than two hundred scholars, among them autograph manuscripts of Mommsen, Kant, Schelling, and the Humboldt brothers. Current research projects include complete editions of the works of Jean Paul, Kant, and Leibniz.

Weinhaus Lutter & Wegner, a once-famous inn on Gendarmenmarkt (whose successor is located behind the Schauspielhaus at Charlottenstrasse 49), was a favorite haunt of the Romantic poet, draftsman, composer, and supreme court councillor E.T.A. Hoffmann, where he caroused with his friend the famous actor Ludwig Devrient. Jacques Offenbach chose the inn as the setting of his only opera, the *Tales of Hoffmann*.

Not far from Gendarmenmarkt, at Mohrenstrasse 37b and 40-41, is the **Mohrenkolonnaden**, built in 1787 by Carl Gotthard Langhans, the only structure of this sort in Berlin to be found on its original site. There were once three others, and their purpose was to conceal the seven-

55

teenth-century fortification trenches. Carl von Gontard's **Spittelkolonnaden** of 1776 were torn down in 1929. A copy was built in Leipziger Strasse in 1980, not far from the Mohrenkolonnaden (see also Königskolonnaden [No. 99]).

At Taubenstrasse 3, on the corner of Glinkastrasse, are the only Baroque residential **buildings** in this neighborhood, built in 1738-39. One of them was the home of the philosopher and theologian Friedrich Schleiermacher (1768-1834).

34 Postmuseum

Leipziger Strasse/Mauerstrasse
Entrance at Leipziger Strasse

The world's oldest museum of postal services, founded in 1872.

Among the museum's holdings are a nearly complete collection of historical telegraph machines, numerous unique items from the early days of the telephone (Philipp Reis's 1860 prototype and Berlin's first phone booth, from 1929), as well as 20,000 historical mail delivery and travel maps. Part of the museum's large stamp collection, the complete series of German postage stamps from 1849 to 1990, is on permanent view.

Designed by Ernst Hake, the building was constructed from 1894 to 1897. The rounded corner is typical of the imposing neo-Baroque style under Wilhelm II. Three-story arcades dominate the domed interior court. The building was severely damaged in 1945, and restoration work has been in progress since 1983.

A branch of this museum (a relic of the divided city) is the Postmuseum Berlin in Urania-Haus in Schöneberg [No. 98].

35 Former Preussischer Landtag, former Preussisches Herrenhaus, former Reichsluftfahrtministerium

Former Prussian Legislature Building, former Prussian Manor, former Air Ministry

Between Leipziger, Otto-Grotewohl- and Niederkirchner Strasse

The remains of the Berlin government district, once located on both sides of Otto-Grotewohl-Strasse (Wilhelmstrasse until the war) between Unter den Linden and Niederkirchnerstrasse, after the bombings of 1944-45 and demolition after the war.

The **former Prussian Legislature** building, erected between 1892 and 1897 and today

the designated seat of the Berlin House of Representatives, is on the south side of the block. On the north side, at Leipziger Strasse 3, is the **former Prussian manor** (1904). Both were designed by Friedrich Schulze in a Palladian style with facades articulated by colossal orders.

Between them is the **former Reichsluftfahrtministerium** (Air Ministry)—its ceremonial court facing Otto-Grotewohl-Strasse—designed by Ernst Sagebiel and constructed in 1935-36, the first of several ostentatious Third Reich buildings in Berlin to be completed. Its function was part of the symbolic "national awakening," in which air travel and the air force played a significant, political role. After World War II the building housed ministries of the German Democratic Republic. The mural in the columned hall on Leipziger Strasse was created by Max Lingner in 1952 in the Socialist Realism style. Most of the complex currently houses the offices of the Treuhandanstalt, the holding company formed to manage and sell off state-owned East German businesses, and it has been named Detlev-Rohwedder-Haus in memory of its first president, who was murdered on April 1, 1991.

The other government buildings that once lined Otto-Grotewohl-Strasse were demolished during and after the war. A documentation of the Third Reich government district and the atrocities committed here is housed in the nearby memorial at Prinz-Albrecht Grounds (Stresemannstrasse 110, [see No. 113]).

36 Friedrichstrasse and Metropol-Theater

Friedrichstrasse 101-2

From Oranienburger Tor in the north to Mehringplatz at Hallesches Tor in the south—Friedrichstrasse is over two miles long and one of the city's busiest avenues.

Its importance in imperial Berlin at the turn of the century when it was a magnificent boulevard with huge hotels and entertainment establishments is supposed to be reestablished by the current redevelopment: on the west side of Friedrichstrasse are the new Grand Hotel and the Hotel Metropol, on the east side the imposing, twenty-five-story International Trade Center, built by a Japanese company in 1978. Building activity has grown to a spectacular frenzy since 1990, with new developments designed by leading architects for international department stores and insurance companies rising everywhere.

Facade of the former Reichsluftfahrtministerium on Otto-Grotewohl-Strasse, once seat of the Nazi Air Ministry, today headquarters of the Treuhandanstalt

The train and S-Bahn station Friedrichstrasse was the only station operating as a regular border crossing to and from West Berlin and West Germany during the years of the Wall. To date, the station has not been redesigned.

Among the older buildings on the street are the **Haus der Journalisten** at No. 101-2, which houses the Journalists' Association and eastern Berlin's most famous cabaret theater, the Distel, as well as the

Some like it hot *at the Metropol-Theater*

Metropol-Theater. The Metropol was built in 1910 by Heinrich Schweitzer and Alexander Diepenbrock as the Admiralspalast—a magnificent swimming pool and ice-skating rink with a richly decorated facade and an interior court. In 1922 it was remodelled as a theater by Wilhelm Cremer and Richard Wolffenstein, and today operettas and musicals are staged here.

37 Berliner Ensemble
Bertolt-Brecht-Platz

Brecht's famous theater company of the post-World War II years.

The former **Theater am Schiffbauerdamm**, designed by Heinrich Seeling with ornate, neo-Baroque interior **furnishings**, was built in 1891-92. In accordance with Max Reinhardt's theater reforms, an orchestra pit and the soon-to-be-famous revolving stage were added from 1903 to 1905. Helene Weigel performed her celebrated Mother Courage on this stage. In 1928 it was the site of the original production of Brecht's *Three Penny Opera*; Brecht's Berlin Ensemble—which moved to the Deutsches Theater [No. 39] in 1949—gave the theater its current name in 1954. Brecht's legacy is kept alive here with performances of his original productions. In front of the theater is a monument to Brecht by Fritz Cremer.

Deutsches Theater and the neighboring Kammerspiele, legendary German stages

38 Neuer Friedrichstadtpalast

New Friedrichstadt Palace
Friedrichstrasse 107

Superlative revue theater, successor building to Hans Poelzig's famous Grosses Schauspielhaus, the stage that Max Reinhardt made legendary.

The **old Friedrichstadtpalast**, built between 1865 and 1868 as Berlin's first market hall and remodelled in 1919 as the Grosses Schauspielhaus, celebrated its greatest successes under Max Reinhardt. In 1985 it was torn down because collapse threatened. The **Neuer Friedrichstadtpalast**, built northeast of the old one by Manfred Prasser and opened in 1984, has over 2,000 seats. Television shows and revues are performed here.

39 Deutsches Theater/Kammerspiele

Schumannstrasse 13 a

A traditional theater and a milestone in German cultural history: it is one of the few preserved theater interiors of the late nineteenth century, and it features a balcony foyer in the Italian Renaissance style. One of the most important German stages.

The Friedrich-Wilhelmstädtisches Theater, as the building was initially known, was built in 1849-50 by Eduard Titz, a Schinkel student. By 1874 the stage had presented premieres of operettas by Albert Lortzing, Jacques Offenbach, and Johann Strauss. In 1883 Adolph L'Arronge founded the private **Deutsches Theater** company. Under Max Reinhardt, who was its director from 1905 to 1920 and 1924 to 1932, the theater gained international renown. He had succeeded Otto Brahm, the man who discovered Gerhart Hauptmann. Reinhardt had the adjoining Emberger Säle (Emberg Halls) converted to the **Kammerspiele** theater. After Reinhardt's emigration in 1932, the theater continued in his spirit under Heinz Hilpert. The magnificence of the building was restored in extensive renovations, completed in 1983 in time for the company's one-hundredth anniversary. Truly magnificent, however, is the roster of its stars: Elisabeth Bergner, Luise Ullrich, Käthe Dorsch, Paul Wegener, Erich Ponto, Albert Bassermann, Fritz Kortner, Ernst Busch, Werner Krauss, and many more of the foremost actors and actresses of the German-speaking stage have performed here.

Bronze busts of Otto Brahm and Max Reinhardt are on the plaza in front of the theater.

40 Charité

Robert-Koch-Platz

Large teaching hospital with an important tradition of instruction and research.

Established as a plague hospital by Frederick I in 1710, the Charité became the University Clinic at the University's foundation in 1809. It had to be virtually completely rebuilt after 1945 due to severe damage sustained in World War II, and

today its grounds cover some thirty-six acres. On the east side of Robert-Koch-Platz is the Surgical Center, a tall structure built between 1977 and 1981. In front of it stands Louis Tuaillon's 1916 monument to Robert Koch (1843-1910). Koch, as well as such renowned scientists as Hufeland, Virchow, von Leyden, Pavlov, Sauerbruch, and von Graefe, gave the clinic its reputation. On Karlplatz is a monument (1906-10) to Rudolf Virchow (1821-1902) by Fritz Klimsch.

At Luisenstrasse 58-60 is the **Akademie der Künste** (Academy of Arts), established in 1950 as the East Berlin successor to the Prussian Academy of Arts founded in 1696 [see No. 52].

41 Tierärztliche Anatomie

Veterinary Anatomy Building

In the park north of
Schumannstrasse, entrance at
Reinhardtstrasse 24

One of the very few eighteenth-century buildings erected for the instruction of veterinary medicine to have survived.

The anatomy building, located behind Ludwig Ferdinand Hesse's 1839-40 former veterinary training school, was built in 1789-90 by Carl Gotthard Langhans, and it is an important example of early neoclassical architecture in Berlin. It is surrounded by park-like grounds crossed by the Panke creek. In its circular **lecture hall**, part of an 1876 addition, benches are arranged amphitheater-style, and in the

tambour overhead are grisaille paintings by Christian Bernhard Rode.

42 Dorotheenstädtischer Friedhof and Brecht-Haus

Dorotheenstadt Cemetery and Brecht House

Chausseestrasse 126

Hallowed ground for the cultural elite of Berlin next to a memorial to one of Germany's greatest writers.

Among those buried in the **cemetery**, laid out in 1762, are the philosophers Johann Gottlieb Fichte (1762-1814) and Georg Wilhelm Friedrich Hegel (1770-1831), the sculptors and architects Karl Friedrich Schinkel (1781-1841), Christian Daniel Rauch (1777-1857), Friedrich August Stüler (1800-1865), and Johann Gottfried Schadow (1764-1850), and the publisher Litfass (died in 1874), inventor of the Litfass-Säule, the ubiquitous outdoor advertising pillar. In more recent years they have been joined by the writers Heinrich Mann (1871-1950), Anna Seghers (1900-1983), Arnold Zweig (1887-1968), and Bertolt Brecht (1898-1956), by Brecht's wife, the actress Helene Weigel (1900-1971), the poet Johannes Robert Becher (1891-1958), the composer Hermann Eisler (d. 1952) and the inventor of political photomontage, John Heartfield (d. 1968).

The **cemetery of the French Reformed congregation**, at Chausseestrasse 127, is partly enclosed by the Dorotheenstädtischer Friedhof; laid out in 1780, it contains the graves of, among others, the actor Ludwig Devrient (1784-1832), the engraver Daniel Chodowiecki (1726-1801), and Friedrich Ancillon (1767-1837), tutor of Crown Prince Friedrich Wilhelm. Ancillon's sarcophagus is based on one of Schinkel's last designs.

The three-story, late neoclassical **Brecht-Haus** (Chausseestrasse 125) adjoins the cemetery. It was the last workplace and residence of Bertolt Brecht and Helene Weigel, from 1953 until her death in 1971. Today it houses the Bertolt Brecht and Helene Weigel Archive.

43 Invalidenfriedhof
Veterans' Cemetery
Scharnhorststrasse 25

After 1961 a symbol of the destruction accompanying the building of the Berlin Wall: numerous gravestones were relocated or destroyed in order to have free sightlines for aiming at those attempting escape.

The **cemetery**, originally laid out in 1748, lies directly along the path of the former Berlin Wall and was ravaged accordingly. Most of those buried here were officers

Museum für Naturkunde, inner court with dinosaur display

and generals from the nearby Veterans' Home. Among the few preserved tombstones is the massive **monument** to Gerhard von Scharnhorst, general of the Prussian army in the Napoleonic Wars and responsible for the army's reorganization, who died in Prague in 1813. The elevated sarcophagus of Carrara marble was designed by Karl Friedrich Schinkel in 1824 and carried out, after reburial of the general in 1826, by Christian Friedrich Tieck (relief frieze), the lion having been cast at the royal iron foundry in 1834 to a model by Christian Daniel Rauch.

44 Museum für Naturkunde
Natural History Museum
Invalidenstrasse 43

A unified ensemble of a central structure with flanking buildings, constructed by August Tiede between 1875 and 1889 in the late neoclassical style of the Schinkel school.

The museum **building**, set back from its surroundings and thus, in the Baroque tradition, made more prominent, has an imposing projecting front bay whose upper floor is reminiscent of Perrault's facade of the Louvre in Paris. Like the buildings to either side—on the left, the Central Geological Institute, on the right, the Agriculture and Botany Faculty—it has a huge, glassed-in **inner court** with arcaded galleries. A **monument** to Albrecht David Thaer (1752-1828), the founder of agricultural science in Prussia, stands in the inner court of the faculty building. It is Christian Daniel Rauch's last work, completed by his student Hugo Hagen in 1859.

A fair distance east on Invalidenstrasse on the left, at Bergstrasse 29, is the **second cemetery of the Sophienkirche** congregation, nicknamed the "Musikerfriedhof" (musicians' cemetery). Buried here are Wilhelm Friedrich Ernst Bach (1759-1845), grandson of Johann Sebastian Bach and court conductor to Queen Luise; the composer Albert Lortzing (1801-1851); Carl Bechstein, founder of the renowned piano factory that bears his name (d. 1900); and Walter Kollo (d. 1940), composer of numerous operettas and "evergreens."

At Invalidenstrasse 3, near the beginning of the street, is the **Elisabethkirche** (St. Elisabeth's Church), a classic Schinkel structure. Burned out in 1945, the building was preserved as a ruin. It is one of four Schinkel-designed suburban churches, this one distinguished by a markedly classical facade.

Neue Synagoge ▷

45 Neue Synagoge

New Synagogue
Oranienburger Strasse 30

*The prime example of the orientalizing
tendency in Berlin's Romantic architecture.*

The massive **building**, begun in 1859 to designs by Eduard Knoblauch and completed
by Friedrich August Stüler in 1866, is one
of the most important examples of the
Moorish style in Berlin. Its picturesque effect is dominated by the facade, its recently regilded 164-foot-high central cupola,
and by the minaret-like side towers. Desecrated in 1938 on "Reichskristallnacht"
and heavily damaged by bombs in 1943,
the ruin has been under reconstruction
since 1988. To be completed in 1995, it will
form part of a Centrum Judaicum.

Nearby—at Oranienburger Strasse 35-
36—is the **former Postal Delivery Bureau**,
designed by Carl Schwatlo and built between 1875 and 1881, one of the most magnificent of Berlin's municipal office buildings, distinguished by rich, prominently
modelled terra-cotta ornament.

46 Sophienkirche

St. Sophia's Church
Sophienstrasse

*An early Baroque church, founded by the wife
of Frederick II. Its tower, the only one in
Berlin to survive in its original state, was
inspired by Schlüter's Münzturm [see No. 10]
and the former Potsdam Garnisonskirche.*

The simple nave was built in 1712, the two
sacristies added in 1834. Its tower—one of
Berlin's most beautiful—was added by
Johann Friedrich Grael between 1732 and
1734. The church was renovated in the
neo-Baroque style in 1892. In the **cemetery** are the tombs of the composer Karl
Friedrich Zelter (1758-1832) and of the
historian Leopold von Ranke (1795-1886).

South of the church on Grosse Hamburger Strasse is the oldest preserved **Jewish cemetery** in Berlin, consecrated in
1672. Here the philosopher Moses Mendelssohn (1729-86) found his final resting
place. Closed in 1827, the cemetery was
levelled by the Nazis in 1943. It was restored as a park after 1945. At the entrance, a bronze **sculpture** by Will Lam-
mert serves as a memorial to the Jewish
residents of Berlin who were brought during the war to a home for the aged that
once stood here, a collecting point for
transport to the concentration camps in
Auschwitz and Theresienstadt.

Tower of Sophienkirche

Tiergarten

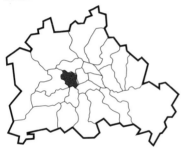

Originally a forested area, the land for the Tiergarten district was purchased in 1527 by Prince Elector Joachim I and converted into a park and game reserve from 1657 to 1659 under Frederick William the Great Prince Elector. First extensive building projects were undertaken in the early eighteenth century, when Frederick William I allotted land to the Huguenots here. They named their settlement after the biblical land of Moab,

"Terre de Moab" or "Terre des Moabites." It was incorporated, as Moabit, in 1861 and put under the jurisdiction of the Tiergarten district in 1920.

It is a district with two distinct faces: one of Berlin's oldest and loveliest parks next to an industrial and working-class residential sector. At a total area of just over five square miles, Tiergarten's population numbers 95,000.

Located at the center of old Moabit, St.-Johannis-Kirche (St. John's Church) is one of the four suburban houses of worship designed by Karl Friedrich Schinkel in 1832. On the grounds is a mass grave where about 550 victims of the Gestapo lie. Down the main street, at Alt-Moabit 48, is the Hansa-Theater, founded in 1963 by Paul Esser as the Berliner Volkstheater. A little farther on, at Alt-Moabit 100, Meierei Bolle (Bolle Dairy) has its headquarters. Established in 1881, Bolle's white, horse-drawn dairy wagons and their drivers' brass bells were known to every Berlin child well into the 1930s. Since its fusion in 1990 with the former East German Konsum markets, Bolle's now owns the largest supermarket chain in Berlin. Right next door is the Berliner Kammerspiele, a theater that stages plays for young people.

47   Former Hamburger Bahnhof
Former Hamburg Station
Invalidenstrasse 50

The oldest passenger station building in the city, with a design that set the standard for all of Berlin's later railroad stations.

Designed in the style of Italian Renaissance palaces by Friedrich Neuhaus and Ferdinand Wilhelm Holz and built between

1845 and 1847, the station was closed less than 40 years later, in 1884. From 1906 to 1945 it housed the Museum of Transportation and Engineering, and since 1988 it has been home to a **branch of the Nationalgalerie**. A model of the original facility, only a fragment of which survived World War II, is displayed in the Museum für Verkehr und Technik (Transportation and Technology) in Kreuzberg [No. 116].

Former Hamburger Bahnhof, today exhibition space for modern art

Kriminalgericht Moabit, the entrance hall

48 Kriminalgericht Moabit

Moabit Criminal Courts

Turmstrasse 91

A belated blossoming of Baroque architectural fantasies, with elaborate facade and magnificent entrance hall, modelled on the more opulent architecture of earlier centuries with the self-confidence of the historical revival.

The **Old Criminal Courts** building was erected between 1877 and 1882. As it soon proved too small, an enormous annex in the neo-Baroque style of Wilhelm II's era by Rudolf Mönnich and C. Vohl was added from 1902 to 1906. The Old Criminal Courts were destroyed in the war, and what remained was razed in 1953.

The annex, now the **Neues Kriminalgericht** (New Criminal Courts), has a huge, pompously magnificent entrance hall designed by Paul Thoemer. Behind the building lies Berlin's best-known prison, built on a star-shaped plan and with a special high-security tract.

Peter Behren's AEG Turbinenfabrik. The photograph was taken shortly after its completion. Today, trees partly obscure the view of the facade

49 AEG Turbinenfabrik

AEG Turbine Factory

Huttenstrasse 12-16

An incunabulum of modern industrial architecture in steel and glass. One of the world's first outstanding functionalist buildings, designed by Peter Behrens, a pioneer of the Modern Movement.

When in 1906 Behrens was named artistic advisor to the German General Electric Corporation, AEG, he became the first artist in history to influence the look of a company's products and buildings. He became the leading industrial architect and industrial designer in the country. In 1909 Behrens built the **assembly shed** for the AEG Turbinenfabrik. Originally 360 feet long, the building was extended to 680 feet at a later date. To ensure ample natural lighting for the interior, the entire facade on Berlichingenstrasse was conceived as a glazed wall rhythmically articulated by steel supports. For the first time in an industrial building, unclad structural components served as visible architectural elements, making the ideal of "form follows function" a reality. The steel structure, its front flanked by rusticated concrete columns, is topped by a projecting, pentagonal gable, echoing traditional architectural forms. Chiselled on the gable is the old, hexagonal AEG logo and the inscription

TURBINENFABRIK. The building now belongs to Kraftwerkunion Berlin (KWU), a power company.

At the end of Beusselstrasse, which crosses Huttenstrasse, lies Berlin's huge west harbor, **Westhafen** (built 1920-27). The original warehouses from the 1920s can be distinguished by their red brick facades. Since 1948 the harbor has been equipped with new storage buildings and a modern crane system, making it, with its three docks and eleven miles of railroad yards, one of the largest inland harbors in Europe, handling about five million tons of goods annually.

50 Tiergarten

Berlin's most popular park and, covering nearly five hundred acres, the largest recreational area in the city.

From 1943 to 1945, bombs rained on the Tiergarten, and in their wake came the Berliners with axe and saw, taking the re-

Tiergarten, Berlin's largest park. An idyllic spot in the center of the city

maining trees for firewood and planting potatoes and turnips in their place.

Reforestation began in 1949, with the symbolic planting of a linden tree by Ernst Reuter, first mayor of West Berlin. Donations of trees from all over West Germany began arriving, and soon over a million saplings and shrubs enlivened the devastated park in happy disregard of its original nineteenth-century layout by Peter Joseph Lenné, who had created an English landscaped garden here. Yet today the Tiergarten again boasts idyllic watercourses, ponds, and meadows, the branching bays of Neuer See (New Lake) with a café and boat rental, and innumerable paths on which you can walk for fifteen miles without retracing your steps.

Dotted around the Tiergarten are a number of **monuments** to past greats of German arts and letters, including the Goethe Monument (1880) by Fritz Schaper, the Lessing Monument (1890) by Otto Lessing, a great-great nephew of the poet, and the Composers Monument (1904) in honor of Haydn, Mozart, and Beethoven by Rudolph Siemering. Gustav Eberlein was the designer of the Wagner Monument (1903) and of the monument dedicated to a native son, the composer Albert Lortzing. On the north side of Strasse des 17. Juni near Brandenburger Tor stands the **Soviet War Memorial**, built in 1945 out of marble salvaged from Hitler's Reich Chancellory, a broad portal bearing the bronze statue of a Red Army soldier.

5I Siegessäule
Column of Victory
Grosser Stern

Symbol of Prussian victories in the campaigns against Denmark in 1864, Austria in 1866, and France in 1870-71. A Berlin landmark.

"Gold-Else" (Golden Elsie), the Berliners call their Victoria with typical irreverence. The platform beneath her feet offers a marvellous view of the Tiergarten and far beyond the Brandenburger Tor.

Plans for the column were begun by Johann Heinrich Strack at the behest of Wilhelm I in 1864, but it was not finished until 1873. The thirty-five-ton, gilded goddess of victory with her laurel wreath and spear is a bronze created by Friedrich Drake. Originally installed in front of the Reichstag building, statue and column were moved in 1939 to Grosser Stern traffic circle, where their height was increased by twenty-one feet.

Siegessäule

The Kaiser having stipulated that war booty be used in the monument, Strack adorned the four (originally three) sections of the fluted column with captured, gilded gun barrels. The column rests on a square socle of red granite and a circular **colonnade hall**. Inside is a glass mosaic (1875) based on a design by Anton von Werner, representing the history of German unity after the Franco-Prussian War of 1870-71. **Bronze reliefs** on the socle illustrate scenes from the Napoleonic Wars. They were removed after 1945, but three of the four have since been restored to their original place; the fourth is apparently irrecoverably lost. Two of them, the reliefs illustrating the Franco-Prussian War, were returned by the French government on the occasion of Berlin's 750-year jubilee in 1987.

A spiral staircase with 285 steps leads up inside the column to the lookout platform, 157 feet above the ground.

On the north side of the traffic circle stands a **statue of Otto von Bismarck**, founder of the German Empire. It was created in 1901 by Reinhold Begas, as were the four bronze groups around the twenty-eight-foot-high pedestal: in front, Atlas; to the left, an allegory of state wisdom resting on the Sphinx; to the right, state power vanquishing the panther of revolt; and at the rear, Siegfried forging the sword of empire. Next to Bismarck are **monuments** (both 1904) to Field Marshal Helmuth von Moltke by Joseph Uphues and to War Minister Albrecht von Roon by Harro Magnussen.

52 Hansa-Viertel
Hansa Quarter

State-of-the-art example of housing and town planning in the 1950s, with contributions by such renowned architects as Aalto, Gropius, Niemeyer, Taut, and Vago.

Located at the northern edge of the Tiergarten, nestled in a large bend of the Spree River between Tiergarten and Bellevue S-Bahn stations, the Hansa-Viertel rose from 1955 to 1957 as the centerpiece of the International Building Exhibition (Interbau), which drew design contributions by forty-eight distinguished architects from thirteen countries. Characteristic of the development is its relaxed mixture of structures—low buildings, four- to six-story apartment buildings, and high rises—and its integration of the Tiergarten's landscaping as a recreational area right at the inhabitants' doorstep. A plaque on each building bears the name of its architect. The quarter begins at the **Berlin Pavillon**, located at S-Bahn station Tiergarten, near Strasse des 17. Juni. Designed by Hermann Fehling, Daniel Gogel, and Peter Pfankuch, the pavilion hosts exhibitions by the Berlin Building Authority on topics related to city planning. A total of thirty-six structures are grouped around Hansaplatz U-Bahn station, including two churches, a kindergarten, a shopping center, the Grips-Theater (Altonaer Strasse 22), a municipal library, and the Akademie der Künste (Academy of Arts); the two last-mentioned buildings were designed by Werner Düttmann.

Hansa-Viertel, exemplary 1950s residential architecture with contributions by 48 leading architects

The **Grips-Theater** is Germany's best-known theater for children and young people, noted for its innovative staging and its willingness to tackle controversial subjects.

The **Akademie der Künste** (Hanseatenweg 20) is not a school but, as its 1954 reinauguration statutes say, "an association of outstanding artists." Founded in 1696 by Prince Elector Frederick III, the Berlin academy was the third of its kind in Europe, after those in Rome and Paris. As Preussische Akademie (until 1945 located at Pariser Platz 4) it became world-renowned; after World War II, in 1950, an independent institution was established in East Berlin. In 1960 funds provided by the American industrialist Henry H. Reichhold, a native of Berlin, were used to build the new West Berlin facilities, which consist of three structures linked by foyers and galleries: the "Blaues Haus" (Blue House), the Exhibition Building, and, at a right angle to the latter, the Studio. In front of the entrance is a group of contemporary sculptures, dominated by Henry Moore's *Large Reclining Woman* of 1956.

The two Berlin Academies of Art were merged in February 1992 by extending membership of the West Berlin Academy to all members of the former East Berlin institution.

Schloss Bellevue, Berlin seat of the Federal President

53 Schloss Bellevue

Bellevue Palace
Spreeweg

Berlin's first early neoclassical palace, dating from the era of Frederick the Great. Today, Berlin residence of the Federal President.

The present site of the palace was occupied, from 1710 onward, by a plantation of mulberry trees for the raising of silkworms. In 1743 Georg Wenzeslaus von Knobelsdorff bought the property and built a residence for himself on the site of the stables and farm buildings. Today's **palace**, designed in the French Baroque style by Philipp Daniel Boumann, was erected in 1785 for August Ferdinand of Prussia, the youngest brother of Frederick the Great. Severely damaged in World War II, the original interiors were lost, except for the oval **banquet hall** of 1791 by Carl Gotthard Langhans. The remaining rooms were redesigned.

The **English Garden** in the western part of the palace park was replanted in 1952, with the aid of the Shropshire Horticultural Society and funds donated by the English Royal Family. The thatched-roofed **Parkcafé** offers a program of changing exhibitions and concerts. At a total area of about fifty acres, the park was considered one of prewar Berlin's most beautiful. It contained a number of small architectural jewels, including a garden house by Schinkel, all of which were destroyed in the war and have not been restored. But even in its present form the park remains a delight.

Kongresshalle. In the reflecting pool, Two Forms *by Henry Moore*

54 Kongresshalle

Congress Hall
John-Foster-Dulles-Allee

The "Pregnant Oyster," one of Berlin's best-known landmarks, now serves as the Center of World Cultures.

Rusting of the steel supports inside the concrete cantilevered roof caused the Kongresshalle to come crashing down in 1980. However, repairs were finished in time for Berlin's 750-year jubilee in 1987. The Kongresshalle was erected in 1957 as the U.S. contribution to the Interbau Exhibition. It was designed by Hugh A. Stubbins (former assistant to Walter Gropius at Harvard University), with the collaboration of Werner Düttmann and Franz Mocken. Its almost square platform rests on a foundation of a thousand concrete piles, needed to support the spacious auditorium (1,250 seats). Located on the lower level, apart from a smaller, four-hundred-seat auditorium, are several conference rooms, an exhibition hall, and a restaurant. An outside staircase above the main entrance leads over a large reflecting pool to the platform. To the left stands a bronze by Henry Moore, *Two Forms*.

Until 1957 the ruins of the legendary **Kroll Opera** could be seen nearby, a palatial amusement center built in 1844 as a restaurant. At various times it housed Reichstag sessions, an opera company, and performances of the German State Opera.

Since 1987 the Kongresshalle has had a neighbor, a **carillon** in the shape of a 138-foot-high tower clad in black granite (its sixty-eight bells are played daily at 12 noon and 6 p.m.).

55 Reichstag Building

Platz der Republik

One of the most elaborate buildings in the historical revival style popular under Wilhelm II, inspired by Italian architecture of the High Renaissance. Since 1894 seat of the parliaments of the Empire, then of the Weimar Republic, and of the Third Reich, and since 1972 a part-time seat of the German Bundestag.

Built to plans by Paul Wallot between 1884 and 1894, the Reichstag, 450 feet long and 318 feet wide, was intended as a visible symbol of the grandeur and power of the new German Empire, proclaimed in Versailles in 1871. The inscription, DEM DEUTSCHEN VOLKE (To the German People) was too democratic as far as the Kaiser was concerned, and had to wait for engraving until 1916. On November 9, 1918, Representative Philipp Scheidemann stood in the second large window to the left of the portal and proclaimed the Republic. Shaken by internal dissent and crises, the Weimar Republic came to an ignominious end when Hitler was named Chancellor on January 30, 1933. The Reichstag fire of February 28, 1933, helped the Nazis obtain a broad majority

Reichstag building, official seat of the German parliament

in the parliament, which from that point on was forced to convene at the Kroll Opera across the way (until 1941; [see No. 54]). The undamaged part of the Reichstag building was meanwhile used for exhibitions. On April 30, 1945, Red Army soldiers raised the Soviet flag on its roof.

Heavily damaged during the war, the building was restored between 1957 and 1972, with the exception of the majestic glass cupola that once rose above its center. The interior, given a functional new design by Paul Baumgarten, contains, in addition to a new plenary auditorium, thirty conference rooms and almost two hundred offices for the parties and committees of the German Bundestag. On October 4, 1990, a day after the official reunification of the two Germanies, the united parliament held its historic first meeting here.

56 Philharmonie

Philharmonic Hall
Matthäikirchstrasse 1

One of the most important buildings of modern Berlin, superb both aesthetically and acoustically; home of the Berlin Philharmonic Orchestra.

The southern margin of the Tiergarten was once occupied by embassies, punctuated here and there by an artist's residence. Largely destroyed in World War II, the district bordered by Potsdamer-, Tiergar-

ten-, and Stauffenbergstrasse has since been gradually redeveloped, beginning with the 1960 to 1963 construction of Hans Scharoun's Philharmonie. It was followed by the Neue Nationalgalerie [No. 60], designed by Mies van der Rohe and built from 1965 to 1968, and Scharoun's Staatsbibliothek [No. 59] of 1967-68. Four years then passed before Scharoun presented a conception for further development of the area into a **Kulturforum** (Arts Forum). In accordance with his plans, the Institut für Musikforschung (Music Research) and the affiliated Musikinstrumenten-Museum (Museum of Musical Instruments [No. 57]), 1973, the Kunstgewerbemuseum (Museum of Decorative Arts [No. 58]), 1975-85, and the Kammermusiksaal (Chamber Music Hall), 1984-87, have been erected.

The altered situation since the fall of the Wall will necessitate a revision of Scharoun's plans for the Kulturforum: a new building for the combined Kupferstichkabinett (Collection of Prints and Drawings) and the Kunstbibliothek (Art Library) will open in 1993; a new building for the combined Gemäldegalerie (Picture Gallery) is planned for 1996.

The **Philharmonie** is a grandly designed and dynamic structure whose shimmering gold facing, added in 1979, further enhances its architectural quality. It was built from 1960 to 1963, to award-winning plans by Hans Scharoun. Nucleus of the building is the **auditorium** with its staggered tiers of seats and pavilion-like ceiling, built on an irregular polygonal plan whose center is occupied by the orchestra podium. Arranged around this focus, as if suspended there by the force of music itself, are 2,200 seats in nine rising terraces. The structure seems to negate the axiom of architectural rectangularity, its facets recalling the sensational zigzag style of the 1920s. The ceiling consists of separate, suspended, sail-like sections that serve to enhance the hall's acoustics. The natural stone floor in the foyer was designed by Erich F. Reuter; Bernhard Heiliger created the sculpture, *Triad*, and Alexander Camaro the four stained-glass windows. Outside, the twenty-foot, wing-like sculpture on the gracefully curving roof is by Hans Uhlmann.

Behind the Philharmonie stands another Scharoun building, the **Kammermusiksaal** (1984-87), also known as the "Little Philharmonie" on account of its mere 1,063 seats. The construction was supervised by Scharoun's assistant and successor, Edgar Wisniewski, and like its neighbor it boasts magnificent acoustics.

Philharmonie

57 Musikinstrumenten-Museum

Museum of Musical Instruments

Tiergartenstrasse 1

Four hundred years of music history as reflected in rare and exemplary instruments. The building is an interesting example of modern museum architecture.

The State Institute for Music Research with affiliated Musikinstrumenten-Museum was part of the plans for the new Kulturforum from the very beginning. Preliminary designs by Hans Scharoun were completed after his death by Edgar Wisniewski in 1973. The cornerstone, however, was not laid until 1979, and construction was finished in 1984.

The museum contains over 2,500 instruments, many of them still in working order, dating from the sixteenth to the twentieth century. Its core was formed by the Collection of Old Musical Instruments established in 1888 at the Royal Academy of Music, which by the 1920s had grown to over four thousand items. The majority of these were lost or destroyed in World War II. Apart from its musicological interest, the museum's art collection—paintings and sculptures illustrating nineteenth-century musical history—makes it well worth a visit.

The modern, functional home of Germany's oldest museum of decorative arts

58 Kunstgewerbemuseum

Museum of Decorative Arts
Tiergartenstrasse 6

The oldest collection of its kind in Germany. Decorative and applied arts from the early Middle Ages to the present day, including a unique collection of medieval goldsmiths' work: the Welfenschatz treasure, Treasure of Enger, and Basel Cathedral Treasure.

The forerunner of this museum was founded in 1867 and housed, from 1881 to 1920, in the Martin-Gropius-Bau [No. 113] and then in Berlin City Palace. During World War II, almost the entire holdings of tex-

tiles, glass, and stained glass were lost or destroyed. After the war the remaining collections were split up, finding new homes in East or West depending on the site of their wartime storage. In West Berlin, a provisional museum was installed at Schloss Charlottenburg until this new **Kunstgewerbemuseum**, designed by Rolf Gutbrod and built across from the Philharmonie between 1978 and 1985, had been completed.

Centerpiece of the department of medieval arts and crafts is the **Welfenschatz** (Guelph Treasure, 11th-15th century), a treasure of reliquaries including

Kunstgewerbemuseum: The portable altar of Eilbertus, part of the Welfenschatz, Cologne, c. 1150

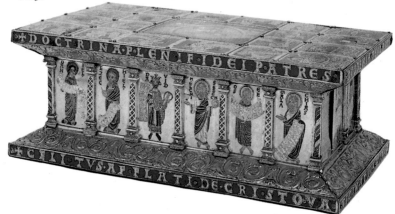

the famous Domed Reliquary (Cologne, c. 1175), portable altars, and the elaborately decorated *Welfenkreuz* (Guelph Crucifix, 11th century). Other high points are a golden reliquary cross (c. 1100), the Baptismal Font of Emperor Frederick I Barbarossa (c. 1160), and the *Heinrichskreuz* (Henry Cross), the reliquary crucifix of Emperor Henry II (early 11th century), part of the **Basel Cathedral Treasure**. The museum also has departments devoted to the decorative arts of the Renaissance, the Baroque period, the eighteenth and nineteenth centuries in Europe and Asia, and finally, on the lower level, to twentieth-century applied art and product design.

The museum holdings that were stored in the East during the war—furniture, jewelry, and porcelain—are now on display at Schloss Köpenick [No. 167].

59 Staatsbibliothek zu Berlin – Preussischer Kulturbesitz (II)
State Library of Berlin
Potsdamer Strasse 33

One of the largest modern library buildings in Europe. A general scholarly library with special collections of world rank.

The former Prussian State Library, which dates back to the year 1661, was divided after World War II into a German State Library (East) [No. 30] and a State Library of Prussian Holdings in the Arts (West). The two institutes were united in 1991, and the holdings, some eight million volumes, are now in the process of being reorganized and redistributed. While the older books are to be housed in the building at Unter den Linden (Haus I), those dating from 1945 and later will be held at Potsdamer Strasse (Haus II).

This ultramodern palace of books, Scharoun's final design, was erected from 1967 to 1978. It is composed of several architectural units housing individual departments. The archives include the papers of over 430 women and men of letters (those of Fichte, Herder, Hegel, Schopenhauer, to name only a few), musical documents (including the Mendelssohn Archive), maps, periodicals, and a picture archive containing over five million photographs and prints. The reading rooms seat six hundred.

60 Neue Nationalgalerie
New National Gallery
Potsdamer Strasse 50

Museum with outstanding Impressionist and twentieth-century art collections, presented in a model specimen of modern architecture by Ludwig Mies van der Rohe.

Erected between 1965 and 1968, the Neue Nationalgalerie building exemplifies Mies's mature style, embodying as it does his conception of a "hall per se" that could be adapted to a variety of functions. The square-shaped ground floor is built into a slope and thus is only partly visible. Above it, as if mounted on a platform, rises the steel and glass main hall, which measures 164 by 164 feet and is 28 feet high. This steel-skeleton glass hall with cantilevered roof was one in a series of similar projects

Neue Nationalgalerie: Edvard Munch, Harry Graf Kessler, 1906   ▷

73

Mies van der Rohe's Neue Nationalgalerie building with a steel sculpture by Alexander Calder. St.-Matthäus-Kirche in the distance

that played a key role in Mies's work. The ground floor, about double the area of the glass hall, houses the actual exhibition rooms, and to the west it opens out along its entire length onto a **sculpture garden**. Sculptures are also installed on the platform around the glass hall. The collection unites those holdings of the old Nationalgalerie [No. 18c] that were returned to West Berlin after World War II, and the Gallery of the Twentieth Century, founded in 1954. Acquisitions of works by artists of international renown have been added over the years. The glass pavilion is de-

Neue Nationalgalerie: Max Beckmann, Death, *1938*

voted principally to exhibitions of modern art.

A delightful contrast to the modern architecture of the Kulturforum is the **St.-Matthäus-Kirche** (St. Matthew's Church), the sole remaining structure of the mid-nineteenth-century town houses and villas of the "Privy Councillors' Quarter." The church, designed by Friedrich August Stüler in the *Rundbogenstil*, or round-arched style, of the Schinkel school, was built from 1844 to 1846. Damaged in the war, its exterior has been restored to the original plans.

Nearby rises the **Wissenschaftszentrum** (Science Center; Reichpietschufer 48-58), a postmodern pasticcio created by the British architect James Stirling and built between 1984 and 1988. Striped in pink and light blue and uniting elements from almost every style of Western architecture, its facade gives a vivacious face to the mundane offices within.

61   BEWAG (former Shell-Haus)

Stauffenbergstrasse 26

The first high-rise building in Germany with a steel skeleton construction.

The former Shell-Haus was built from 1930 to 1932 by Emil Fahrenkamp. The **facade** on Reichpietschufer is aesthetically pleasing with its staggered ground plan and variegated roof line rising in steps from six to eleven floors. Between 1965 and 1967 the complex was extended with two annexes designed by Paul Baumgarten. Although these also have steel skeletons, they are clad with enamelled aluminum panels around the steel-frame windows, while the original building has a facing of Roman travertine set to emphasize the horizontal articulation.

Since 1952 it has served as headquarters of BEWAG (Berlin Power and Light Corporation).

BEWAG, the former Shell-Haus, by Emil Fahrenkamp

Exhibition in the Gedenkstätte Deutscher Widerstand

62 Gedenkstätte Deutscher Widerstand

Monument to the German Resistance
Stauffenbergstrasse 13-14

Documentation of the German resistance movement against Hitler, displayed in historical rooms.

The former Reichsmarineamt (Imperial Navy Office), a Baroque revival building of 1911 to 1914 by the renowned Berlin architects Heinrich Reinhardt and Georg Süssenguth, was one of the last great construction projects of the imperial era. As headquarters of the Wehrmacht High Command from 1935 to 1945 it is an ap-propriate place to honor those who resisted the Nazis and their war machine.

In the courtyard, the **Monument to the Victims of July 20, 1944** (1953) by Richard Scheibe commemorates the Wehrmacht officers Schenk von Stauffenberg, von Quirnheim, von Haeften, and Olbricht, who were executed on this spot after their failed attempt on Hitler's life. On the second floor of the building, in historical rooms once occupied by the General Staff, is the permanent exhibition on "Resistance to National Socialism."

63 Bauhaus-Archiv
Klingelhöferstrasse 14

A late work by pioneer modernist architect Walter Gropius, founder of the Bauhaus. Inside, a unique survey of one of the major design schools of the twentieth century. Outstanding special exhibitions.

Designed in 1964, the building was originally intended for Darmstadt, a city in Hesse then home of the Bauhaus-Archiv, but could not be realized there. When the building went up in Berlin in 1979, ten years after his death, Gropius's wish to see his legacy displayed in his home town was belatedly fulfilled. Main feature of the **structure** is a lucidly articulated white concrete facade with north-facing skylights arranged in a rigorous row. The play of volumes and the emphasis on exterior forms are characteristic of the later years of Gropius's career, contrasting sharply with

Bauhaus-Archiv building, designed by Walter Gropius

Zoologischer Garten, the Elephant Gate on Budapester Strasse

his earlier, purely functional approach. Apart from Gropius, the staff of the Bauhaus, which moved from Weimar to Dessau in 1925 and thence, in 1932, to Berlin (where it was forcibly closed in 1933), included the architects Meyer, Mies van der Rohe, and Breuer, and such artists as Kandinsky, Itten, Klee, Moholy-Nagy, and Feininger. The archive contains a comprehensive **collection** of architectural models, designs, paintings, and drawings, as well as furniture and other craft and industrial products that poignantly illustrate the influence of the Bauhaus on contemporary design.

64 Zoologischer Garten and Aquarium

Hardenbergplatz 8
Side entrance: Budapester Strasse
(Elephant Gate)

An oasis of nature in the midst of the big city. A zoo of superlatives, Germany's oldest and most popular, boasting more species than any other in the world, a fascinating nocturnal-animal house, and an aquarium famous for its collection of crocodiles and other armored lizards.

Only ninety-one of the **zoo**'s almost ten thousand animals survived World War II, including a hippopotamus bull called Knautschke (Squeaky), born in 1943, and an elephant. Today the animal population of the eighty-six acre refuge numbers nearly 13,800 and represents over 1,400 species. The **aviary** covers an area of 35,500 square feet. Adjacent is a **predatory bird annex** and a **pheasantry**, which houses rare gallinaceous birds, doves, and bustards. Berlin has had a pheasantry, with ostriches and exotic species of deer, since 1670.

In its present form the zoo was established in 1841 by the naturalist Martin Lichtenstein, with Alexander von Humboldt and landscape architect Peter Joseph Lenné, and opened to the public in 1844.

From Budapester Strasse one enters through Elephant Gate, a reconstruction of the 1899 original. Nearby is Fritz Behn's monument to Bobby, an enormous gorilla that was the first ever to be born in captivity. The zoo is open daily from 9 a.m. to 6:30 p.m., 5 p.m. in winter.

The **aquarium**, well worth a visit, harbors about 10,000 animals representing 656 species: fish, reptiles, amphibians, spiders, snails, scorpions, and insects.

All around the Center

Charlottenburg

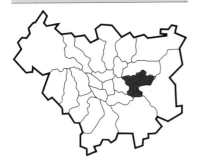

When Queen Sophie Charlotte died in 1705, the palace built for her by the first king of Prussia, Frederick I, was rechristened from Lietzenburg to Charlottenburg, along with the village of Lietzow where it stood. In spite of its diminutive population (less than 100), Charlottenburg received city status, and thus became one of the eight towns to be incorporated, in 1920, into Greater Berlin. By the end of World War II, only 604 of its 11,075 residential buildings remained undamaged. As Berlin's center became part of East Berlin after the war, a new downtown for West Berlin developed in Charlottenburg. Today Charlottenburg has an area of over eleven and a half square miles, of which forty-two percent is built up, and a population of 185,000.

65 Bahnhof Zoologischer Garten
Zoo Station
Jebenstrasse 8/Hardenbergplatz

During the division of the city, from 1961 to 1989, West Berlin's sole main line station.

Bahnhof Zoo is once again what it was before World War II—a busy junction of long-distance rail traffic between the western and eastern capitals of Europe and, in the inner-city system, one of the busiest interchanges between S- and U-Bahn lines and numerous bus lines.

The terminal was erected from 1934 to 1936 to the plans of Fritz Hane, on the site of an earlier station; the restaurant terrace on Hardenbergplatz, designed by Horst Engel, was added in 1957. The station was completely renovated and fitted with clear glass walls between 1987 and 1990. A new travel center is opening in 1992.

66 Breitscheidplatz with Weltkugelbrunnen
Breitscheid Square with World Globe Fountain

Piccadilly Circus and Hyde Park Corner rolled into one, this is western Berlin's most prominent plaza.

Flanked on the west by Kaiser-Wilhelm-Gedächtniskirche (Memorial Church [No. 67]), on the east by the Europa-Center [No. 68], and gripped in an incessant flow of cars, buses, and pedestrians to north and south, busy Breitscheidplatz has become a favorite meeting point since its redesign in 1983.

The **Weltkugelbrunnen**, unveiled in summer 1983 and affectionately known to Berliners as the "Wasserklops" (Wet Meatball), is a creation of the sculptor Joachim Schmettau. The sixteen-foot pink

Bahnhof Zoo, busy station for long-distance and inner city trains

◁ *Kaiser-Wilhelm-Gedächtniskirche, a symbol of the desire for freedom during the years of the Cold War*

Bustling Breitscheidplatz with Weltkugelbrunnen, a favorite meeting point

granite fountain sculpture symbolizes the political state of the world at the time of its design. The overall planning of the plaza, including hydraulic engineering and lighting, was carried out by Ivan Krusnik and Oskar Reith.

Located at Budapester Strasse 44-48 is an art museum, the **Staatliche Kunsthalle**, which holds exhibitions of twentieth-century art. During the annual Berlinale film festival the premises are used as a press and information center.

67 Kaiser-Wilhelm-Gedächtniskirche

Kaiser Wilhelm Memorial Church
Breitscheidplatz

One of the city's best-known landmarks: its ruined steeple and modern tower and chapel are an unforgettable reminder of the futility of war.

Designed by Franz Schwechten and built between 1891 and 1895, the neo-Romanesque church was severely damaged in an air-raid on November 22, 1943, then reduced to rubble by artillery fire during the final days of the war. Its fate was the sub-ject of fierce debate in the postwar years, and finally it was decided to erect a **new building** while retaining the 207-foot-high ruin of the originally 370-foot-tall western tower. Egon Eiermann of Karlsruhe won the design competition. His solution: a flat-roofed octagon of pierced, glazed concrete slabs; a 174-foot hexagonal steeple and bell-tower with six bells; a rectangular sacristy built around an inner court; and a foyer with a library. The stained glass for the new buildings was made in Chartres. A covered walkway links the tower ruin, which serves as a memorial hall, with the chapel and new church tower. At every full hour the **bells** in the old tower ring out a melody by Prince Louis Ferdinand, great-grandson of the last Kaiser.

The furnishings of the **Memorial Hall** demonstrate, very much in the spirit of Kaiser Wilhelm II, the unity of throne and altar in Protestant Prussia. In addition to a large, damaged statue of Christ by Fritz Schaper, and several mosaics and marble reliefs, there is an outstanding piece titled *Fürstenfries* (Princes' Frieze) with portraits of the Hohenzollern rulers from Prince Elector Frederick I (reigned 1414-1440) to

A sidewalk café on Kurfürstendamm

the last German crown prince, Friedrich Wilhelm (died 1951), and his wife, Cäcilie.

The Risen Christ over the plain altar in the new chapel is a chased-metal piece by Karl Hemmeter. The Karl Schuke Organ, installed in 1962, has 5,100 pipes and sixty-three registers, and soars twenty-eight feet in height.

Diagonally opposite the church, at Hardenbergstrasse 29a, is the **Zoo-Palast**, Berlin's largest cinema and main venue of the annual film festival, the Berlinale.

68 Europa-Center

Breitscheidplatz

At 282 feet one of the tallest buildings in the city. Over a hundred shops, and a marvellous view of Berlin from the observation platform at the top.

Designed by Helmut Hentrich and Hubert Petschnigg with the artistic and town-planning assistance of Werner Düttmann and Egon Eiermann, the Europa-Center was built from 1963 to 1965. The black steel structure takes its architectural cues from the Gedächtniskirche opposite. Its attractions include a cabaret, **Die Stachelschweine** (Hedgehogs), located downstairs; a casino, the **Spielbank Berlin**, on the second floor (accessible from Budapester Strasse); and the **Verkehrsamt** or tourist office (entrance on Tauentzienstrasse).

69 Kurfürstendamm

Berlin's favorite shopping street and promenade.

In the sixteenth century the 2¼-mile thoroughfare was a bridle path to Jagdschloss Grunewald [No. 141]. The development of the Ku'damm, as Berliners call it, took place from 1883 to 1886 at the behest of Otto von Bismarck. Only a very few of the original, opulent, turn-of-the-century buildings survived World War II and have been faithfully restored. Examples are houses No. 14-15, No. 48-50, and No. 59-60, the Iduna Building, whose verdigris cupolas enliven the corner of Leibnizstrasse, and the buildings at Nos. 201, 213-16, and 218.

Next-door to the Wertheim Department Store is the **Ku'damm Eck** (Kurfürstendamm 227-228, corner of Joachimsthaler Strasse), a shopping center designed by Werner Düttmann that contains eighty shops, restaurants, and cinemas as well as

81

Panorama of western Berlin looking west. Kaiser-Wilhelm-Gedächtniskirche is in the foreground; behind it, Kurfürstendamm veers to the left, Hardenbergstrasse to the right

a skittle and a bowling alley. In a wax museum on the third floor, the **Berliner Panoptikum**, four hundred royal, political, athletic, and cinema celebrities imperturbably receive visitors. A Medizinisches Kabinett (Medical Gallery) exhibits authentic anatomical models dating to the 1890s.

On the other side of the street, at Kurfürstendamm 18-19, the renowned **Café Kranzler** offers a chance to enjoy the bustle of Berlin's busiest corner over a leisurely cup of coffee. Founder of the establishment was Johann G. Kranzler, an Austrian confectioner attached to the Prussian court, whose original café at Unter den Linden, founded in 1825 and demolished during World War II, opened this branch on Kurfürstendamm in 1931.

Located just down the street (at Kurfürstendamm 27, corner of Fasanenstrasse) is Berlin's most celebrated grand hotel, **Bristol Hotel Kempinski**. The name Kempinski recalls the culinary tradition of the house: Berthold Kempinski (1845-1910), proprietor of a wine restaurant, came from Posen (today in Poland), as did many entrepreneurs of the post-1871 boom years who made their fortune in the young capital. Today's hotel was built in several stages, beginning in 1952, by Paul Schwebes. Architecturally noteworthy is the natural stone facing, whose buff color is effectively set off on the ground floor by black-framed opaque glass windows.

At No. 206-208 rises **Ku'damm Karree**, with 215,000 square feet of floor space the second largest shopping and entertainment center in the downtown area. The two boulevard theaters, the **Theater am Kurfürstendamm** and the **Komödie**, both associated with the name of the great producer and director Max Reinhardt, have long been located here; the building complex was added from 1971 to 1974 by Sigrid Kressmann-Zschach. A special attraction is the **flea market** held here every Sunday. The main shopping arcade leads from Kurfürstendamm to **"Sperlingsgasse"** (Lietzenburger Strasse 82-84), where thirteen bars and restaurants welcome guests from 7 p.m. to the early hours of the morning.

70 Käthe-Kollwitz-Museum

Fasanenstrasse 24

The life's work of Germany's most important twentieth-century woman graphic artist and sculptor, displayed in a stately town house. [For the eastern Berlin milieu where the artist spent her life, see No. 108.]

Built in 1871 and refurbished in the neo-classical style in 1897, the museum building has more recently received a new domed roof. It is part of an ensemble of three villas from the *Gründerzeit*, the post-1871 boom years, that were restored in the last decade. Museum director is Professor Hans Pels-Leusden, an artist and art dealer, who donated his collection of one hundred prints, seventy drawings and posters, and a number of sculptures by Käthe Kollwitz (1867-1945) to the museum.

The **Grisebach Villa** (1891-95) next door, at Fasanenstrasse 25, named after its architect, Hans Grisebach, houses Pels-Leusden's gallery. No. 23 has, since 1986, been home to the **Literaturhaus**, where Berlin's literary scene convenes. The **Tucholsky Room** there is furnished with pieces from that writer's house in Hindas, Sweden, where he lived in exile.

71 Jüdisches Gemeindehaus

Jewish Community House
Fasanenstrasse 79-80

A meeting house and memorial. Cultural center of the largest Jewish community in Germany, whose history goes back over three hundred years.

This was the site of a Reform **synagogue**, built in the Byzantine style by Ehrenfried Hessel in 1911-12, which was desecrated and set fire to by a Nazi platoon on November 9, 1938. Its ruins remained until 1958. The portal of the old synagogue has been used as the main entrance to the new community center, which was designed by the architects Dieter Knoblauch and Heinz Heise and erected from 1957 to 1959.

A pair of columns from the main facade of the destroyed synagogue stands as a memorial adjacent to the two-story building. A wall in the rear courtyard serves as a **commemorative site**, dedicated to the Jewish citizens of Berlin whose lives were taken during the Third Reich.

The lobby of Theater des Westens

72   Theater des Westens
Kantstrasse 9-12

Modern entertainment behind venerable old walls: Berlin's operetta and musical stage.

Erected by Bernhard Sehring in 1895-96 in the historical revival style popular in the period of Wilhelm II's reign, the **theater** provides an ideal setting for the classical operetta and lighter musical entertainment its stage has presented for most of the building's history. From 1945 to 1961 it served as a provisional home of the Municipal Opera. In 1978 the structure was remodelled and restored, then modernized once again in 1984. Under its present artistic director, Helmut Baumann, the stage has become a lively venue of modern musical theater.

Tucked away in a tiny annex is the **Vaganten-Bühne**, which calls itself "Berliner Kellertheater" (Basement Theater) and seats, at a pinch, an audience of one hundred.

Two blocks down Kantstrasse to the west, in a neighborhood with Old Berlin charm, lies **Savignyplatz**. The square is flanked by some fine examples of nineteenth-century residential architecture. It is a book-lover's paradise and an attraction for hungry night owls (boasting about fifty restaurants offering various national cuisines in the near vicinity). The building at Savignyplatz 5 bears a memorial plaque to the artist George Grosz, who died here in 1959, only a few days after his return from the United States. The delightful bronze sculpture on the north side of the square, *Knabe mit Ziegenbock* (Boy with Billy-Goat), was created by August Kraus in 1928.

73   Hochschule der Künste
College of Art
Hardenbergstrasse 33

An elaborate neo-Baroque palace in the style popular under Wilhelm II, flanked by a modern concert auditorium, Berlin's second largest.

The Hochschule der Künste was founded in 1975 with the merger of the College of Visual Arts, the College of Music and the Performing Arts next door (entrance at Fasanenstrasse 1), the Teachers College, and the Institute of Church Music (Hardenbergstrasse 44). The main building was erected between 1898 and 1902 to plans by Heinrich Kayser and Karl von Grossheim.

Modern annexes to the College of Music house the **Konzertsaal** (concert hall; main entrance on Hardenbergstrasse) and the **Studiobühne** theater. The two original wings were destroyed in the war and rebuilt, partly on the existing foundations, by Paul Baumgarten. The Konzertsaal, whose 1,360 seats make it the second-largest music auditorium in Berlin next to the Philharmonie [No. 56], was completed in 1955, while the Studiobühne opened its doors in 1975.

In the late 1960s the College of Art as well as the cafeteria of the Technical University next door and Steinplatz across the street were a key focus of the campus revolt in West Berlin.

74 Technische Universität
Strasse des 17. Juni 135

Once Germany's largest and most renowned engineering school. Houses an important collection of plans relating to the history of Prussian and Berlin architecture of the nineteenth and twentieth centuries.

The origins of today's Technische Universität (TU) go back to an 1879 merger of the Architecture Academy and the Trades Institute. These were augmented, in 1916, by the Academy of Mining (established 1770). A humanities faculty was added in 1950, an agriculture faculty in 1951, and a department of electronic engineering in 1955.

The **main building**, a Renaissance revival design by Richard Lucae, Friedrich Hitzig, and Julius Raschdorff carried out from 1878 to 1884, suffered severe bomb damage in World War II. Its north wing has since been replaced by a modern ten-story **high rise** with aluminum cladding (architects: Kurt Dübbers and Carl-Heinrich Schwennicke). The low, windowless, projecting structure in front is the **Auditorium Maximum**, which seats 1,200.

The new building is flanked on the west by an **extension** constructed from 1900 to 1902 and later enlarged. In its stairway stands a monumental statue of the industrialist Alfred Krupp (1899) by Ernst Herter, a counterpart to the bronze statue of Werner von Siemens created by Wilhelm Wandschneider in 1899, which stands in front of the Institute of Electronic Engineering in the northern part of the campus.

Walking in the direction of Hardenbergstrasse from the main campus, one passes the Student Union and enters the **Mensa** (Commons), a cube-shaped concrete building designed by Werner Düttmann and erected in 1965-66. The TU has twenty-two departments and a student body of 25,000, including 4,600 foreign students.

Technische Universität, Institute of Mathematics building on Strasse des 17. Juni

75 Staatliche Porzellanmanufaktur KPM
National Porcelain Manufactory
Wegelystrasse 1

Finest quality china manufactured by one of Germany's oldest firms, whose blue scepter mark is a guarantee of exquisite taste and traditional quality.

KPM goes back to an enterprise established by a private businessman, Wilhelm Kaspar Wegely, in 1750. After overcoming initial difficulties with the help of model maker Friedrich Elias Meyer and several talented decorators from the famous manufactory at Meissen, the firm became one of the leading porcelain producers in the country. In 1763 it was made a royal enterprise, **Königliche Porzellan-Manufaktur Berlin (KPM)**, and was permitted by Frederick the Great to use the Brandenburg scepter that has been its trademark ever since. The company was transferred to state ownership in 1918.

Severely damaged in World War II, KPM resumed operations in 1954. Today it supplies fine chinaware and decorative porcelain goods of the highest quality to clients around the world.

Its creations of the neoclassical period first established the company's reputation far beyond the borders of Prussia. Technical improvements have also contributed to

85

Porcelain vase with a view of Berlin,
KPM Berlin, c. 1830

its fame, such as the Seger Process, which permitted the use of unprecedentedly brilliant colors beneath the glaze and thus made possible some of the marvellous effects seen in Art Nouveau china.

KPM has **shops** at Wegelystrasse 1 and at Kurfürstendamm 26a. A permanent **exhibition** comprising five hundred items that delightfully illustrate the company's

history is on view at the Belvedere [see No. 81]. KPM china may be seen as well in the Bröhan-Museum [No. 84], at Schloss Köpenick [No. 167], and in the Märkisches Museum [see No. 13].

76 Ernst-Reuter-Platz

One of the biggest plazas in the city, and among its busiest traffic intersections.

Five main traffic arteries converge here to encircle an island whose water basin is enlivened by the play of forty-one fountains.

The buildings on the two blocks to the east of the plaza house institutes of the Technische Universität: the **Department of Architecture** building (1968) by Bernhard Hermkes and the adjacent **Institute of Urban Planning** (1970) by Hans Scharoun in front of which stands a bronze sculpture by Bernhard Heiliger, *The Flame* (1961), dedicated to Ernst Reuter, the first postwar mayor of Berlin; the **Institute of Mining and Metallurgy** by Willy Kreuer (1955-59); and the adjacent **Institute of Physics** (Hardenbergstrasse 35).

Across the street, at Hardenbergstrasse 6, is the **Renaissance-Theater**, constructed in an existing building by Oskar Kaufmann in 1922. The theater put on its first play in war-torn Berlin only nineteen days after the capitulation. The intimate atmosphere of its original auditorium with elaborate wood-inlay panelling by César Klein (restored in 1985) make the theater well worth a visit.

Window display at the KPM store on Kurfürstendamm

Berlin's largest and most popular flea market, held Saturdays and Sundays on Strasse des 17. Juni

On the southwestern side of the square is a sculpture by Gerhard Marcks, *Capering Stallions* (1975).

Berlin's largest flea market is held every Saturday and Sunday from 8 a.m. to 3:30 p.m. on Strasse des 17. Juni, a few hundred yards east of Ernst-Reuter-Platz.

77 Schiller-Theater

Bismarckstrasse 110

The main stage of Berlin's national repertory company, the Staatliches Schauspielhaus, noted equally for its performances of classical and modern drama.

The present structure is the third version of this theater, but its core is still made up of parts of the original **building** by Max Littmann and Jacob Heilmann, erected here from 1905 to 1907. It was expanded in 1937-38, then largely destroyed in the war, and reconstructed in 1950-51, incorporating the parts that had remained intact. Architects Heinz Völker and Rudolf Grosse fitted it with a smooth ashlar facade interrupted only by the projecting curve of a glazed wall above the entrance. The reliefs in the foyer are the work of Bernhard Heiliger, while the plaster-and-inlay murals along the stairways leading to the up-

Friedrich von Schiller's Räuber *performed at the Schiller-Theater*

Deutsche Oper. To the right is Hans Uhlmann's steel sculpture, popularly known as "Schaschlik" (shish kebab)

per foyer were created by Hans Kuhn. Ludwig Peter Kowalski designed the eighty-two-foot-long and seventeen-foot-high engraved glass wall in the upper foyer.

Located in a wing off the main building is the **Schiller-Theater Werkstatt**, an experimental drama workshop with 197 seats that opened on September 28, 1959, with a performance of Edward Albee's *Zoo Story*. Another branch is the **Schlosspark Theater**, a charming little playhouse at Schloss Steglitz [No. 134].

78 Deutsche Oper Berlin
Bismarckstrasse 34-37

A venerable institution in modern architectural costume, home to famous singers and conductors—one of the leading opera companies in the world.

Opened in 1912 as the Deutsches Opernhaus Charlottenburg, the original building was intended as a demonstration of the autonomy of the city of Charlottenburg with respect to the Staatsoper on Unter den Linden [No. 27]. Twelve years later, however, the house came under the authority of Berlin and was rechristened Städtische Oper (Municipal Opera).

The first director of the Charlottenburg Opera was conductor Bruno Walter, followed in 1925 by Heinz Tietjen (who held the position again from 1948 to 1954), and from 1931 to 1933 by Carl Ebert (also 1954-61). In 1943 the building was reduced to ruins in an air raid.

After occupying a provisional home at the Theater des Westens [No. 72], the company moved into its present home in 1961—a modern auditorium with 1,885 seats, built on the original site by Fritz Bornemann. Over the years, the orchestra has been honed to excellence by the likes of Ferenc Fricsay, Eugen Jochum, Lorin Maazel, and Giuseppe Sinopoli. Tatjana Gsovsky established the superb ballet, led today by Peter Schaufuss.

The building's **main facade**, about 230 feet in length, is clad with pebbled concrete slabs that serve to dampen the noise of the busy street outside. The **lateral facades** are entirely glazed, revealing the steel skeleton construction. The abstract **sculpture** at the entrance, a sixty-foot-tall untitled piece in black steel by Hans Uhlmann, was erected in 1961.

Inside, the panelled walls of the **main foyer** are graced by a large, abstract composition (1961) by Ernst Wilhelm Nay. The two sculptures in the foyer are *Hierarchy*, by Kenneth Armitage, and *Seated Figure*, by Fritz Wotruba.

Rathaus Charlottenburg. Its tower is a district landmark

79 Rathaus Charlottenburg
Charlottenburg City Hall
Otto-Suhr-Allee 96-102

An impressive example of the Berlin historical revival style, combining elements of the Baroque, neoclassicism, and Art Nouveau.

Following Otto-Suhr-Allee from Ernst-Reuter-Platz in the direction of Schloss Charlottenburg, one passes, at No. 18, the **Tribüne**, a small, private theater with 375 seats built in 1918-19. The **Rathaus**, designed by Heinrich Reinhardt and Georg Süssenguth, was erected between 1899 and 1905 on the site of the old town hall of 1791. Expanded from 1911 to 1913 by Heinrich Seeling, it suffered extensive bomb damage during World War II and was restored after the war. The 290-foot-

high tower with its copper-clad peak is a landmark of the district, visible from a great distance. The **Bürgersaal** (community meeting hall) inside was redesigned in 1957 by Werner Düttmann.

Opposite the Rathaus, at Otto-Suhr-Allee 89, is the oldest building on the street, dating from 1820. The inscription, which translates "Apothecary to the Royal Court, anno 1799," commemorates the **Hofapotheke** (Royal Apothecary) that was once located adjacent to the Rathaus.

Further down the street, proceeding in a northwesterly direction, is the **Luisen-kirche** (1716), the former parish church of Charlottenburg. Originally Baroque in style, the building went through several alterations before it was redesigned by Karl Friedrich Schinkel from 1823 to 1826. It was heavily damaged in the war; during subsequent restoration the tower received the present squat, pyramidal roof.

Monument to Frederick William the Great Prince Elector in the front court

80 Schloss Charlottenburg

Charlottenburg Palace
Luisenplatz

The most significant historic building in the western part of the city, a superb example of Baroque architecture. Home of exquisite collections, including paintings by Watteau, Friedrich, Schwind, Runge, and Spitzweg. Elaborate Rococo interiors. In the courtyard, the finest Baroque equestrian monument in all Germany.

Owing to the extensive destruction of historical buildings in Berlin during the war and its aftermath (entailing the loss of the city palaces in Berlin and Potsdam), Schloss Charlottenburg today is one of the very few examples of large-scale court architecture built under the Hohenzollerns.

The **central tract** was begun in 1695 by Johann Arnold Nering as a summer residence for Sophie Charlotte, the second wife of Prince Elector Frederick III, in what was then still a rural area. It was completed in 1699 by Martin Grünberg. Over the next hundred years the palace acquired its present form and extent.

The first annexes were built soon after Prince Elector Frederick III crowned himself King Frederick I of Prussia, in 1701. In 1702 Johann Friedrich Eosander von Göthe, a Swedish architect trained in Paris, added the two lateral wings and the central **court**.

Originally the palace was called Lietzenburg, after the nearby village of Lietzow. After the death of Sophie Charlotte in

1705 it was renamed in her honor. Building continued, and by 1713 the 157-foot-high **cupola tower**, crowned by a weathervane in the shape of a gilded Fortuna, had risen above the central tract. The western wing was extended with the **Orangery**. Under Frederick the Great, from 1740 to 1747, the **Knobelsdorff Wing**, which is named after its architect, was erected to the east of the main tract. Then, under Friedrich Wilhelm II, came the **Schlosstheater**, a 1788-91 extension to the Orangery by Carl Gotthard Langhans that increased the overall length of the palace to 1,657 feet.

In the wake of an air raid in 1943, Schloss Charlottenburg was almost completely gutted by fire. After decades of restoration work, it now presents an aspect both inside and out that approaches its original state. The graceful Fortuna that catches the breeze above the cupola is a recreation (1977) by Richard Scheibe.

The **Equestrian Monument to Frederick William the Great Prince Elector** in the central court originally stood on Lange Brücke, a bridge in Mitte district since renamed Rathausbrücke [see No. 16]. During World War II an attempt was made to save the statue by loading it onto a barge and taking it away. It got as far as Tegel Harbor, where it sank, barge and all. It was salvaged in 1950 and erected in 1952 in front of Schloss Charlottenburg. The pedestal is a replica; the original is in the

Bode Museum [No. 18d]. The monument, one of the most impressive of its kind, is the work of Andreas Schlüter, who modelled it in 1696-97 at the behest of Prince Elector Frederick III. In 1700 it was cast by Johann Jacobi in a single piece and unveiled in 1703 adjacent to the Berlin City Palace.

Also by Schlüter is the **Monument to Prince Elector Frederick III**, his patron, of which a bronze cast stands in front of the Knobelsdorff Wing. The original was located from 1802 to the end of World War II at Königsberg Palace in East Prussia, but has since disappeared without trace.

Space permits mention of only a few of the **reconstructed rooms** of the palace: the

monarch as a dining and throne room, and the 138-foot-long **Goldene Galerie**, which leads to the **Konzertzimmer**. This part of the palace was almost completely gutted in 1943. Since restored to their original splendor, the rooms are fine examples of Rococo interior design from the period of Frederick I and Frederick the Great.

The walls of the **Weisser Saal** are clad in pink imitation marble. A new ceiling painting (1972-73) by Hann Trier replaces Antoine Pesne's *Marriage of Peleus and Thetis* of 1742, which was lost. Thanks to Frederick's penchant for French Rococo painting, one can now marvel in his apartments at eight pictures by **Watteau**, perhaps the finest collection of works by

Galerie der Romantik in Schloss Charlottenburg: Caspar David Friedrich,
The Solitary Tree, *1822*

Oak Gallery on the ground floor of the central tract, in which chamber music concerts are occasionally held; the **Porcelain Chamber**, westernmost room in the Eosander von Göthe annex, with a superb display of seventeenth- and eighteenth-century Chinese and Japanese porcelain; and, behind a mirror-door there, the splendid **chapel**.

Located on the upper floor of the Knobelsdorff Wing are the **apartments of Frederick the Great**, consisting of rooms right next to the grand staircase overlooking the park, and rooms at the eastern end. In between lie the banquet halls created by Knobelsdorff and Johann August Nahl: The **Weisser Saal**, which served the

the painter anywhere. It includes early canvases such as *The Fair* (c. 1705) and *Bridal Procession* (c. 1709), as well as *The Concert* (c. 1715), the remarkable shopsign for the art dealer Gersaint (*Enseigne de Gersaint*, 1720), and the second, 1718 version of *Embarcation for Cythera* (the first version is in the Louvre). Among the many other artists represented in the collection are Lancret, Chardin, and Pesne.

The **Galerie der Romantik**, a department of the Nationalgalerie located for the time being on the ground floor of the Knobelsdorff Wing, contains, with twenty-three works, the world's largest collection of paintings by Caspar David Friedrich (1774-1840). The famous *Monk by the Sea*

Schloss Charlottenburg, Goldene Galerie

(1808-10), *The Solitary Tree* (1822), and *Woman at the Window* (1822), in which his wife, Caroline Bommer, is shown looking out over the Elbe River from the window of his Dresden studio, are among the works in the collection. Also on view are fifteen landscapes and architectural capriccios by Karl Friedrich Schinkel (1781-1841), including the characteristic *Gothic Church on a Cliff by the Sea* (1815). Carl Blechen is represented by twenty-three paintings, most notably the colorful *Interior of the Palm House*, painted for King Friedrich Wilhelm III on Pfaueninsel (Peacock Island [No. 148]) in 1832. His *Neustadt-Eberswalde Rolling Mills* (1834) is one of the earliest depictions of an industrial plant in the history of art.

The collection includes works by most important artists of the German Romantic movement. Eduard Gaertner's large *View of Unter den Linden* (1853) leads into the department devoted to Biedermeier art. This period is represented foremost by Carl Spitzweg (1808-1885), notably his *Poor Poet* and *The Love Letter*.

The Orangery in the western wing houses major art exhibitions, and, further west, the Langhans building, formerly the Schlosstheater, is currently home to the **Museum für Vor- und Frühgeschichte** (Pre- and Early History). The **collection** is divided into four departments, with as many rooms, in which finds from the Old and Middle Stone Ages (5,000-2,500 B.C.) to the Iron Age of the early medieval period are displayed. A highlight of Room 2 is the Collection of Trojan Antiquities. Each

Tomb of Queen Luise by Christian Daniel Rauch, 1811-14

93

room includes excavation finds made in and around Berlin, such as the bronze statuette of a cow (third century A. D.) discovered in the district of Schöneberg.

The museum has its origins in the collections of art and antiquities assembled by the Hohenzollerns. It moved several times in the hundred years before World War II and had its last prewar home in the Martin-Gropius-Bau [No. 113]. Despite wartime storage of the collection, many valuable pieces were lost, including the Treasure of Priamos and the Gold Treasure of Eberswalde, named after the town in Brandenburg province where this largest find of Bronze Age golden implements ever made in Germany was unearthed. Numerous acquisitions have since been made, especially of finds from excavations in the Berlin area and of major pieces from the Near East, particularly Syria.

Those parts of the original collection that were stored in the East during World War II are now in the Museum für Vor- und Frühgeschichte currently in storage at the Bode Museum [No. 18d].

Belvedere

81 Schlosspark Charlottenburg
Charlottenburg Palace Park

A jewel of European landscape design, combining the geometry of French Baroque with the freedom of the English landscape garden. Its mausoleum commemorates a key phase of Prussian history.

The **garden** directly behind the palace was restored after the war to its original form—a French Baroque layout with ornamental beds, hedges, and an octagonal basin with a fountain. Set on herme pedestals along the garden side of the Orangery and the Knobelsdorff Wing are twenty-four marble busts of Roman emperors and their wives, created by Kaspar Günther for Schloss Oranienburg around 1663.

An avenue of firs leads from the Langhans Wing to the **Mausoleum** of Queen Luise, designed by Karl Friedrich Schinkel shortly after her death on July 19, 1810. The original sandstone of the Doric front has since been replaced by reddish granite. The interior was largely the work of Heinrich Gentz. A chapel was added to the mausoleum in 1841, then expanded in 1890-91. The marble sarcophagus of Queen Luise, a major work of nineteenth-century German sculpture, represents the queen asleep. It was created in Italy by Christian Daniel Rauch from 1811 to 1814. Berliners still come here on the anniversary of the queen's death to lay flowers at the foot of her tomb. Buried beside her are King Friedrich Wilhelm III (d. 1840), Prince Albrecht (d. 1872), and Princess Liegnitz, the king's second wife (d. 1873). The heart of King Friedrich Wilhelm IV (d. 1861) is interred in a stone capsule between his parents. The marble sarcophagi of Kaiser Wilhelm I (d. 1888) and his wife Augusta (d. 1890) are by Erdmann Encke. The Mausoleum is closed in the winter months.

Adjacent to the palace to the northeast, near the Spree River, stands the **Schinkel-Pavillon**, named after the architect who designed it for Friedrich Wilhelm III as a summer house. Built in 1824-25 under the supervision of Albert Dietrich Schadow, it was based on Villa Chiatamone in Naples, where the king had resided in 1822. A gallery with loggias on all four sides leads around the upper floor. The charming pavilion, a mere fifty-nine by fifty-four feet in area, contains paintings, sculptures, and objects of decorative art from Schinkel's era.

The paths along the Spree pass the Carp Pond and lead to the **Belvedere**, a three-story tea pavilion designed by Carl Gotthard Langhans in 1788. With its oval ground plan, domed roof, and curved projecting bays, the structure is a delightful example of early neoclassical architecture enlivened by reminiscences of the Baroque. Today the Belvedere houses a collection of Berlin porcelain of the eighteenth and nineteenth centuries.

◁ *Bird's-eye view of Schlosspark Charlottenburg. The twin buildings across from the palace on both sides of Schlossstrasse, at the top of the photograph, house the Ägyptisches Museum (left) and the Antikensammlung (right).*

95

82 Ägyptisches Museum

Egyptian Museum
Schlossstrasse 70

One of the world's major collections of Egyptian art. New superlatives will be in order when, as a result of German reunification, it is combined with the important Egyptian collection now in the Bode Museum downtown [No. 18d]. Definitely the most popular attraction: the limestone bust of Queen Nefertiti.

Directly across from Schloss Charlottenburg, where Schlossstrasse begins, stand two imposing, symmetrically arranged, column-and-dome topped buildings that, oddly enough, were originally barracks for a guards regiment (1851-59; architect Friedrich August Stüler). On the island separating the two traffic lanes of Schlossstrasse, Prince Albrecht of Prussia (1809-1872) rides toward the palace in a 1901 **equestrian statue** by Eugen Boermel and Conrad Freyberg. The building to the east and the adjoining former stables are the home of the **Ägyptisches Museum**.

Masterpieces of the collection are exhibited in the main building, arranged according to artistic significance instead of the usual, chronological presentation. This quite unorthodox display has proved extremely popular. By concentrating on highlights, it conveys an overwhelming impression of the refined culture and aesthetic diversity of ancient Egypt. Its prime attraction is the **Bust of Queen Nefertiti**, a limestone sculpture excavated in 1912 at Tell el-Amarna. The same area yielded the plaster head of her husband, King Echnaton (both c. 1340 B.C.).

Other works of the period include a piece known as *Strolling in the Garden*, which represents a young royal couple, and the Stele of Chief Sculptor Bak and His Wife. The *Statues of a Seated Married Couple* are dated to the Fifth Dynasty (c. 2400 B.C.) and the *Statue of Seated Hetepni* to the Sixth Dynasty (c. 2150 B.C.). The *Berlin Green Head* (c. 500 B.C.) is extraordinary in its sculptural quality, as are the many vivid **animal sculptures**, such as the Lion's Head from the temple of Pharaoh Niuserre (c. 2450 B.C.).

The Kalabsha Gate, displayed in the passage to the Marstall (former stables), is a gift of the government of Egypt to the Federal Republic. Its reliefs depict Emperor Augustus as pharaoh offering sacrifices to the Egyptian deities Isis, Osiris, and Mandulis.

In the **Marstall**, the collection is arranged according to cultural and historical

Ägyptisches Museum: Queen Nefertiti, Egypt, 18th dynasty, c. 1340 B.C.

criteria, the objects grouped under such headings as writing implements and manuscripts.

The history of the museum goes back to the late-seventeenth-century collections established by the prince electors of Brandenburg. Prewar home of the museum was the Neues Museum on Museumsinsel [No. 18b]. The collection was split during the war and stored outside the city. Those holdings later returned to West Berlin became the foundation of this museum. The holdings returned to the East make up the Ägyptisches Museum currently exhibited in the Bode Museum [No. 18d]. It is planned to reunite the two branches in their former home when the Neues Museum has been rebuilt, sometime in the late 1990s.

83 Antikensammlung

Collection of Antiquities
Schlossstrasse 1

The decorative arts of ancient Greece and Rome in outstanding examples. A highlight: the finest collection of Scythian gold outside the Community of Independent States (formerly Soviet Union).

The Antikensammlung Charlottenburg is housed in the other former army barracks built by Friedrich August Stüler from 1851 to 1859, twin of the Ägyptisches Museum, at left. Recently reunited, at least administratively, with the Antikensammlung in the Pergamon-Museum [No. 18e], from which it has been separated since World War II, this museum is renowned for its holdings of antique vases. About half the collection of over four thousand vases is here in Charlottenburg, as well as about half of the bronzes and a smaller proportion of the fourteen thousand or so gems and cameos. Most of the collection of antique glassware was lost in the war and has had to be replaced by new acquisitions. The Charlottenburg museum also contains a number of sculptures and ancient weapons. On display in the **Schatzkammer**, or Treasury, in the basement are the finds of Scythian Gold from Vettersfelde, and the Hildesheim Silver Treasure, as well as jewelry from ancient Rome and Byzantium, Roman coins, and mummy portraits. The oldest finds—from Crete and Ancient Greece—bear witness to the heyday of Minoan culture (c. 2200 B.C.).

The holdings may be moved or rearranged in the future.

Bröhan-Museum: Paul Börner, Odalisque with Tucan, *1912. Meissen Porcelain Manufactory*

84 Bröhan-Museum
Schlossstrasse 1 a

Antikensammlung: Amphora of Andokides: Wrestlers in a Palaestra, *c. 525 B.C.*

Art Nouveau and Art Deco in unusual range and quality.

The building in which the museum was inaugurated in 1983 was constructed in 1893 as an infantry barracks. Its precious contents, donated to Berlin by Professor Karl H. Bröhan, were assembled by him from 1966 to 1975—a truly astonishing collection of *objets d'art*, china, glassware, paintings, furniture, and industrial designs in the Art Nouveau and Art Deco styles. The paintings, drawings, and prints are all examples of the Berlin Secession movement, which included the artists Baluschek, Hagemeister, and Jaeckel, as well as Corinth, Leistikow, and Ury.

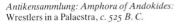
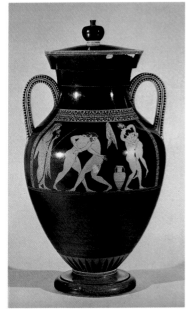

85 Gustav-Adolf-Kirche
Gustav Adolf Church
Brahestrasse/Herschelstrasse

An exemplary specimen of the Neue Sachlichkeit *(New Objectivity) style in Protestant church architecture.*

Architect Otto Bartning made effective use of the corner building site, conceiving the ground plan in the form of an arc segment that converges toward the altar at the south end, where the tower sets a dominant exterior accent. Bartning, who made his reputation with non-traditional ecclesiastic architecture, designed this church in 1925 but had to wait until 1932 to 1934 to see it built. Severely damaged in World War II, it was reconstructed under his supervision from 1950 to 1960.

86 Kirche Maria Regina Martyrum

Church of Maria Regina Martyrum
Heckerdamm 230

A moving memorial to victims of Nazism, designed by two of Germany's finest postwar church architects.

A Catholic "memorial church to those who shed their blood for freedom of religion and conscience between 1933 and 1945," Maria Regina Martyrum was erected from 1960 to 1963 to plans by Hans Schädel, Master Builder of Würzburg Cathedral, and Friedrich Ebert. It consists of a **double church**, an open court with an altar, a community room, and a bell tower. The church is surrounded by high, dark-gray basalt slabs that recall prison walls. A gateway in the **bell tower** leads to the open-air court, which has a capacity of 10,000 worshipers. On the eastern wall of the courtyard, abstract bronze figures by Otto Herbert Hajek symbolize the Fourteen Stations of the Cross. Above the portal of the upper church is a sculpture of the Virgin, *The Woman of the Apocalypse and*

the Seven Serpents, by Fritz Koenig, who also created the Pietà in the **lower church**. In front of the Pietà are the graves of Bernhard Lichtenberg, Provost of Berlin Cathedral, who died in Nazi confinement in 1943, and Erich Klausener, head of the Catholic Action resistance movement, who was murdered in 1934. A third grave is symbolically dedicated to "all martyrs whose final resting place remains unknown." The **upper church** is dominated by Georg Meistermann's mural behind the altar, which represents the vision of the New Jerusalem and the Lamb from the Revelations of St. John.

87 Gedenkstätte Plötzensee

Plötzensee Memorial
Hüttigpfad

A reminder to the living of those who died at this most notorious of Nazi execution sites.

From 1933 to the final days of the war, hundreds of political prisoners and resistance fighters from all over Europe were hung or beheaded in a brick shed near the present site of the **Plötzensee-Jugendstrafanstalt** (Juvenile Penitentiary). A fifty-nine-foot-long wall erected there bears the inscription "Dedicated to the victims of Hitler's dictatorship 1933-1945." To the right of the wall is an urn containing earth from every concentration camp.

In the **Evangelisches Gemeindezentrum** (Protestant Community Center; Heckerdamm 226), drawings by Alfred Hrdlicka on sixteen panels, the *Plötzenseer Totentanz* (Dance of Death, 1970), commemorate the victims.

Gedenkstätte Plötzensee, a memorial to those who died at the hands of the Nazis

Lietzenseepark. At right is the Hotel Seehof

88 Lietzenseepark
Neue Kantstrasse

An urban refuge with all the desirable elements: a lake, lawns, trees, playgrounds, and romantic paths; an example of beautiful landscaping in a constricted area.

Designed by Erwin Barth in 1919-20, the park follows the sinuous path of an Ice Age trough. On the southwestern shore of the lake rises the **Evangelische Kirche am Lietzensee** (Protestant Church on Lietzensee; Herbartstrasse 4-5), built by Paul Baumgarten in 1959, which makes effective use of the inclined terrain. The church, constructed like a tent on a pentagonal ground plan, is shielded from the street by a wall but opens out to the lake at the back, its glazed curtain wall revealing the beauties of the changing seasons. A man-made cascade flows into the lake on the south shore.

Although the park is bisected by Neue Kantstrasse, there is a pedestrian underpass that connects both sections. Idyllically located on the eastern shore is the **Hotel Seehof**, which offers fine dining on a lakeside terrace.

The imposing neo-Baroque building on Witzlebenstrasse, near the park, is the former Imperial Military Court. Built from 1908 to 1910 to plans by Heinrich Kayser and Karl von Grossheim, it now houses the Berlin section of the **Federal Supreme Court.**

St. Canisius, a Catholic church at Witzlebenstrasse 27-29, was the first new church built in Berlin after the war (1954-57; architect Reinhard Hofbauer). Interesting features are a nave that tapers stepwise toward the choir, the free-standing 164-foot-tall bell tower topped by a cross, and the unusual roof construction. The stained-glass windows by Egbert Lammer suffuse the space with mystical light. Berlin's annual Corpus Christi Day processions begin at St. Canisius.

89 Internationales Congress Centrum (ICC)
Messegelände

A huge, imposing structure housing a convention hall that attracts about 400,000 fair and congress participants every year from all parts of the world.

Whatever one's opinion about this idiosyncratic, oblong block measuring 131 by 1,050 by 262 feet and clad entirely in silvery aluminum, the ICC does represent an architectural landmark in Berlin somewhat comparable to the Centre Pompidou in Paris, which was built at about the same time. Designed by Ralf Schüler and Ursulina Schüler-Witte, it was erected between 1973 and 1979.

From the foyer on the north side of the main building, blue and red light paths lead the visitor past a light sculpture to the main stairway and the eighty rooms of various sizes where conferences and meetings are held. Congress Auditorium (Saal 1) seats 5,000, and a second auditorium (Saal

Internationales Congress Centrum and the Funkturm

2) on the other side of the central stage building has a capacity of 2,200. The seats can be raised to the ceiling, leaving a free space for banquets and parties of three to four thousand people. Cultural events take place in a theater equipped with state-of-the-art stage technology. On the plaza to the north is a monumental sculpture, *Alexander the Great Before Ekbatana* (1980), by Jean Ipoustéguy. A three-story bridge connects the ICC with the exhibition park buildings on the opposite side of Messedamm.

90 Messegelände and Sommergarten
Exhibition Park
with Summer Garden
Hammarskjöldplatz

Large exhibition facility hosting international trade shows that attract record attendances.

Almost half a million visitors throng the twenty-five exhibition buildings in late January every year when the International Green Week, Europe's largest food, farm-ing, and gardening show opens its doors. Nearly as many, close to 450,000, come every two years at the end of August to the International Broadcasting Exhibition, a media extravaganza in which purveyors of consumer electronics equipment as well as German and foreign radio and television stations participate. Numerous other annual or biannual fairs are held here (see pp. 183-84.).

The first exhibition halls were built here before World War I. After a fire in 1935, Richard Ermisch designed new buildings that, despite heavy bomb damage during the war, still dominate the grounds today. Further halls were added after 1950. The facility covers a total area of some forty-seven acres, about half of which is indoor exhibition space. Of the grounds, about ten acres are suitable for outdoor exhibitions and shows. The centrally located, oval **Sommergarten** was laid out by Hans Poelzig in 1930 as an extensive flower display. At the north entrance, on Hammarskjöldplatz, stands a monument to Dag Hammarskjöld, winner of the Nobel Peace Prize in 1961, by Werner Düttmann.

its function as transmission tower for West Berlin broadcasting stations to the 755-foot-high mast erected on Scholzplatz, some two miles to the west, and since then it has been used only by police and fire departments.

Right at its base, the **German Radio Museum** (Hammarskjöldplatz 1) was opened in 1967. The history of German broadcasting began in Berlin, when, on October 29, 1923, the country's first radio station transmitted its first wireless announcement from this very site. The museum's seven departments offer a review of the technological development of broadcasting since its inception, supplemented by an amateur radio station and a dummy head recording studio.

92 Haus des Rundfunks
Broadcasting House
Masurenallee 8-14

Germany's earliest broadcasting building, an architecturally convincing, functional, early-1930s structure that is still in use.

Hans Poelzig's 1929 to 1931 broadcasting building has retained its validity to this day. At present the headquarters of the radio division of Sender Freies Berlin (SFB), it was occupied from 1945 to 1956 by the Soviet Military Administration, who established their Berliner Rundfunk here. The ensuing renovation left Poelzig's clinker facade intact and also retained the

91 Funkturm and Deutsches Rundfunkmuseum
Radio Tower and German Radio Museum
Messedamm 11

A Berlin landmark with an observation platform that offers a magnificent panoramic view of the city. Historical site with a small but interesting museum.

"Langer Lulatsch" (Spindly Beanstalk), as the **Funkturm** (490 feet high including antenna) is affectionately known, was erected from 1924 to 1926 for the Third German Broadcasting Exhibition by Hein, Lehmann & Co. to plans by Heinrich Straumer. Sited at the northeastern edge of the exhibition park, it served as a radio mast, an observation tower with restaurant, and an illuminated marker for air traffic. While Berlin's Eiffel Tower is only about half as high as its model, it did set new technical standards in terms of minimal ground area (66 by 66 feet) and low weight (400 tons, as compared to 9,500 for the Eiffel Tower). A lift provides access to the two-floor **restaurant** 180 feet above the ground and to the **observation platform** at 410 feet. In 1962 the structure relinquished

Rundfunkmuseum at Funkturm: the 1930s radio store display

Hans Poelzig's heart-shaped Haus des Rundfunks

Georg-Kolbe-Museum: Georg Kolbe, The Dancer Nijinsky, 1913-19

basic configuration of a heart-shaped complex whose two inwardly curving wings meet at an obtuse angle. Behind the spacious entrance hall, which extends upward over five floors and often hosts art exhibitions, is the Grosser Sendesaal (Grand Auditorium). A two-level bridge links the building with the SFB television studios next door.

93 Friedhof Heerstrasse

Heerstrasse Cemetery
Trakehner Allee 1

One of the most beautifully landscaped cemeteries in Berlin and last resting place of famous artists and writers.

The wooded, terraced grounds of the cemetery surround idyllic **Sausuhlensee** lake. Among the famous Germans buried here are the art dealer Paul Cassirer, the poets Theodor Däubler, Arno Holz, and Joachim Ringelnatz, the writer Maximilian Harden, the actresses and actors Tilla Durieux, Grete Weiser, Victor de Kowa, and Paul Wegener, the playwright Curt Goetz, the architect Werner Düttmann, the artist George Grosz, the conductor Leo Blech, and the sculptor Georg Kolbe.

South of the cemetery, at Sensburger Allee 25, is the **Georg-Kolbe-Museum**. Its comprehensive collection documents the work of the sculptor who once lived here as well as the work of other early twentieth-century Berlin sculptors. Installed outside, in the **Georg Kolbe Grove**, are five larger-than-life bronzes, casts of the artist's plaster models: *Large Kneeling Woman* (1942-43), *Reclining Woman* (1939-41), *Dionysus* (1932), *Large Falling Man* (1939-43), and *Mars and Venus I* (1940). Somewhat farther east, at the corner of Heerstrasse and Preussenallee, is Hugo Lederer's colossal bronze of 1908, *The Wrestler*, standing on a pedestal of shell limestone.

94 Le Corbusier House
Reichssportfeldstrasse 16

"Unité d'habitation"—a landmark of modern housing design by one of the most influential twentieth-century architects.

After Marseille and Nantes, Le Corbusier built his third "housing unit of appropriate size" here in Berlin. The seventeen-story, reinforced-concrete structure, 184 by 443 by 75 feet, was erected from 1956 to 1958 for the Interbau Building Exhibition [see No. 52].

It has 557 apartments of various sizes and arrangement (single or two-level with interior staircase) that are accessible by means of nine "streets" within the building. The 1,500 or so occupants make up a small town of their own, with autonomous power plant, a post office, and a shopping mall. Characteristic of Le Corbusier's anti-rational style is the employment of brilliant primary colors on the balconies and the articulation of the facade by means of continuous balcony railings.

95 Olympia Stadion
Olympischer Platz

Site of the XI Summer Olympics in 1936, and still, at a seating capacity of 96,000, Germany's largest sports stadium. Imposing example of Nazi architecture.

Constructed by Werner March with the collaboration of his brother, Walter March, the stadium was the focus of the *Reichssportfeld* laid out for the 1936 Summer Olympic Games. This was the first sports complex on the European continent designed to encompass all of the athletic disciplines of the day.

The **stadium** with its huge oval (984 by 755 feet) of reinforced-concrete grandstands clad in shell limestone originally had over 85,000 seats and standing room for 35,000. That its exterior height is a mere fifty-four feet at this enormous capacity is explained by the fact that the sports field lies thirty-nine feet below ground level. Two tall pillars mark the Olympic Gate to the east. Installed in front of the south entrance is the old, cracked Olympic Bell, made of ten and a half tons of steel.

Adjacent to the stadium to the north is the **Swimming Arena** (7,600 seats), and farther north, the German Sports Forum

Le Corbusier House. Despite its daring design it shows the limits of Bauhaus ideology

Olympia Stadion. Its sunken playing field permits a low exterior height

of 1926-28, with sculptures by Georg Kolbe, Arno Breker, and Josef Thorak, among others.

The western part of the complex is occupied by the **Maifeld**, open-air festival grounds with a capacity of 500,000, including grandstands for 70,000 spectators. Its 250-foot-high **bell tower** affords a wonderful view of the stadium, the city, and the Havel river and lake district meandering toward Potsdam in the distance.

The **Waldbühne** (Forest Theater), constructed at the same time as the Olympia Stadion in a dell in the Murellen Hills west of the Maifeld, is one of Europe's largest open-air theaters, at a seating capacity of 20,000. It was designed by Werner March along the lines of ancient Greek amphitheaters. Site of Nazi ritual and ceremony in the 1930s and 1940s, it today hosts the blither entertainments of jazz and rock concerts.

Waldbühne, a favorite jazz, pop, and classical music stage in the summer months, with outdoor seating for 20,000

Schöneberg

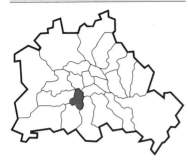

The first written mention of the village of Sconenberch dates to the year 1264, when it figured in a deed of gift from Margrave Otto III to the Benedictine nuns of Spandau. In 1751 Frederick the Great established a settlement for Bohemian weavers next to the old village, the colony of Böhmerberg or Neu-Schöneberg. By 1898 the population of Schöneberg had burgeoned to 75,000, and it received municipal by-laws. When it was incorporated into Greater Berlin in 1920, Schöneberg was merged with the village of Friedenau, founded in 1871. At an area of 4¾ square miles, its present population is 156,000.

Located at Munsterdamm 90 on the "Insulaner," a 250-foot-high, landscaped hill built of war rubble in southern Schöneberg, is the Wilhelm Foerster Observatory. The associated Planetarium at the foot of the hill is one of the most modern in Europe with a dome forty-three feet in diameter.

The famous actress Marlene Dietrich lies buried in the Third Schöneberg cemetery, on Stubenrauchstrasse in Friedenau.

96 Kaufhaus des Westens (KaDeWe)

Tauentzienstrasse 21

The biggest department store on the Continent, with a sales area of 460,000 square feet, where about 80,000 customers a day spend over one and a half million Deutsche Marks.

When Johann Emil Schaudt's building went up in 1906-7, the area around Wittenbergplatz was still purely residential. The store was bought in 1927 by entrepreneur Hermann Tietz of the Hertie chain. It was expanded several times and formed the nucleus of a new shopping district in West Berlin. KaDeWe's food department on the sixth floor is worth a visit by itself. It offers exotic delicacies from all over the world, and anything not in stock can be ordered. KaDeWe's original 1920's exterior is currently being restored.

97 Nollendorfplatz

Two men made this plaza famous—theater director Erwin Piscator and the Anglo-American writer Christopher Isherwood.

Erwin Piscator, director of the Theater am Nollendorfplatz (est. 1906) from 1927 to 1930, rang in a chapter of theater history here that has since become inseparably associated with his name. From 1939 to 1951 he taught his revolutionary technique at the Dramatic Workshop, part of the New School in New York.

The famous KaDeWe food department, a gourmet's paradise

Christopher Isherwood lived from 1919 to 1933 on Nollendorfplatz, at Nollendorfstrasse 17. His novel *Goodbye to Berlin* (1935) provided the basis for the play *I am a Camera* and for the hit musical *Cabaret*.

The former theater, today called **Metropol**, is now one of the largest discotheques in Europe, and a venue of the Jazz festival held in Berlin every November. The square is dominated by the viaduct of U-Bahn Line 1, which is elevated from here to its terminal station at Schlesisches Tor. In the hotel at Motzstrasse 7, Germany's most important Expressionist poet, Else Lasker-Schüler, lived in a tiny back room from 1924 until her emigration to Jerusalem in 1933.

98 Urania

Kleiststrasse 13

A science center with a museum devoted to the history of postal and telephone technology.

The Urania, originally founded in 1888, is dedicated to the dissemination of scientific knowledge in an accessible form. A private association with about 5,000 members, its facility has club rooms, lecture halls, and exhibition space. The Urania hosts lectures, slide shows, and film screenings on scientific research, art, culture, technology, travel, and space exploration.

Located on the first floor is the **Postmuseum Berlin**, the postwar western pendant of the Postmuseum in Mitte district [No. 34]. Highlights of the collection are the telegraph department, broadcasting technology, stamps, a video conference studio, and an exhibition illustrating the history of postal services in Prussia.

99 Heinrich-von-Kleist-Park

Potsdamer Strasse

A delightful little park whose gate, the Königskolonnaden, is a fine example of early Berlin architecture.

Originally, the site of the **park** named after the famous writer was a kitchen garden, which existed here from 1506 to 1679. Next, the Botanical Garden was located here, until it received its present site in 1897 [No. 135].

The **Königskolonnaden** (King's Colonnades) were designed by Carl von Gontard, architect of the towers of the French and German cathedrals on Gendarmenmarkt [No. 33]. Built from 1777 to 1780 to adorn a bridge on Alexanderplatz in Mitte district, they had to make way for automobiles in 1910 and were moved here to provide an impressive foil for the neo-Baroque Kammergericht (Supreme Court) then under construction (1909-13; architects Paul Thoemer and Rudolf Mönnich).

Heinrich-von-Kleist-Park, Gontard's Königskolonnaden frame a view of the Kammergericht

Rathaus Schöneberg. A replica of the Philadelphia Liberty Bell hangs in the tower

The **Kammergericht** (entrance at Elssholzstrasse 32) was the site of the notorious show trials at which members of the July 20, 1944, resistance group that tried to kill Hitler were condemned to death. Headquarters of the Allied Control Council from 1945, the building witnessed the signing, in 1971, of the Four Power Agreement, which proved so crucial to the security of West Berlin. The bronze statues in front, *Horse Tamers*, are by Peter Jakob Clodt von Jürgensburg. They were presented in 1842 by Czar Nicholas I to his brother-in-law, Friedrich Wilhelm IV, and stood until 1945 on the Lustgarten side of Berlin City Palace.

100 Rathaus Schöneberg
Schöneberg City Hall
John-F.-Kennedy-Platz

Imposing headquarters of the former city of Schöneberg and from 1948 to 1990 seat of the West Berlin government.

A bronze plaque by Richard Scheibe at the main entrance commemorates American President John F. Kennedy's visit to Berlin in 1963. The four-story neoclassical building housing some 340 offices was erected from 1911 to 1914 to the plans of Peter Jürgensen and Jürgen Bachmann. Above the main portal rises a 230-foot-high, square clock tower, which houses a 1950 replica of the famous Liberty Bell in Philadelphia. At eleven and a quarter tons, it is the largest bell in Berlin.

101 Schöneberg Village Church
Hauptstrasse

Sole remaining witness to the reconstruction of Schöneberg after its devastation in 1760 during the Seven Years' War.

The original church, probably medieval in origin, was replaced from 1764 to 1766 by a simple, rural Baroque structure with a dome-capped tower. Burned out in World War II, the interior was renovated in 1955. Adorning the altar is the tombstone of Grand Commander Claus von Bach, a significant piece of 1521 from Nuremberg that was originally located in the Franciscan Monastery Church in Mitte district [No. 11].

Wilmersdorf

The name derives from that of a noble family, the von Wilmestorffs, who owned the village and neighboring community of Schmargendorf in the fifteenth century. In about 1650 it came into the possession of Prince Elector Joachim Frederick, who moved a school he had founded in 1607, the Joachimsthal Gymnasium, to Wilmersdorf, where it remained until 1912. The former school building (Bundesallee 1-12) with its attractive facade is a fine example of Schinkel-school late neoclassicism, enlivened by stylistic borrowings from Italian Renaissance villas and palaces. It was erected between 1876 and 1880 to plans by Johann Heinrich Strack. Wilmersdorf received municipal by-laws in 1906 and was incorporated into Greater Berlin in 1920. Forty-three percent of the district's total area of thirteen and a quarter square miles is open space, covered by woods and parks.

102 Schaubühne am Lehniner Platz
Kurfürstendamm 153

Brilliant star of the German drama scene, an experimental stage with actors and directors of international repute.

The story of the Schaubühne is indissolubly tied to its first dramatic and artistic director, Peter Stein (who since 1985 has appeared here as guest director only). It began as a group of students who, in opposition to Berlin's state-owned theaters, established themselves in 1962 in an old building in Kreuzberg to put on von Horváth, Fleisser, Sperr, Hacks, Lange, Weiss—and above all, Brecht, who at the time was still very much a pariah in West Berlin.

Stein joined the troupe in 1970, bringing with him gifted young unknowns like Bruno Ganz, Edith Clever, Jutta Lampe, and Otto Sander—actors and actresses now at the top of their profession. The troupe needed a home, and in 1975 the city fathers agreed to a conversion of the former Universum Cinema on Lehniner Platz (1926-28), a building by the famous architect Erich Mendelsohn. The outward form of the cinema was retained by installing the three separate stage areas divided by hydraulic partitions in a deep underground space. Completed in 1981, the Schaubühne's flexibility with respect to

Schaubühne, one of Germany's finest theater companies

stage and auditorium configuration is perhaps without parallel anywhere in the world, and as far as the quality of its acting and productions goes, the troupe has become a byword in theater circles.

103 Freie Volksbühne
Schaperstrasse 24

A theater with an unusual past, spawned by the labor movement and long associated with the political avant-garde. Its premiere of Hochhut's The Representative, *directed by Erwin Piscator, made drama history in the year the theater opened.*

This theater shares part of its history with the Volksbühne [No. 8] in Mitte district. Founded in 1890 with the aim of creating stage productions that would reflect the interests of working people, the company was originally located on Rosa-Luxemburg-Platz. The theater association was forcefully disbanded in 1933. In 1947 it was reestablished in West Berlin as Freie Volksbühne (Free People's Theater).

Fritz Bornemann designed the new facility in 1962-63 along lines similar to those of his building for the Deutsche Oper [No. 78]—an unadorned, rectangular structure with steel and concrete skeleton and glazed facade.

104 Evangelische Kirche am Hohenzollernplatz
Protestant Church on Hohenzollernplatz
Hohenzollerndamm 202-3

A superb example of Expressionist church architecture.

The church was erected from 1930 to 1933 to plans by Fritz Höger. Höger was one of the most important proponents of Expressionism in German architecture and is best known for his Chile-Haus in Hamburg. This church, a concrete skeleton construction with a copper-clad roof and slender, angular spire, caused a sensation when it was built. Höger's predilection for hardfired brick is very much in evidence in the facade design, which is enlivened by decorative elements such as gilded bricks and joints. The rigorously geometric exterior contrasts sharply with the interior, which is dominated by thirteen Gothic-inspired pointed arches. Its solemn, even mystical atmosphere distinguishes it from the austere plainness of most Protestant church interiors of the period.

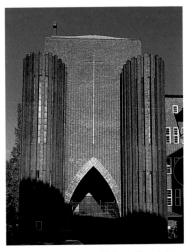

Evangelische Kirche am Hohenzollernplatz

105 Christi-Auferstehungs-Kathedrale
Christ Resurrection Cathedral
Hohenzollerndamm 166

Berlin's metropolitan character has long been reflected in the diversity of its religious congregations and the unique styles of their church architecture.

The **Russian Orthodox Church of Christ's Resurrection**, a central-plan structure with a round, domed tower in the center and onion domes at the corners, was designed in the old Russian Novgorod style and consecrated in 1938.

West front of the Russian Orthodox Christi-Auferstehungs-Kathedrale

Nearby, at Brienner Strasse 7-8, stands the **Mosque** of the Pakistani Ahmadiyya Congregation. Topped by an onion dome and two minarets, it was built by H. A. Herrmann from 1924 to 1927 in the Indian Moghul style. The building is accessible to non-Moslems.

106 Teufelsberg

Teufelsseechaussee

Popular winter-sports center and one of Berlin's highest hills (377 feet).

It took nearly nine hundred million cubic feet of war rubble to construct this 270-acre artificial landscape in Grunewald Forest. The north slope of Teufelsberg (Devil's Mountain) offers two ski jumps equipped with snow-making gear and a sled run. The neighboring, 361-foot hill is popular with hang-gliding enthusiasts in the summer months. From the foot of Teufelsberg it is about a fifteen minute walk in a southwesterly direction to **Teufelssee**, a beautiful lake and nature preserve.

The signals and radar base on top of Teufelsberg

Also in Grunewald Forest, farther west on the riverside road Havelchaussee, is the **Grunewaldturm** (Grunewald Tower), from whose lookout 345 feet above the Havel River you can see all the way to Potsdam and Spandau in clear weather (once you have braved the 204 steps to the top). The brick structure was erected on 260-foot-high Karlsberg in 1897, in memory of Kaiser Wilhelm I. Its designer, Franz Heinrich Schwechten, based it on the medieval city towers once common in the region. A further attraction is a terrace restaurant to which special excursion buses ply from Bahnhof Zoo in the summer season.

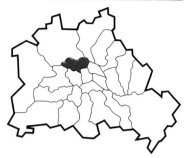

Wedding

A factory and working-class residential district dominated by the plants of companies like Osram (light bulbs) and Schering (pharmaceuticals). The German General Electric Corp., AEG, also once had its headquarters here; its plant, including Peter Behrens's pioneering industrial buildings of 1910-12, still stands southeast of Humboldhain Park. Shut down in 1983, the buildings now house other companies. A sight of interest on Brunnenstrasse is a factory gate of 1896, designed by Franz Heinrich Schwechten in the style of the northern German *Backsteingotik* (Brick Gothic) and characterized by pointed towers flanking the arched gate. The Gesundbrunnen district, part of Wedding today, was once a spa, built in the eighteenth century on a natural spring supposedly discovered by King Frederick I. The spa closed in the late nineteenth century when the healing waters ceased to flow.

The villages of Wedding and Gesundbrunnen have been part of Berlin since 1861. In 1920 they and their outlying communities were incorporated as Wedding district into Greater Berlin. During the 1920s the two German labor parties, SPD and KPD, were so strongly represented here that they earned the district the nickname of "Red Wedding." Not without its amenities, the district boasts one of the city's largest and loveliest parks, Volkspark Rehberge, which extends over an area of 212 acres.

107 Nazarethkirche

Nazareth Church

Leopoldplatz

The only suburban church by Karl Friedrich Schinkel whose exterior has survived in its original state.

Nazarethkirche is one of four small Schinkel-designed churches built from 1832 to 1835 in the rapidly expanding industrial suburbs of northern Berlin. His Elisabethkirche in Mitte district was destroyed in World War II, though its ruins still stand [see No. 44]. The others are Paulskirche, on the corner of Bad- and Pankstrasse in the Gesundbrunnen section of Wedding district, and St.-Johannis-Kirche, on Alt-

Nazarethkirche

Prenzlauer Berg

With a population of 143,000 and an area of four and a quarter square miles, the Prenzlberg, as it is also called, is the most densely populated district in former East Berlin. At the beginning of the nineteenth century only a hundred people lived here: small farmers who worked the loamy soil.

Like nearby Wedding, Prenzlauer Berg developed into a typical working-class district with five-story tenement blocks made up of a front and one or more rear buildings separated by courtyards. Beginning in the 1960s the district became a haven for young dissidents, writers, artists, and bohemians—a Berlin Montmartre. Old, abandoned buildings were converted into studios, galleries, and alternative performance spaces.

The three main thoroughfares slicing through the district in a northerly or northeasterly direction are the Greifswalder Strasse, Prenzlauer Allee, and—the most interesting one, since it is the main commercial avenue of the district—the Schönhauser Allee, planted with linden and chestnut trees in 1743.

Moabit in Tiergarten district. Unlike them, Nazarethkirche has not been enlarged or had its exterior significantly altered since its construction. An unpretentious masonry structure with round-arch portal and projection pediment, it conveys an unadulterated impression of Schinkel's inimitable sense of proportion. The round arches in the nave and the semicircular apse reveal the stylistic influence of North Italian Romanesque architecture. The church serves as a community center, and its interior has been altered for this purpose. Services are held in the new Nazarethkirche to the rear, which was designed by Max Spitta between 1889 and 1893.

Sidewalk racers in Prenzlauer Berg

Interior of the Synagogue on Rykestrasse

The Jewish Cemetery on Schönhauser Allee

Typical facades on Wörtherstrasse

108 Schönhauser Allee

Today as in the Middle Ages the main link to the villages of Pankow and Nieder-schönhausen and to the palace there, the onetime residence of Frederick the Great's wife.

A monument (1892) on **Senefelderplatz**, a square near the intersection with Kollwitz-strasse, is dedicated to Alois Senefelder, the inventor of lithography. On the east side of Schönhauser Allee, just beyond Senefelderplatz, is the **Jüdischer Friedhof** (Jewish Cemetery), designed by Friedrich Wilhelm Langerhans, and laid out in 1827. Well-known personalities from politics, business, and the arts and sciences of nineteenth- and twentieth-century Berlin are buried here, such as the composer Giacomo Meyerbeer (1791-1864), the publisher Leopold Ullstein (1826-1899), the literary historian Richard Moritz Meyer (1860-1914), and the painter Max Lieber-mann (1847-1935).

Nearby, in a park on Belforter Strasse, stands one of the district's symbols, a round **water tower** that was part of Berlin's first waterworks, built between 1853 and 1856 and used until 1915. Slightly to the north, in the rear court of Rykestrasse 53, is a **synagogue**, built in 1903-4 by Johann Hoeninger. It is one of the few that was not completely destroyed during the pogrom on the night of November 9, 1938. At Kollwitzplatz, one block west of the

synagogue, stands the **Käthe Kollwitz Monument**, created by Gustav Seitz in 1958 from one of the artist's self-portraits. A limestone copy of Kollwitz's sculpture *The Mother* stands in front of Kollwitz-strasse 25, site of the house where the politically engaged artist and her husband, who was a doctor to the poor in the district, lived from 1891 to 1943.

The **U-Bahn** along Schönhauser Allee, which opened in 1913, emerges from below ground beyond Senefelder Platz station and continues as an elevated railway on a steel track, colloquially referred to as "the magistrate's umbrella" because of its distinctive look. The elevated **stations** Eberswalder Strasse and Schönhauser Al-lee, designed by Alfred Grenander and J. Bousset, have essentially survived in their original form.

109 Gethsemanekirche

Gethsemane Church
Stargarder Strasse 77

One of the important sites in Berlin's most recent history: Meeting place of dissidents who led the uprising against the Communist regime in 1989.

Erected by August Orth between 1891 and 1893 in the Rhenish style of the thirteenth century, this cruciform church has a star-tlingly massive octagonal interior, enclosed by arcade-supported stone galleries.

Gethsemanekirche on Stargarder Strasse

The **Augustinuskirche** at Dänenstrasse 17-18, built in 1927-28 by Josef Bachem and Heinrich Horvatin, has an unusual choir and an expressive color scheme.

110 Zeiss-Grossplanetarium
Zeiss Planetarium
Prenzlauer Allee 80

One of the technologically best-equipped planetariums in Europe.

Located not far from the S-Bahn station Prenzlauer Allee, the Planetarium was built from 1985 to 1987. Its exterior dome is some ninety-eight feet in diameter and encloses a projection dome that is over seventy-five feet in diameter. It can accommodate 292 visitors in its astronomy demonstrations.

On Greifswalder Strasse, in the park named after him, is a **monumental bust** of Ernst Thälmann, a 1986 work by the Russian sculptor Lew Kerbel. Thälmann, a Communist leader, was assassinated by the Nazis in 1944. This bust was the last large monument of a political nature to be put up in the former German Democratic Republic.

111 Fruchtbarkeitsbrunnen
Fountain of Fertility
Arnswalder Platz

Monumental, late-1920s fountain.

Hugo Lederer's red, porphyry fountain, created between 1927 and 1934, faces a congested bypass road, Breitscheidstrasse. The figural groups symbolizing fertility culminate in two powerful bulls, giving the fountain its popular name "Stierbrunnen" (bull fountain). The monumentality of the installation recalls the artist's famous Bismarck Monument in Hamburg.

The Zeiss-Grossplanetarium, one of the most modern facilities of its kind in Europe

Friedrichshain

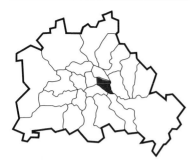

At 3¾ square miles the smallest district in former East Berlin, Friedrichshain was a working-class neighborhood housing a population of 350,000 until World War II, when more than half of the area was destroyed. Today only about 108,000 people live here. The district extends east from downtown Berlin, between the northern bank of the Spree and the northern edge of Volkspark Friedrichshain. The main east-west axis is the long avenue formed by Karl-Marx-Allee and its continuation, Frankfurter Allee. At the edge of the district is the neo-Gothic Bartholomäus-kirche (St. Bartholomew's Church, Friedenstrasse 1), built between 1854 and 1858 to designs by Friedrich August Stüler, and reconstructed in a simplified form after World War II.

Postwar construction along Karl-Marx-Allee reflects the transformations in the Communist view of architecture: from the purely functional to a historical revival mode and back again to rational construction. The conspicuous towers on Strausberger Platz typify Stalinist architecture; the fountain (1967) in the middle of the square is by Fritz Kühn. The Kosmos-Film-Theater at Karl-Marx-Allee 131a, built in 1961-62, is characteristic of the period that followed the historical revival. The high-rises across the street, with their projecting rotundas facing the Frankfurter Tor, on the other hand, were influenced by the Berlin neoclassical tradition of Gontard's domed cathedral towers on Gendarmenmarkt [No. 33]. They were built between 1957 and 1960.

Karl-Marx-Allee and Frankfurter Allee (pre-1961 site of a Stalin monument and called Stalin-Allee) document the rigorous implementation of large-scale urban planning, inspired by Russian models, at the expense of the historic, smaller structures. Karl-Marx-Allee was the setting for official parades in the German Democratic Republic up to the fortieth anniversary ceremonies of the country just before its demise in 1989.

---

112 Volkspark Friedrichshain
Friedrichshain People's Park
Am Friedrichshain

A public garden rich in tradition, newly laid out after its destruction in World War II.

The park was begun in 1840 to commemorate the one-hundredth anniversary of Frederick the Great's accession to the throne. Conceived as an eastern counterpart to the Tiergarten, the 128-acre park is the largest and also the oldest in the eastern city center. Its western section was laid out between 1846 and 1848 by Peter Joseph Lenné, the eastern section by his pupil Gustav Meyer between 1874 and 1876. On the western edge of the park is the neo-Baroque **Märchenbrunnen** (Fairy Tale Fountain). Created in 1913 by Ludwig Hoffmann, it displays characters drawn from Grimm's fairy tales. The extravagant installation is characteristic of the grandeur popular during the reign of Wilhelm II.

Postwar additions to the park include two hills created from war rubble and offering fine views. The park borders on a twenty-acre sports and recreation center.

South of the park is a **cemetery** for those who died in the revolutions of March 18, 1848, and November 1918.

Volkspark Friedrichshain, the Fairy Tale Fountain

Kreuzberg

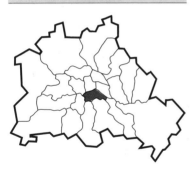

With a population of 154,000 and an area of four square miles Kreuzberg is the most densely populated district in all of Berlin. Crowded as it is today, it is difficult to imagine what Kreuzberg was like in 1939 when it had more than twice as many inhabitants, some 332,000. Kreuzberg is Berlin's most colorful district. Thirty percent of the population is made up of native Turks, Greeks, and Yugoslavs. They live among the students, artists, bohemians, and others who were drawn to Kreuzberg's relatively inexpensive tenement apartments and lively counterculture scene.

Topographically, Kreuzberg is characterized by the elevated tracks of U-Bahn Line 1 and by the Landwehr Canal, which cuts through the entire length of the district. Also typical are the many erstwhile factory lofts in back tenements that have been converted into studios and experimental theaters. Kreuzberg is the site of many buildings erected as part of the IBA International Building Exhibition in 1984/87 that drew such noted architects as Aldo Rossi, Peter Eisenman, Charles Moore, and James Stirling.

II3 Martin-Gropius-Bau
Stresemannstrasse 110

Important late Schinkel-school building and one of Berlin's most beautiful exhibition spaces, site of historical collections and major international travelling exhibitions.

Built for the Royal Museum of Decorative Art, this superbly proportioned neo-Renaissance building by Heino Schmieden and Martin Gropius, a great uncle of the famous Walter Gropius, was erected from 1877 to 1881. The building suffered considerable bomb damage in World War II and was painstakingly restored from 1979 to 1981. Schinkel's Bauakademie (Architecture Academy; no longer extant) served as a model for Gropius's design.

Center of the structure is a spacious interior court surrounded by arcaded galleries. Present occupants of the museum are the **Berlinische Galerie**, which concentrates on the history of Berlin art and culture from the nineteenth century to the present day; the **department of Judaica** of the Berlin Museum [No. 118]; and the **Werkbund-Archiv**, a collection of twentieth-century design.

Adjacent to the Martin-Gropius-Bau on the rubble lot of **Prinz-Albrecht grounds** is a documentation of the sites nearby where, from 1933 to 1945, several Nazi terror organizations had their headquarters: the Gestapo in the former School of Applied Art, the SS in the Prinz Albrecht Hotel, and the Reich Security Bureau in Prinz Albrecht Palace. The buildings have all been demolished, but the Gestapo cellars, where countless people were tortured, have been excavated and preserved as a reminder of a moral and political nadir in German history of the not-so-distant past. The documentation **"Topographie des Terrors"** is housed here.

Martin-Gropius-Bau

Martin-Gropius-Bau, interior court

Ruins of the Anhalter Bahnhof

II4 Former Anhalter Bahnhof

Anhalt Station
Askanischer Platz

Ruins of the main entrance are the sole witness to what was once Berlin's largest and most famous rail terminal, setting of red-carpet receptions for emperors and tyrants.

Anhalter Bahnhof was built from 1874 to 1880 to the plans of Franz Schwechten, a collaborator of Martin Gropius. It was an imposing, arcaded Renaissance-revival structure, whose design was based on the station that set the standard for all of Berlin's railway terminals, Hamburger Bahnhof in Tiergarten district [No. 47].

Heavily damaged during the last war, the station ruins were demolished in 1961, leaving only the truncated portal. The future use of the huge lot, which became a prime downtown site when the Wall went down, is still under discussion.

II5 Hebbel-Theater

Stresemannstrasse 29

Berlin's sole remaining Art Nouveau theater.

Hungarian-born architect Oskar Kaufmann designed three theaters for Berlin: the Hebbel-Theater (1907-08), the Volksbühne [No. 8], and the Renaissance-Theater [see No. 76]. With the Hebbel-Theater he created a pure Art Nouveau building whose soaring facade conceals a series of small, intimate rooms (box office, ground-floor and main foyers, auditorium). Their warm atmosphere is underscored by panelling in a variety of woods. The beautiful auditorium seats 800, and owes its continued existence to the donations of a dedicated group of theatergoers.

II6 Museum für Verkehr und Technik

Museum of Transportation and Technology
Trebbiner Strasse 9

One of Germany's best technological museums, located on the site of old Berlin railroad yards.

The museum's fine collections cover road and rail transport as well as practically every branch of technology from household appliances to heavy machinery (the latter, when necessary, in the form of fine models). Special attractions are the **Versuchsfeld**, an experimental lab on the first floor of the main building where various apparatus are available for hands-on operation, and the impressive collection of steam engines. First opened in 1983, the museum continues to expand. A large **mural** on the side wall of the building shows how the complex will look when it is completed.

Museum für Verkehr und Technik

117 Checkpoint Charlie
Zimmer-/Friedrichstrasse

Until 1989 crossing point from West to East Berlin for non-Germans, Allied military personnel, and diplomats.

Relics of the Wall line the street, though they give only a very incomplete impression of the erstwhile barrier with its wire fences and guard towers overlooking a desolate no-man's-land. It is planned to leave sections of the Wall standing at other points in town, as protected national monuments, while the Haus am Checkpoint Charlie, at Friedrichstrasse 44, is a museum on the history of the Wall. The post-modern building at the corner of Kochstrasse that houses part of the museum was built by the American architect Peter Eisenman for the 1984/87 IBA International Building Exhibition.

118 Berlin Museum
Lindenstrasse 14

A lovely Baroque building erected during the reign of Frederick William I. A welcome architectural accent in a district now under redevelopment, and the perfect place for a review of Berlin history.

Erected in 1734-35 to plans by Philipp Gerlach, the three-winged Baroque structure initially served as Berlin's first administrative headquarters. Its original purpose is reflected in the personifications of Justice and Mercy on the pediment of the main facade. Until 1913 the building housed the Royal Supreme Court (which then moved to new premises on Kleist-Park, see No. 99), where the famous writer and composer E. T. A. Hoffmann served as a councillor. Severely damaged in World War II, it was reconstructed from 1965 to 1967.

Museum für Verkehr und Technik: Locomotive 17008, Type S 10, by Schwartzkopff, 1911

Berlin Museum

The Berlin Museum, founded in 1962, opened its doors here in 1969. Conceived as a complement to the Märkisches Museum on Köllnischer Park [see No. 13], its collections illustrate many facets of Berlin's history from the sixteenth century to the present day. Part of the museum's collection of Judaica is shown here, the other part is exhibited in the Martin-Gropius-Bau [No. 113] until a planned extension is built. A merger of the Berlin Museum and the Märkisches Museum is under discussion.

Berlin Museum: Lovis Corinth, Self-Portrait, *1900*

119 Mariannenplatz
Mariannenplatz

Center of "Little Istanbul," as Kreuzberg is also known: the district is the largest Turkish city outside Turkey.

The lovely oblong **park** was designed in 1853 by Peter Joseph Lenné, and it has been restored according to his original plan. On its western side, at Mariannenplatz 2, is the **Künstlerhaus Bethanien**. A hospital until 1970 (designed by Ludwig Persius and Theodor Stein and built from 1845 to 1847), today it serves the Kreuzberg district as an arts center, with studios, a printmaking workshop, and exhibition spaces. The **Fontane Apotheke**, a room in the former hospital named after the writer Theodor Fontane who worked here as a young druggist in 1848-49, houses the District Archive (Heimatarchiv) and the Namik Kemal Library, the only Turkish library in Berlin.

   St.-Thomas-Kirche, on the north side of the park, is an attractive historical revival church, a fine example of the mixing of styles popular at the time of its construction, from 1864 to 1869. It was designed by Friedrich Adler, a student of Schinkel. Severely damaged in World War II, its reconstruction was completed in 1963.

   Among the statues in the park is the Monument to the War Dead of the Berlin Fire Department (1960), by Dietrich Wolff and Guido Jendritzko.

Facades on Chamissoplatz ▷
A Turkish wedding
A second-hand store

Mehringplatz, modern architecture around a Baroque circle

120 Mehringplatz

Synthesis of Baroque layout and modern residential architecture.

This circular plaza, laid out in 1730 at what was then the southern edge of the city, was originally the junction of three streets converging from the north (Wilhelm-, Friedrich-, and Lindenstrasse). To commemorate the victory over Napoleon, Christian Gottlieb Cantian created the sixty-two-foot-high **column** (1843) topped with a bronze Victory by Christian Daniel Rauch that rises at the center of the roundel. To the south stand two neoclassical female figures, *Peace* (1879) by Albert Wolff and *Clio Recording the History of the Wars of Liberation* by Ferdinand Hartzer.

Postwar reconstruction of the plaza was carried out from 1969 to 1975 by Werner Düttmann, based on an award-winning design by Hans Scharoun. The resulting **circular residential development** consists of a three-story inner ring and a five-story outer ring of buildings. The high-rise to the west, a staggered structure reaching fifteen stories, houses an insurance company (architects Scharoun and Bodo Fleischer).

121 Amerika-Gedenkbibliothek
American Memorial Library
Blücherplatz 1

With over 1.2 million books lent annually, the largest central library of its kind on the Continent.

The Amerika-Gedenkbibliothek is Berlin's central public library. It was established by a foundation to thank the United States for the Berlin Airlift, which saved the city during the blockade of 1948-49. Inspired by British and American libraries, it was designed by Fritz Bornemann, Gerhard Jobst, Willy Kreuer, and Hartmut Wille and built from 1952 to 1954. The library holds over a million volumes, including sheet music, records, and tapes.

122 Cemeteries at Hallesches Tor
Zossener Strasse

Several adjoining cemeteries, the most important burial grounds in the western part of the city: resting place of famous men and women of the eighteenth and nineteenth centuries, with gravestones in early neoclassical to Art Nouveau styles.

Amerika-Gedenkbibliothek, Berlin's main public library

Cemeteries at Hallesches Tor: fine old tombstones and graves of famous Berliners.
E. T. A. Hoffmann's grave (left)

The oldest cemetery, Jerusalemkirchhof I, was laid out in 1735 as a paupers' graveyard for the Friedrichstadt Congregation and a burial ground for the Bohemian Congregation. Stone walls separate the individual cemeteries of the extensive complex, those of the Dreifaltigkeits-(Trinity), the Jerusalem and New Church, Böhmische (Bohemian), and Brüder (Brethren) congregations, a total of about 80,000 graves.

To list only a few of the famous persons buried here: the architect David Gilly; poets Adelbert von Chamisso and E. T. A. Hoffmann; composer Felix Mendelssohn-Bartholdy as well as his parents and his sister Fanny with her husband, the artist Wilhelm Hensel; Henriette Herz, who was famed for her literary salon; theater architect Carl Ferdinand Langhans; and the writer-couple Karl August and Rahel Levin Varnhagen von Ense. A memorial commemorates the two most important artists at the court of Frederick the Great, architect Georg Wenzeslaus von Knobelsdorff and painter Antoine Pesne.

Riehmers Hofgarten, elegant 19th-century residential architecture

123 Riehmers Hofgarten
Yorckstrasse 83-86

Fine example of late-nineteenth-century Berlin residential architecture, with multiple interior courts and access drives that make the complex a small city unto itself.

After the founding of the German Empire, Berlin began to burst at the seams, its population burgeoning from 823,000 in 1871 to 1.9 million in 1900. The result was a building boom in which tenements with as many as three back buildings rose overnight, especially in the Kreuzberg district. Master mason Wilhelm F. A. Riehmer built about twenty four- and five-story apartment houses for the well-to-do between 1881 and 1892, first on Hagelberger Strasse, then along Grossbeerenstrasse, and finally on Yorckstrasse. The buildings are grouped around landscaped courtyards connected by interior drives. A particularly fine facade with a decorative round-arched portal is to be seen on Yorckstrasse.

124 Victoriapark and Kreuzberg Hill
Kreuzbergstrasse

None of Karl Friedrich Schinkel's architectural or sculptural creations has inspired as much patriotic sentiment or been infused with more sacred symbolism than the hilltop monument in this park.

Rising at the peak of the 217-foot-high Kreuzberg, the **National Monument in Commemoration of the Wars of Liberation** (1813-15) is a Gothic tabernacle in miniature, cast by the Royal Iron Foundry and erected from 1818 to 1821. At a mere sixty-six feet in height, it is small in relation to the Gothic cathedral Schinkel had originally planned for the site. Its material recalls the financial sacrifices made by the population under the motto "I gave gold for iron" during the Napoleonic Wars, and its form evokes a reliquary shrine. The twelve niches contain statues by Rauch, Tieck, and Wichmann that represent military commanders and members of the royal family, and at the same time symbolize key battles. The name of both hill and district—Kreuzberg—derives from the Iron Cross at the peak of the monument. **Victoriapark** was laid out around the hill between 1888 and 1894 with a waterfall, sled run, and enclosures for animals. Statues of patriotic poets and writers are placed around the slope, and at the foot of the waterfall is a bronze group, *The Rare Catch*; all date from the 1890s.

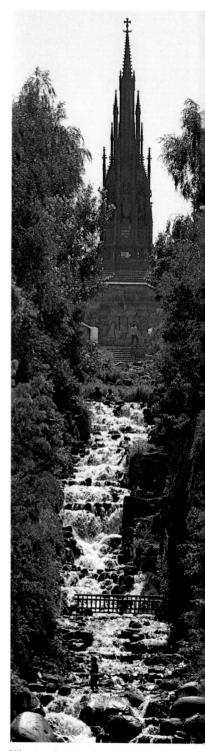

Viktoriapark at Kreuzberg: the National Monument and man-made waterfall

Outer Districts

Neukölln and Tempelhof

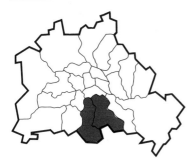

Both of these districts are primarily residential—from urban tenements and high-rises to vestiges of rural villages—with a bit of industry mixed in. They have similar histories, both districts having been settled in the Middle Ages. The district of Neukölln is home to 307,000 people, who live in the former town of Neukölln or one of the

former villages: Britz, Buckow, and Rudow, all settled in the thirteenth century. Neukölln, for its part, was founded in 1874 from an amalgamation of two villages, one of which was sold to the cities of Berlin and Cölln in 1435 by the Knights of St. John. The other was founded in 1737 by Bohemian Hussites. The total area of the district is 17¼ square miles, 31.8 percent of which is built up; nearly 1,500 acres are used agriculturally. The district's largest park is on Mohriner Allee in the southwest: Britzer Garten, a landscaped terrain with artificial lakes and charming cafés built for the 1985 national garden show.

Tempelhof, as well as its incorporated former villages of Mariendorf and Marienfelde, was founded by the Knights Templar Order in the early thirteenth century. The dissolution of the order in 1312 brought the territory into the possession of the Knights of St. John, who sold it in 1435 to Berlin-Cölln. In 1920 Tempelhof, Mariendorf, Marienfelde, Lichtenrade, and the western part of Buckow were incorporated as Tempelhof district into Greater Berlin. 188,000 people live here today in an area of 15¾ square miles.

125 Flughafen Tempelhof and Luftbrückendenkmal
Tempelhof Airport and Airlift Monument

Berlin's main airport from 1923 to 1975—a historic site. Supply base during the 1948-49 blockade and Airlift.

In the final years of the nineteenth century these grounds witnessed some of man's earliest attempts to fly, and in 1908 the Wright Brothers demonstrated the world's first motorized aircraft here. The present facility, a typical example of Third Reich architecture, was built to plans by Ernst Sagebiel between 1936 and 1939. It was one of the largest and most significant airports in Germany after 1945 and a hub of European commercial aviation. From 1923 to 1975 almost all of Berlin's civilian and military air transport was based here. Since Tegel Airport went into operation in 1975, traffic at Tempelhof has decreased.

The striking sculpture on the plaza in front of the terminal is the **Airlift Monument**, designed in 1951 by Eduard Ludwig. The three westward-pointing arcs symbolize the three air corridors across Soviet-controlled territory to West Berlin. In 1948-49 the Western Allies replied to

Tempelhof Airport and Airlift Monument

Volkspark Hasenheide, a favorite public garden

the Soviet government's eleven-month blockade of the city by instituting an air-lift, in the course of which some 250,000 cargo transports landed and took off at Tempelhof—often at intervals of ninety seconds or less.

126 Volkspark Hasenheide
Hasenheide People's Park

A popular park, made famous in Germany by the man who introduced open-air gymnastics here.

Originally a prince's rabbit preserve, Hasenheide was transformed into a land-scaped park by Peter Joseph Lenné in 1838. His lovely gardens were used as an army firing range for a while, and from 1936 to 1939 Hasenheide was made over into a public park with playgrounds, animal enclosures, rhododendron beds, and an open-air theater. Erdmann Encke's 1872 **bronze statue** hints at the reason the park is famous in Berlin: it commemorates Friedrich Ludwig Jahn (1778-1852), known as the Father of German Gymnastics, who opened the country's first public athletic field here in 1811 with the intention of "steeling the national physique" to resist French occupation. A notable feature of the monument is the pedestal, which consists of stone blocks donated by German athletic clubs all over the world.

From **Rixdorfer Höhe**, a 228-foot hill within the park that was built of war rubble, a fine view is to be had of Tempelhof Airport and most of the Kreuzberg and Neukölln districts. Katharina Singer's *Trümmerfrau* sculpture (1955) at the Graefestrasse entrance to the park, a larger-than-life-size seated figure in lime-stone, recalls the countless Berlin women who combed and sorted the rubble of the

devastated city after World War II and without whose backbreaking effort Berlin's reconstruction would hardly have been possible. A companion piece stands in front of Berlin Rathaus [No. 4].

127 Druckhaus Tempelhof
(former Ullstein-Haus)
Tempelhof Printing Building
Mariendorfer Damm 1-3

Landmark of the Tempelhof district and a model of early modern high-rise architecture.

Visible from afar, the thirteen-story, 253-foot-high tower of the Druckhaus Tempelhof was erected from 1925 to 1927 to a

Druckhaus Tempelhof

design by Eugen Schmohl. It was built by Europe's mightiest newspaper and magazine publishers of the day, Ullstein-Verlag. The structure, the first high rise in Berlin to be "cast" in reinforced concrete, is clad entirely in hard-fired brick and accented with details in carved stone. Extended in the 1950s, the building houses several businesses and offices today.

128 Tempelhof and Mariendorf Village Churches
Reinhardtplatz
Mariendorfer Damm

Thirteenth-century churches built by the Order of the Knights Templar.

The village church is the oldest building in the former village of **Tempelhof**, a settlement founded by the Knights Templar in the early thirteenth century. A rough-hewn granite structure with long nave and semicircular apse dating from the latter half of that century, it stands on the foundations of an earlier church from the charter period. Part of the former commandery, it stands some distance away from the village green. A highlight of the furnishings is a 1596 copy by Daniel Fritsch of the St. Catherine Altarpiece in Dresden, painted by Lucas Cranach the Elder in 1506.

Farther south, in **Mariendorf**, the Knights Templar built another ashlar church, this one based on the typical four-part Romanesque plan—apse, choir, nave, and tower—built in the early thirteenth century. The Baroque spire extension was added in 1737. About the mid-sixteenth century three columns and vaulting were

added to the nave. The panels depicting Old Testament scenes (sixteenth to seventeenth century) were originally located in the Heiliggeist-Kapelle in Mitte district [see No. 5].

129 "Hufeisensiedlung"
"Horseshoe Settlement"
Fritz-Reuter-Allee

Berlin's most unusual housing development, a unique configuration designed in the 1920s by Bruno Taut.

The "Hufeisensiedlung," the expansive company town of Siemensstadt in Charlottenburg, "Weisse Stadt" in Reinickendorf, and "Onkel Toms Hütte" in Zehlendorf [No. 143], exemplify public housing design of the 1920s in Berlin. A solution to the acute housing problems of the day was found in row construction which, replacing multistory tenements flush with the street, permitted the building of smaller units with yards and plenty of light and fresh air.

The "Hufeisensiedlung" was nicknamed after the shape of its central structure, a three-story apartment building extending in horseshoe form around a small pond. City building councillor Martin Wagner and architect Bruno Taut collaborated from 1925 to 1927 on a total of 1,027 apartments, 427 of them in single-family houses.

In 1930-31 the development was extended by Taut and Bruno Schneidereit, then expanded again in the 1950s by Eduard Ludwig and Werner Weber, whose structures provide a transition to Gropiusstadt [No. 130].

A facade in the "Hufeisensiedlung," an exemplary 1920s housing development

Gropiusstadt, a controversial public housing development of the 1960s

I30 Gropiusstadt
Fritz-Erler-Allee

A gigantic development with over 17,000 apartments, housing 50,000 people. A collaboration of several renowned architects, it is representative of housing design in Germany during the 1960s.

This huge satellite city of 640 acres was built in several phases from 1964 to 1975. Although based on plans drawn up by the famous Bauhaus architect Walter Gropius in 1960, the final result varies in many respects from his original conception.

Thanks to its horizontal extension and greater architectural diversity, Gropiusstadt does not look quite as forbidding as the equally gigantic Märkisches Viertel in Reinickendorf district to the north. U-Bahn Line 7 has four stations in Gropiusstadt, each with its own shopping center and other amenities. Beginning at the westernmost station, **Johannisthaler Chaussee**, points of interest are a shopping mall (architect Wils Ebert), Martin Luther King Church (Karl Otto), and Am Regenweiher Elementary School (Norman Braun). Near **Lipschitzallee** station are a multipurpose building by Anatol Ginelli, St. Dominicus Catholic Church by Hans Schädel and Hermann Jünemann (1977), and apartment buildings by Gropius himself. A second, multistory shopping center (architect Hans Bandel) is located at **Wutzkyallee** U-Bahn station, as are Helmholtz High School and Martin Lichtenstein Elementary School (Kurt Brohm and Wilhelm Korth). North of Fritz-Erler-Allee is a vivaciously designed elementary school appropriately named after Walt Disney, a reinforced concrete structure by Gerd and Magdalena Hänska. Gropiusstadt ends at **Zwickauer Damm** station.

131 Britz and Buckow Village Churches
Dorf-/Backbergstrasse
Alt-Buckow

Traces of two old Berlin villages surrounding thirteenth-century churches: a glimpse of the region's past.

Both villages were for centuries the property of the von Britzke family. **Britz**, with its village church by a pond, the neoclassical priory, and the schoolhouse, has an interesting historical ensemble at its center. The church, probably dating from the latter half of the thirteenth century, is built on a rectangular plan with a tower and a straight-walled choir to the east. A sepulcher was added to the choir in 1776. The Baroque pulpit-altar, a combination of the two peculiar to the region, is a donation dating from 1720. The modern windows in the choir were added during postwar renovations.

The village church in **Buckow** is one of the loveliest in Berlin. The hamlet and its church, a fieldstone building with long nave and intact, castle-like tower, had its origins in the mid-thirteenth century. Three columns installed at a later date divide the nave into two aisles whose groin vaults are adorned with late-Gothic frescoes depicting scenes from the Passion.

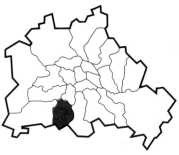

Steglitz

The most popular attractions in this largely residential district are the Schlossstrasse shopping area with its numerous large department stores, and the splendid Botanical Gardens. The first written mention of Steglitz, in 1375, is in the land register of Emperor Charles IV. Yet it wasn't incorporated as a village until 1806, when it had 157 inhabitants. By 1909 Steglitz had grown to a population of 83,000. In 1920 it was combined with the villages of Lichterfelde, Lankwitz, and the suburban development of Südende (est. 1872) to form a district of Greater Berlin with a total area of 12¼ square miles. The present population of Steglitz is 190,000.

The old village green of Lichterfelde along Hindenburgdamm is surrounded by late-nineteenth-century villas. At its northern end is Schloss Lichterfelde (Hindenburgdamm 20, illus. p. 130), a fine neoclassical palace with a pretty park.

132 Marienfelde Village Church
Alt-Marienfelde

Berlin's oldest village church. Stylistically unadulterated late-Romanesque structure on one of the prettiest and best-preserved village greens in the city. Surrounded by fine old farmhouses.

Founded by the Order of the Knights Templar, the rough-hewn granite church is composed of a rectangular nave, an indented choir with semicircular apse to the east, and a broad transept with tower to the west. The saddle roof of the tower is capped with a weather vane dating from 1595. While the church is thought to have been built in 1220, the choir annexes date from the fourteenth and fifteenth centuries. The vestibule at the western portal and the wooden barrel vaults that replaced the original beamed ceiling were added in 1921. Key features of the **furnishings** are a baptismal font of 1624 bearing the red eagle insignia of the city of Cölln, and a globe chandelier dating from the seventeenth century.

133 Lilienthal-Gedenkstätte
Lilienthal Monument
Lilienthalpark

One of the sites where aviation history began: the first man-made airfield in the world.

When Otto Lilienthal and his brother built a fifty-foot-high mound in 1894 and took off in their glider to sail some 110 yards, little did they know that they were creating their own monument. Still, it was not here that the daring engineer met his death, but in the Stöllner Mountains, when he attempted a 330-yard flight. His artificial hill was transformed in 1932 into a cone-shaped monument topped by a globe on which key historical flights are traced. The circular opening in the roof above the globe symbolizes the connection between earth and sky.

The actual **Lilienthal Memorial**, however, is located one and a half miles northwest of here on the eastern banks of the Teltow Canal near Bäkebrücke—a winged Icarus on a twenty-foot pyramidal pedestal created by Christian Peter Breuer in 1914.

Rathaus Steglitz

I34 Schloss Steglitz

Steglitz Palace
Schlossstrasse 48

One of the aesthetically most significant mansions in Berlin.

Architects David Gilly and Heinrich Gentz built the noble neoclassical manor in 1804 for Privy Councillor Carl Friedrich von Beyme. A lovely meander frieze demarcates the two stories of the court facade. At the rear is a portico with four Doric columns topped by a balcony that projects out from the facade in front of a semicircular window. The manor is also known as **Wrangelschlösschen**, named after the popular Prussian Field Marshal von Wrangel (1784-1877), who spent many a

summer here. Restoration is currently under way.

Next door is the intimate **Schlosspark Theater** (476 seats), also by Gentz, originally conceived for musical plays and rustic farces. At present the theater hosts performances by the Schiller-Theater ensemble [No. 77].

Located nearby, at the corner of Schlossstrasse and Grunewaldstrasse, is **Steglitz Rathaus** (City Hall), a brick neo-Gothic medley of pinnacles and bays, battlements and niches designed by Reinhardt and Süssenguth and erected from 1896 to 1898. South of the Rathaus is **Hermann-Ehlers-Platz**, enlivened by a light-and-space sculpture, *Day and Night* (1975), by the English artist Peter Sedgley. The entire area is dominated by the thirty-story office building at the south end of the plaza, Sigrid Kressmann-Zschach's **Steglitzer Kreisel**, which in the 1970s achieved notoriety when its offices proved unrentable.

I35 Botanischer Garten

Botanical Garden
Königin-Luise-Strasse 6-8 and Unter den Eichen 5-10

A 104-acre marvel of landscaping, combining imaginative garden design with scholarly acumen. Germany's largest and most popular botanical garden, with the most extensive plantings arranged by geographical origin in the world.

Berlin has had a botanical garden for over 300 years. More precisely, since 1646, when rare trees and shrubs were planted in the Lustgarten, opposite Berlin City Palace [see No. 15]. From 1679 to 1897 the

Schloss Lichterfelde on Hindenburgdamm (see p. 129)

Botanischer Garten, the Great Tropical House

Botanical Garden was located in Schöneberg, in today's Kleist-Park [No. 99].

The present garden was laid out by Adolf Engler between 1897 and 1903. Economic considerations played a role in the decision to abandon the old site, since Germany's acquisition of African colonies necessitated research on tropical crop plants, and the old botanical garden had no space to build greenhouses.

Devastated during the war, the Botanical Garden's former glory has by now been fully restored. Its renowned **Geographical Section** is a botanical tour around the world: the path begins among the plants of Europe, the German forests, swamp and aquatic plants, and the flora of moors, dunes, and heaths. Then it leads across miniature mountain ranges, from the Pyrenees and the Alps to the Carpathian Mountains, the Himalayas and the Central Asian Altai, each with its typical native plants. Similarly, the flora of Northeast Asia, South Africa, China and Japan, Australia, and the Americas can be explored.

Other attractions are: the **Italian Garden** in front of Victoria-Haus with its delightful fountain; a new **Garden for the Blind** with plants that can be experienced by touch and smell; and the sixteen display houses containing many of the garden's 18,000 species—the orchids, cacti, and car-nivorous plants are particularly popular. The largest greenhouse—the **Großes Tropenhaus**—was destroyed in the war, but has since been rebuilt. 92 feet in height, 197 feet long and 98 feet wide, it is one of the biggest in the world and features a real waterfall and miniature lake inside.

Another point of interest is the **Arboretum**, a plantation of trees and shrubs arranged by genus and family, which is located in the southwestern section of the grounds.

Twenty-nine cultivation houses are devoted to the raising and study of various plant species, with sections for protected species and for useful plants. There are nurseries and a **Botanisches Museum** (entrance on Königin-Luise-Strasse), founded in 1815. Alongside such unusual holdings as plant finds from ancient Egyptian graves, the museum contains a comprehensive specialty **library** and the **General Herbarium**, a collection of over two million prepared plant specimens. Also displayed here are a 4.5-ton slice of an almost 800-year-old California redwood, and a "Tree Organ," designed to help visitors identify Berlin trees by their leaves. Display cases and dioramas illustrate the development and distribution of vegetation across the globe. The Botanical Garden is visited by about 300,000 people annually.

Zehlendorf

Margraves Johann I and Otto III sold the village of Cedelendorp to the Cistercian Monastery of Lehnin in 1242, receiving 300 silver marks. First prosperity came to the village in 1838, when it became a station on the Berlin-Potsdam railroad. At a population of 98,500, Zehlendorf is one of the least populous and least densely settled districts in western Berlin; only 28.5 percent of its 27¼ square miles are built up. The remainder is covered by woods, lakes, parks, and gardens, and 427 acres are used agriculturally.

In 1920 the former village of Dahlem, first mentioned in the records in 1275, was made part of Zehlendorf district. In the possession of the von Wilmestorff family from 1671 to 1799, it was acquired by the Crown Land Office in 1841. Dahlem's autonomous character is most in evidence at the site of its former common (around the Alter Krug Inn), in its fine private homes, superb museums, and the scientific research facilities of the Freie Universität, Technische Universität, and Max-Planck-Gesellschaft.

The southern section of Grunewald Forest (total area 12¼ square miles) is also a part of Zehlendorf, while the northern section lies in Wilmersdorf district. The forest is about three and a half miles wide and five and a half miles long, extending from Heerstrasse in the north to Wannsee in the south.

Grunewald Forest is bisected by the Avus, a freeway opened in 1921 as Germany's first automobile racetrack and subsequently the site of spectacular speed records. The circuit average speed record of 171 mph was established by Bernd Rosemeyer in 1937, and Rudolf Caracciola hit a top speed on the straights of almost 250 mph. The Avus consists of two straight sections some five miles in length and 26 feet in width, connected by the South Curve; the famous, steeply inclined North Curve was sacrificed for the construction of the inner-city *Autobahn* in 1967. Today the Avus is part of Berlin's freeway network, and speed limits have been imposed, prompting many protests. The fastest racetrack in the world, and they expect us to creep along at sixty? Yes, they do, on account of another and sadder Avus record—the accident rate.

East of the Avus, an idyllic chain of lakes extends all the way to Potsdam: Hundekehlsee (18 acres), Grunewaldsee (43 acres), Krumme Lanke (38 acres), and Schlachtensee (77 acres), all connected by a system of canals.

Botanischer Garten,
the Great Tropical House

Museum Dahlem, new wing on Lansstrasse

I36 Freie Universität (FU)
Free University
Boltzmann-/Garystrasse

Germany's first postwar university, established to rival Humboldt Universität in East Berlin.

When the new university began its first courses on Nov. 15, 1948—Berlin's hallowed old Humboldt Universität lay to the east, beyond the demarcation line—its facilities comprised a few abandoned private homes placed pell-mell at the disposal of its departments. The school's various institutes and departments are still scattered all around Dahlem today. A Ford Foundation grant financed the 1952 to 1955 construction of the **Henry Ford Building** (architects Sobotka and Müller), providing an Auditorium Maximum with 1,300 seats, a President's Office, and the University Library. The FU's first new building was the **Mensa** (Commons; Van-t'Hoff-Strasse 6), a rectangular, three-story, steel-and-concrete structure by Fehling and Pfankuch that opened in 1952. The university has expanded since; more recent facilities include the irreverently nicknamed **"Rostlaube"** (Rust Arbor), a complex of intricately connected pavilion-style buildings housing the humanities faculty (Habelschwerdter Allee) that was based on the award-winning design of the Paris architects Candilis, Josic and Woods and erected from 1967 to 1972. Its nickname derives from the brown steel facade. When the second section went up between 1972 and 1979, this time with a shiny aluminum skin, students were quick to dub it the **"Silberlaube"** (Silver Arbor).

The FU has a student body of about 50,000, enrolled in 22 departments and numerous separate institutes.

I37 Museum Dahlem
Arnimallee 23-27/Lansstrasse 8

One of the greatest art collections in Europe, with special collections of world rank.

The Museum Dahlem houses the West Berlin branches of the Gemäldegalerie, the Skulpturensammlung, the Kupferstichkabinett, the Museum für Islamische Kunst, the Museum für Ostasiatische Kunst, the Museum für Spätantike und Byzantinische Kunst, as well as the Museum für Völkerkunde and the Museum für Indische Kunst.

The oldest part of the **museum building** was erected from 1914 to 1921 to designs by Bruno Paul. Before World War II it served merely as a storeroom for the

Museum für Völkerkunde. In 1950 West Berlin installed its art collections here, those objects from the former royal collections housed on Museumsinsel that had been returned to the West after wartime storage. Annexes by Wils Ebert and Fritz Bornemann were built in the 1960s.

The reunification of the Dahlem holdings with those on Museumsinsel [No. 18], decided upon when Berlin was reunified in 1990, will bring a redistribution of the collections throughout the city in its wake. Rearrangement plans, where known, have been listed with each collection.

In front of the Arnimallee entrance stands a bronze Centaur Group (1881) by Reinhold Begas, and at the corner of Arnimallee and Fabeckstrasse, a bronze sculpture of Hercules with the Nemean Lion (1897), by Max Klein.

The **Gemäldegalerie** owns some 1,350 works of European painting from the thirteenth century to the Rococo period, about 700 of which are on display. Exhibited on the ground floor of the old building (entrance on Arnimallee) are thirteenth- to sixteenth-century German, Early Netherlandish, and Italian painting, as well as

Gemäldegalerie: Albrecht Dürer, Hieronymus Holzschuher, *1526*

Skulpturensammlung: Tilman Riemenschneider, St. Matthew from the Münnerstädt Altarpiece, 1490-91

eighteenth-century French and English painting. The upper floor is devoted to Baroque Flemish and Dutch painting, and French and Italian painting of the Baroque and Rococo. Highlights of the museum are the collections of Rubens, Rembrandt (with 21 works, one of the most significant in the world), Raphael, Titian, and of French artists of the eighteenth century, most notably Watteau and Chardin. The other branch of the Gemäldegalerie is housed in the Bode Museum [No. 18d]. Eventually the two branches will be reunited in a new building in the Kulturforum [see No. 56].

The **Kupferstichkabinett** contains one of the world's largest collections of graphic art. It comprises about 35,000 drawings and 380,000 prints dating from the Middle Ages to the present day, 104 illuminated manuscripts, over 400 eleventh- to sixteenth-century miniatures, 190 heraldic albums and sketchbooks, and approximately 1,500 illustrated books of the seventeenth to the twentieth century. In addition, it houses the most extensive Rembrandt collection in the world (150 drawings), and a unique collection of Dürer's drawings and engravings. The Altes Museum [No. 18a] on Museumsinsel currently houses the other branch of the Kupferstichkabinett.

A reunification in new quarters in the Kulturforum [see No. 56] is planned for 1993.

The **Skulpturensammlung** is Germany's finest collection of sculpture. The Museum Dahlem, with about 3,500 objects, houses two-thirds of the original stocks of the pre-war collection, the other holdings are in the Bode Museum [No. 18d], once home of the entire collection. The Dahlem works are arranged in four departments: the **Museum für Spätantike und Byzantinische Kunst** (Late Antique and Byzantine Art); sculpture of 800 to 1800 originating north of the Alps; the Italian Collection, including Gothic marbles and Renaissance and Baroque bronzes; and the Nineteenth-Century Collection, including pieces by Schadow, Rauch, Begas, and others.

The **Museum für Völkerkunde** (entrance on Lansstrasse), the only one of the Dahlem collections that was not originally housed on Museumsinsel, is one of the largest and most interesting ethnological museums in the world. It contains about 453,000 items (393,000 objects of ethnographic interest and 60,000 audio recordings), 141,000 documentary photographs, and 1,000 ethnological films. Officially established in 1873, the museum goes back even further, to the famous Chamber of Art and Rarities founded in the seventeenth century by Frederick William the Great Prince Elector. The museum is divided into eight regional departments: South Seas (Melanesia, Australia, New Guinea, Micronesia, and Polynesia); American Archaeology (Latin America from Mexico to Peru and Northwest Argentina, from about 2000 B.C. to the Spanish conquest in the first third of the

Museum für Islamische Kunst: Stele in the shape of a female head, Yemen, 1st century B.C.

sixteenth century); Indigenous American Peoples (over 50,000 specimens of North and South American Indian art); Africa, Western Asia, Southern Asia, Eastern Asia, and Europe (with the exception of German-speaking regions). There is also a Department of Music Ethnology and a Didactic Division (museums for children and the blind).

Museum für Völkerkunde: permanent exhibition on Africa

135

The **Museum für Indische Kunst** (Indian Art; entrance on Lansstrasse) is the youngest of the State Museums. Founded in 1963, it took over the stocks of the Museum für Völkerkunde in the fields of Indian, Indochinese, Indonesian, and Central Asian art. At about 15,000 specimens it has since become the largest collection of Indian, Nepalese, Tibetan, and Thai art in Germany.

A highlight of the museum is the Turfan Collection, objects discovered in Buddhist caves and temples in Chinese Turkestan during four expeditions carried out from 1902 to 1914. Also noteworthy are the Gandhara works, Greek Buddhist stone reliefs and sculptures dating from the first to the fifth century A.D. and originating from monasteries and chapels in Gandhara, on the Afghanistan border. Not to be missed is the oldest extant bronze statue of the God Vishnu, found in Pakistan and dating from the seventh century A.D.

The **Museum für Islamische Kunst** (Islamic Art; entrance on Lansstrasse) was established by Wilhelm von Bode in 1904. Most of its collection of decorative art is exhibited here, while the architectural fragments and archaeological finds can be seen in the Pergamon Museum [No. 18e]. Postwar acquisitions have substantially enriched the collection, and today the Dahlem museum is considered the most important collection of Islamic art outside the Muslim countries. A move of this branch to the Pergamon Museum is planned.

The **Museum für Ostasiatische Kunst** (East Asian Art; entrance on Lansstrasse) displays art from China, Japan, and Korea. Established in 1906, this department suffered greater war losses than any of the other Berlin State Museums. The collection began after the war with a mere five percent of the prewar holdings. These thankfully included almost the entire collection of Chinese and Japanese painting, a total of 155 works, and large portions of the collection of Korean and Japanese tea ceramics from the bequest of art dealer Tadamasa Hayashi. In 1965 the museum succeeded in acquiring a collection of 150 bronzes from the Ordos region in China (fifth century B.C. to third century A.D.) which is probably unique in Europe. 7,000 works of East Asian graphic art have been transferred here from the Art Library collection. The holdings of the Museumsinsel branch, exhibited in the Pergamon Museum [No. 18e], will be transferred to Dahlem in late 1992.

138 Museum für Volkskunde
Museum for Folklore
Im Winkel 6

Apart from that in Nuremberg, the only folklore collection in Germany of more than regional scope.

A museum of folk art and life in rural Germany: furniture, ceramics, costumes, household goods, textiles, jewelry, as well as models of workshops, such as bakeries, dairies, and spinning rooms, are exhibited here.

Rudolf Virchow, the renowned physician and anthropologist, founded the

Museum für Volkskunde: Chest, Minden-Ravensberg, 1783

Museum of Folk Costume and Household Products, as it was called then, in 1889. His collection was supplemented in 1893 by the objects of popular art that had been brought together for display at the Chicago World's Fair. About 80 percent of the museum's abundant holdings (45,000 items) were lost in World War II. The present museum had its beginning in 1959, when 40 crates containing nearly 3,600 valuable objects were returned to West Berlin from their storage site in Thuringia, formerly East Germany. New acquisitions have increased the scope of the collection, and in 1976 it moved into its current facilities, the former storage tract of the Secret State Archive of Prussian Cultural Holdings.

139 St.-Annen-Kirche
St. Anne's Church
Pacelliallee/Königin-Luise-Strasse

Brücke-Museum: Ernst Ludwig Kirchner, Otto Mueller with a Pipe, 1913

Lovely medieval church with cemetery, in the midst of a well-preserved village core. After 1933, center of the Confessional Church in Germany, under Martin Niemöller.

A simple brick structure on a fieldstone foundation dating from the thirteenth to fourteenth century, St.-Annen has a late-fifteenth-century groin-vaulted choir with large tracery windows that was probably influenced by the choirs of the St. Nikolai churches in Spandau [No. 152] and Berlin [No. 1]. Fragments of frescoes with scenes from the life of Christ and St. Anne, dating from the end of the fourteenth century, were uncovered in 1893. The furnishings include a carved altarpiece with depictions of the Virgin, Child, and St. Anne, and a Crucifixion, originating from the Franziskaner-Klosterkirche in Mitte district [No. 11] and ascribed to the Master of the Dance of Death, a fresco in Marienkirche [No. 5]. The pulpit dates from 1679.

Among those buried in the **cemetery** are Rudi Dutschke, a leader of the 1968 student protests (d. 1979), and the poet Volker von Törne (d. 1980).

Apart from St.-Annen, the well-preserved village center includes the Domäne Dahlem, an old estate turned into a farm museum; Dahlem-Dorf U-Bahn station, a 1913 half-timbered structure with thatched roof in the Lower Saxon style; the Alter Krug (Old Tankard Inn); and the **village green**, on which a small rise shows the position of a vaulted ice cellar built in 1709.

Since the turn of the century Dahlem has developed into Berlin's most prestigious residential district, and it boasts numerous suburban houses—known here as villas—by renowned architects such as Hermann Muthesius (Bernadottestrasse 56-58, 1906; and Pacelliallee 18-20, 1911-12), Bruno Paul (Clayallee 34-38, 1924-25), and Walter Gropius (Am Erlenbusch 14a, 1933).

140 Brücke-Museum
Bussardsteig 9

Fine works by the artists of the Brücke *housed in a small masterpiece of modern architecture, a successful synthesis of aesthetics and functionality.*

Werner Düttmann built the museum in 1966-67 at the prompting of artist Karl Schmidt-Rottluff (1884-1976), who envisioned it as a memorial to a group of Expressionist artists, *Brücke*, active in Dresden and Berlin from 1905 to 1913. A flat-roofed structure at the edge of the Grunewald Forest, it is successfully integrated into the landscape with its expanses of glass and shimmering concrete walls at the entrance. On display in its four well-lit exhibition rooms grouped around an interior court is a collection of about 150 paintings by *Brücke* artists, with an emphasis on Schmidt-Rottluff and Erich Heckel, cofounders of the group, who not only bequeathed a large part of their oeuvres to the city but contributed to the construction costs of the museum. Their work is supplemented by superb oils, watercolors, and sculptures by Ernst Ludwig Kirchner, Otto Mueller, and Max Pechstein.

Also located on the grounds, behind the museum, is the gigantic studio in which Arno Breker produced the monumental and muscular figures that made him a favorite artist of the Nazis.

141 Jagdschloss Grunewald

Grunewald Hunting Lodge
Southeast shore of the
Grunewaldsee

A hunting retreat in a delightful lakeside setting, now the repository of an exquisite art collection.

An inscription below the relief at the entrance gives the name and date of the lodge—"Zum grünen Wald" (At the Green Woods), 1542. The Renaissance main building was designed by Caspar Theyss for Prince Elector Joachim II, a passionate hunter. The stables and outbuildings were added over the course of several centuries. The three-story main building was altered and enlarged in the early eighteenth century as well, and most of the interiors date essentially from this period. Only the vestibule and stairwell have survived in their original form.

Today the lodge houses a **collection** of about 200 works by German and Netherlandish masters of the fifteenth to the nineteenth century, including Blomaert, Bruyn, Jordaens, Rubens, Cranach the El-

der, and Cranach the Younger, who is represented with a Portrait of Prince Elector Joachim II (c. 1551). The long building across from the lodge, built in 1770 by Frederick the Great to store hunting equipment, was converted in 1977 into a small Hunting Museum, with weapons, hunt paintings, and trophies.

142 Waldfriedhof Dahlem

Dahlem Forest Cemetery
Hüttenweg 47

Last resting place of several famous people.

Buried in this simple rural cemetery are, among others, the poet Gottfried Benn, the sculptress René Sintenis, artists Carl Hofer and Karl Schmidt-Rottluff, revolutionary and author Erich Mühsam (murdered in 1937 at Oranienburg Concentration Camp), racing driver Bernd Rosemeyer, architect Heinrich Tessenow, composer Franz Schreker, actor O. E. Hasse, and dancer La Jana.

143 Onkel-Toms-Hütte

Uncle Tom's Cabin
Argentinische Allee

Pioneering housing development of the 1920s.

The development was built in several stages from 1926 to 1932 on either side of Onkel-Toms-Hütte U-Bahn station and shopping center on the edge of Grunewald Forest. Architects were Bruno Taut, Hugo

Jagdschloss Grünewald

Jagdschloss Grünewald: Lucas Cranach the Elder, The Fountain Nymph, *c. 1515*

Häring, and Otto Rudolf Salvisberg. While consisting primarily of single-family row and duplex houses, the development is punctuated by two-, three-, and four-story apartment buildings. The rows of buildings perpendicular to Argentinische Allee are arranged in pairs in order to maximize lot utilization and avoid a monotonous appearance. This rhythmical articulation was underscored by Taut's bright color scheme (restored in the 1980s). A model for its period, the development offered a number of amenities, not the least of which was its abundance of mature trees.

144 Zehlendorf Village Church
Potsdamer Strasse

Small octagonal chapel.

Frederick the Great had this chapel built in 1768 on the foundations of a medieval structure. Closed for many decades, the unusually shaped chapel was reopened for church services in 1953. Two panels of the winged altarpiece (c. 1480), originally adorned the Franziskaner-Klosterkirche in Mitte district [No. 11]. The eleven panels illustrating biblical scenes came from the Baroque choir balustrade of the Heiliggeist-Kapelle [see No. 5], also in Mitte.

145 Museumsdorf Düppel
Düppel Museum Village
Clauertstrasse 11

A reconstructed medieval village that spirits the visitor back over 800 years to everyday life in the region in the thirteenth century.

Located on a 12¼ acre site on a former marsh called Machnower Krummer Fenn, the museum village is a recreation of an actual settlement here. Archaeologists discovered the twelfth-century village from the period of German colonization of the region in 1940, and excavation was begun in 1967. The village was apparently abandoned by its inhabitants as early as 1220, for its marshy ground was poor by comparison to the clay soils of Zehlendorf, a new settlement nearby. Alongside the finished museum buildings, reconstruction of the medieval village continues with the aid of archaeologists and historians.

About a mile to the east is a cluster of interesting **residential buildings**: at Potsdamer Chaussee 48 and 49 (near Am Rehsprung) are the two most significant residences designed by Hermann Muthesius, the main proponent of the arts and crafts movement in Germany; No. 49 dates from 1906-7 and was formerly his own home. An important building ensemble by Muthesius is the **Mittelhof**, a block to the north at Kirchweg 33, constructed in 1914 and 1915. Just west of the *Autobahn*, at Dreilindenstrasse 30, is a private **residence** (1921-22) by Mies van der Rohe.

Museumsdorf Düppel, a reconstructed medieval village

146 Grosser Wannsee
Wannsee Lake

Strandbad Wannsee, Berlin's Lido, is a water sports and recreation paradise, a sandy beach 260 feet wide and nearly a mile long in a lovely wooded setting.

A public beach since 1907, the eastern shore of Wannsee was converted in 1930 by Martin Wagner and Richard Ermisch into Berlin's largest outdoor swimming facility. The **Grosser Wannsee**, actually a bay in the Havel River, is about three-quarters of a mile wide and up to thirty-three feet deep, and it is a sailing center par excellence. North of the beach, the Wannseeterrassen Restaurant offers a wonderful view of the lake and woods.

The house at Strasse Am Grossen Wannsee 56-58 on the western shore was the site of the notorious **Wannsee Conference** of January 20, 1942, at which the "final solution to the Jewish question"—the Holocaust—was settled. On the fiftieth anniversary of the conference, in 1992, the building was turned into a Holocaust memorial.

In a grove on the south side of the smaller, sister lake, **Kleiner Wannsee**, right near the bridge at Bismarckstrasse 3, is the grave of the famous poet and playwright Heinrich von Kleist, on the spot where he and his companion, Henriette Vogel, committed suicide on November 21, 1811. In 1861 the author's weathered gravestone was replaced by a marble monument bearing an inscription by the Berlin physician and writer Max Ring: "He lived, sang, and suffered/In dark, difficult times;/He sought death here/And found immortality." In 1936, the author of the inscription being a "non-Aryan," the stone was removed and replaced by the present one, whose inscription translates "Now, O Immortality,/art Thou entirely mine" (a quotation from Kleist's play, *The Prince of Homburg*). No mention is made of the woman who died at his side.

147 Nikolskoe
Nikolskoer Weg

Little Russia in the Grunewald Forest, and one of the most charming restaurants on the outskirts of Berlin.

Located on a terrace laid out by Peter Joseph Lenné in the early eighteenth century with a superb view of the Havel, Nikolskoe is a Russian-style log house originally built in 1819 by Friedrich Wilhelm III for his daughter, Charlotte, and her husband, who later became Czar Nicholas I. The name Nikolskoe (pronounced Nee-kóls-koae) accordingly means "Nicholas, his own." A tenant of the house was the czar's chief coachman, who ran the equivalent of a speakeasy here, the purveying of alcoholic beverages being illegal at the time. In 1984 the house fell victim to arson, but has since been rebuilt to the original plans and now offers excellent food and drink.

To the east lies Friedrich August Stüler and Albert Dietrich Schadow's **Kirche St. Peter und Paul** (1834 to 1837), a plain, single-aisle brick church with semicircular apse and a Russian-style onion dome. The two eighteenth-century Roman mosaic medallions on the pulpit, representing the church's patron saints, were a gift of Pope Clement XIII to Frederick the Great. Every hour on the hour the carillon in the tower plays the hymns "Lobe den Herren" and "Üb immer Treu und Redlichkeit."

148 Pfaueninsel

Peacock Island

Also known as the "Pearl in the Havel Sea," the island is a masterpiece of German garden design and a model of Romantic landscaping, with evocative artificial ruins and fine neoclassical architecture.

Just under a mile long and about a third of a mile wide, this island in the Havel River was used for rabbit raising centuries ago. Today, still graced by ancient trees and abundant bird life, it is Berlin's loveliest nature preserve. From 1685 to 1689 it was owned by the alchemist Johann Kunckel von Löwenstern, who produced precious ruby glass here for Frederick William the Great Prince Elector.

In the eighteenth century the island was used for agricultural purposes. King Friedrich Wilhelm II purchased it in 1793 and had a small **palace** built for himself and his mistress, Countess Wilhelmine von Lichtenau. Designed by Potsdam royal carpenter Johann Gottlieb Brendel, the 1794 to 1797 structure is a neo-Gothic mock

ruin featuring two towers connected by a bridge. Sadly, the king died in 1797 and was unable to make use of his love nest. His son, Friedrich Wilhelm III, however, spent most of his summers with Queen Luise here.

The bridge between the towers, originally of wood, was replaced in 1807 by a cast-iron one, an early product of the Berlin Iron Foundry. The trompe l'oeil landscape mural in the arched niche on the main facade, giving the impression of an open gateway onto the park beyond, was restored in 1975 in the course of general restoration work on the palace.

The **interiors**—four rooms each on lower and upper floors—have retained their original furnishings and provide superb examples of the neoclassical style popular during the reign of Friedrich Wilhelm II. Rich stuccowork, wall and ceiling murals, and parquet floors of precious woods create the ambience.

In 1822 Peter Joseph Lenné established a **Menagerie** on the island, which later formed the core of the Berlin Zoological Garden [No. 64]. He also transformed the larger part of the island into an English-style **landscape garden**, planting exotic trees and shrubs including a palm collection in a palm house (no longer extant).

In the middle of the island is the **Kavalierhaus** (Gentry House), a former farm redesigned by Karl Friedrich Schinkel from 1824 to 1826, concurrently with the building of his **Schweizerhaus** (Swiss

View of the Havel from Nikolskoe

Pfaueninsel, a palace in the style of a Romantic ruin

House) at the southern tip of Pfaueninsel. The south tower of the former structure is faced with fragments from the late-Gothic facade of a demolished fifteenth-century patrician mansion that Schinkel had brought here from Gdansk.

South of the Kavalierhaus, the **Voliere**, an aviary of 1824, houses a great variety of bird species. Close by is the **Winterhaus** for exotic birds, dating from 1828. About sixty peacocks still roam the island.

The **Meierei** (Dairy) at its northern end is an artificial ruin like the palace, a Gothic capriccio erected by Brendel in about 1795. Southeast of it stands the **Memorial Temple** for Queen Luise, built in 1829.

149 Schloss and Park Kleinglienicke

Kleinglienicke Palace and Park
North of Königstrasse

A marvellous neoclassical creation with landscape and architecture uniquely complementing one another. One of Schinkel's masterpieces.

A small, early neoclassical country house was the nucleus of a twenty-five-year project (from 1824 to 1850) that transformed this rural site near the city line with Potsdam into a work of art. Its initiator was the third son of King Friedrich Wilhelm III, Prince Karl of Prussia, who made the house his summer residence in 1824. He commissioned Karl Friedrich Schinkel to convert the existing buildings into a palace and design a number of auxiliary structures for the grounds, assisted by his students Ludwig Persius and Ferdinand von Arnim. Peter Joseph Lenné was entrusted with the layout of the 287-acre **park**, having proved his skills in his 1816 design of an English-style **Pleasure Ground** commissioned by the previous owner. The prince himself, an art aficionado who had collected Greek, Roman, and Italian sculptures and architectural fragments on his journeys to Pompeii and Carthage, also contributed to the unique character of the estate.

The gilded Lion Fountain in front, framing a lovely view of the **central tract**, is a replica of a fountain in the Villa Medici, Rome. The fountain in the inner garden court was based on the antique Ildefonso Group (Sleep and Death) now in the Prado, Madrid. The rear facade of the building is decorated with fragments and inscriptions dating from Greek and Roman antiquity.

Schloss Kleinglienicke, central tract with the Lion Fountain

Between 1825 and 1828 Schinkel added the northeast tract—the third wing of the palace—and a tower to the Gentlemen's Quarters. These additions were followed, from 1835 to 1837, by the **Grosse Neugierde** at the southwest corner of the park, a circular temple on Corinthian columns whose roof is adorned with a replica of the Lysikrates Monument in Athens. The site was chosen for the lovely view it provides of the Havel River and beyond to Potsdam in the south. West of the Lion Fountain, adjacent to Königstrasse, is the **Kleine Neugierde**, a tea house redesigned by Schinkel in 1825 and decorated with sarcophagus reliefs and fragments of Pompeian mosaics and frescoes. Located on the road skirting Jungfernsee is a further repository of the prince's antiques, the **Kasino**, a former billiard house with terraces and extended pergolas that Schinkel added in the course of his 1824 conversion. The **Jägerhof** (Hunting Lodge) in the northern section of the park, whose battlements and Tudor arches were borrowed from English Gothic, was created by Schinkel in 1828.

Palace and park were acquired by the city of Berlin in the 1930s. The Pleasure Ground was reconstructed from 1978 to 1984, and in 1986 restoration work on the interiors was begun. The former servants' quarters now house a garden restaurant.

150 Jagdschloss Glienicke
Glienicke Hunting Lodge
South of Königstrasse

Site of international youth conferences in a neo-Baroque setting.

Erected by Charles Philippe Dieussart for Frederick William the Great Prince Elector in 1683, the hunting lodge was converted by Ferdinand von Arnim in 1862 into a mansion in the French Baroque style. The work was commissioned by Prince Karl of Prussia, owner of Schloss Kleinglienicke across the street, who bought the hunting lodge for his son. His grandson, Prince Friedrich Leopold, commissioned Albert Geyer to build a further extension in 1889. Geyer gave the palace its present appearance, reminiscent of early Baroque architecture in southern Germany. Max Taut modernized the building in 1963 and turned it into a conference facility (the building is accessible to invited guests only). The bronze figure in front of the main entrance, *Reclining Woman* (1963), is by Richard Scheibe.

143

Spandau

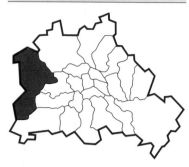

The town of Spandau is older than Berlin itself. Its citadel stands on the site of a Slavic settlement of the eighth century. The town received municipal by-laws in 1232. In the eighteenth and nineteenth centuries Spandau was a center of the national armaments industry. The Siemens Company was founded here in 1897, and in subsequent decades it built its own district of employee housing, Siemensstadt, east of the Havel River. Spandau and the adjacent communities of Staaken, Gatow, Kladow, Pichelsdorf, and Tiefwerder were incorporated as Spandau district into Greater Berlin in 1920, but the town retains a separate identity in its medieval core. With an area of 33 square miles, Spandau not only has more industry than any other Berlin district, but more agricultural land as well (2,520 acres).

151 Gatow Village Church
Alt-Gatow

A simple fourteenth-century church in a rural village center.

The village of Gatow was first mentioned in written records in the year 1272, as a property of a nunnery in Spandau. The core of the old village has survived to this day. The church, a fieldstone building of the early fourteenth century, has been repeatedly altered, its interior most recently in 1953. The altarpiece (c. 1495), a Lamentation of Christ from the school of Michael Wohlgemut, was originally part of the tomb of Martin Wins in Marienkirche [No. 5] in Mitte district. South of the church rises the austerely rectangular **St.-Raphaels-Kirche**, a Roman Catholic house of worship designed by Rudolf Schwarz of Cologne and built in 1960.

152 St.-Nikolai-Kirche and Spandau Altstadt
St. Nicholas' Church and Spandau Old Town
Reformationsplatz

Berlin's sole medieval town parish church and a fine example of the Brandenburg brick Gothic style, located in the midst of Spandau's charming Old Town.

The earliest history of the church and the circumstances of its founding are not known. The year 1210 is the earliest recorded date, but archaeological finds indicate that an ecclesiastical building must have occupied the site as early as the latter half of the twelfth century. The Gothic hall church with steep saddle roof and massive west tower (1467-68, upper story 1740-44) was erected from 1410 to 1450. Gutted by fire in 1944, it was restored in 1988. The spacious interior, a nave with two side aisles, a polygonal choir and ambulatory, culminates in the original vaulting, groined in the nave, giving way to stellar vaulting toward the choir.

To name only the most important of its many fine **furnishings**: the twenty-six-foot-high Renaissance altarpiece made of painted limestone and tuff, donated to the church in 1581 by Count Rochus zu Lynar, builder of the Zitadelle [No. 153]; the Baroque pulpit (c. 1700), a donation by King Frederick William I to the chapel of

Spandau Old Town. The tower of ▷
St.-Nikolai-Kirche is at center

the City Palace in Potsdam and installed here in 1904; and the early sixteenth-century carved wood Crucifixion above the entrance to the north chapel.

In front of the west portal stands an 1889 monument to Prince Elector Joachim II, by Erdmann Enke. The War Memorial north of the church was designed by Karl Friedrich Schinkel in 1816.

Reformationsplatz and the nearby Marktplatz form the nucleus of the **Altstadt**, streets and lanes in which the past still seems very much alive. Several of its houses are registered national historical monuments, including the Gasthof zum Stern (Carl-Schurz-Strasse 41), an inn dating from the early eighteenth century; a house of about 1800 at Breite Strasse 20, with a neoclassical facade from the school of David Gilly; and on the banks of the Havel River, at Behnitz 5, the Heinemann Haus, a half-timbered building with late-Baroque elements, erected in 1795. Points of interest on Kolk are, at No. 3, the Alte Kolkschänke of 1750, and the Roman Catholic Marienkirche. A simple basilica built in 1848 by Julius Manger, it was severely damaged during World War II and restored in 1964.

At Charlottenbrücke there is a boarding point for excursion boats down the Havel.

Zitadelle: gate house and Juliusturm

153 Zitadelle and Juliusturm

Citadel and Julius Tower

Am Juliusturm

The oldest large secular structure in Berlin, and one of the most important surviving sixteenth-century fortifications in northern Europe.

Located at a strategic point north of the confluence of Spree and Havel rivers, the original castle was evidently built around 1160 under Margrave Albert the Bear, and was first recorded in 1197. The circular donjon probably also dates from this period; it was given the name **Juliusturm** in 1584, after Duke Julius von Braunschweig-Wolfenbüttel. The battlements (with lookout platform) were rebuilt to plans by Karl Friedrich Schinkel in 1838. The former main residential tract next to the tower, which now houses the **Spandau Historical Museum**, dates from the fourteenth century. Its walls contain thirteenth and fourteenth-century gravestones taken from the Spandau Jewish Cemetery, evidence of the persecution of Jews around 1350. Conversion of the complex into a citadel began in about 1560

under Prince Elector Joachim II, probably based on plans by the Venetian architect Francesco Chiaramella Gandino, who employed two hundred of his countrymen on the project. It was completed between 1578 and 1594 by Count Rochus zu Lynar, also an Italian, who had been active in France as a builder of fortifications but had been expelled on account of his Huguenot faith. A number of restorations followed, the most recent from 1962 to 1965.

The core of the complex is formed by a square, 656 feet on a side, with a pointed bastion at each corner. The **bastions** are known as King (SW), Queen (SE), Crown Prince (NW), and Brandenburg (NE); they are connected by curtain walls.

Access to the Zitadelle is from the south, by way of a causeway and a bridge through the **gate house**. The commander's quarters, adorned by a segmented archway of about 1700, are on the upper floor of the gate house. Its facade is from 1839. The dungeon of the Juliusturm was once used to house the Imperial War Treasure of 120 million gold marks, part of the five billion that France was compelled to pay as reparations in 1871.

Until 1878 a prison was located in "Crown Prince" Bastion. Its inmates included Anna Sydow, mistress of Joachim II; Benjamin Raule, fleet admiral of the Great Prince Elector; and Mr. Jahn, the father of German gymnastics [see No. 126].

East of the Zitadelle stands the plant of the Bayerische Motoren-Werke, better known as BMW (Am Juliusturm 14-38), the largest motorcycle factory in Europe.

Reinickendorf

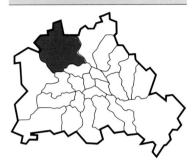

Many visitors to Berlin arrive in Reinickendorf, at Tegel Airport. Reinickendorf is typical of the outer districts in its land use: residential developments, ranging from luxury villas to high-density, low-cost projects, some industry, and plenty of forest, lakes, and fields. First recorded in the year 1375, the district figured as one of Berlin's domains, achieving autonomy in 1852. It was incorporated into Greater Berlin in 1920. Toward the close of the nineteenth century the Borsig Machinery Company and Iron Foundry established its factory here and with it a whole company town, Borsigwalde. A feature of interest is the 1898 gate to the plant on Berliner Strasse, designed along the lines of medieval castle gates by Konrad Reimer and Friedrich Körte; right behind it is Berlin's first high-rise building, a twelve-story office tower (1922-24) by Eugen Schmohl.

Märkisches Viertel, a development housing 50,000 people at the northeastern periphery of the district, built by architects Werner Düttmann, Georg Heinrichs, and Hans Müller from 1963 to 1974, is one of Germany's most notorious large 1960s housing projects. But the district also has open spaces: the area bordering the Tegeler Fliess, a brook that meanders through the district from the former village of Lübars to Tegel, is lovely.

154 Schloss Tegel

Tegel Palace
Karolinenstrasse

"Humboldt's Little Manor," another masterpiece by Schinkel. Memorial to German intellectual history and neoclassical setting for Wilhelm von Humboldt's collection of Greek and Roman antiquities.

The original country house dating from about 1550 was acquired by the von Humboldts, a leading family of Berlin intellectuals, in 1765. Wilhelm von Humboldt, founder of Humboldt-Universität, and his wife, Karoline, commissioned Karl Friedrich Schinkel to enlarge the building, which he did from 1820 to 1824. He turned it into a three-story manor house with corner towers, adorned with reliefs representing eight gods of the winds made by the workshop of Christian Daniel Rauch. The **main facade**, on the garden side, was lent the desired classical character by means of Doric pilasters and projecting cornices, as well as by the marble replicas of famous Greek and Roman statues displayed in four niches on the side elevations. The **interiors** abound with originals and replicas of such sculptures, which von Humboldt collected during his service as Prussian ambassador to Rome.

In 1990 the von Humboldt collection was restored to the palace in its entirety. Schinkel's interior decorations have been especially well preserved in the vestibule, the library, the Blauer Salon, and in the Antiquities Room (Antikensaal). The **atrium** features the most important piece in the collection, the marble Fountain of St. Calixtus from the second century A.D.

Schloss Tegel. Karl Friedrich Schinkel enlarged this country home for the von Humboldt family

Tegel Harbor. The American architect Charles Moore designed the library (left) and the fish sculpture for the 1984/87 IBA International Building Exhibition

In the **park** to the west of the manor, a magnificent lane of linden trees planted in 1792 leads past the 400-year-old Alexander von Humboldt Oak to the tomb of the von Humboldt family. It was designed by Schinkel after the death of Karoline (1829); the statue on the granite column is a replica of Danish sculptor Bertel Thorvaldsen's *Hope* (1817).

The terrain descends gradually to **Tegeler See**, the largest and most beautiful of the Havel lakes. Seven small islands dot the water; a school farm is located on the largest. In the course of the 1984/87 IBA International Building Exhibition a number of projects by contemporary architects rose on Tegel Harbor nearby, including a **phosphate filtering plant** by Gustav Peichl (1980-82; corner of Karolinen- and Buddestrasse), and a **cultural and recreation center** (1988-; Karolinenstrasse) designed by Charles Moore, only partially constructed to date.

Greenwichpromenade, along the northern shore of the lake, is a boarding point for boat excursions to Spandau and Wannsee. The harbor bridge at the western end of the promenade leads to **Freizeitpark Tegel** (Tegel Recreation Park) and to the fine restaurant, Seepavillon, from whose terraces one enjoys a marvellous view of the lake. A water-sports paradise, including a beach, of course, the lakeside park offers an abundance of opportunities for walks to various popular destinations. Walking along the western shore one passes the Reiherwerder peninsula, site of **Villa Borsig**, a palatial neo-Baroque manor house built from 1911 to 1913 and now headquarters of the German Foundation for International Development, and the ferry to the school farm, Scharfenberg.

155 Reinickendorf and Wittenau Village Churches

Alt-Reinickendorf
Alt-Wittenau

Two late-fifteenth-century single aisle churches.

The earliest record of the old village of **Reinickendorf** dates to the year 1375. In the midst of its village green, which is lined by single-story nineteenth-century farmhouses, stands a small **fieldstone church** with a rounded apse dating from the fifteenth century. Its squat tower was added in 1713. A winged altarpiece (c. 1510) with paintings of eight scenes from the Passion based on woodcuts by Albrecht Dürer, and two carved wooden female figures (late fifteenth century) are complemented by modern furnishings.

The old village of **Wittenau**, northeast of Alt-Reinickendorf, also has a well-preserved village green and a number of fine nineteenth-century farmhouses. Its church, built of rough fieldstone, is a simple hall dating from the close of the fifteenth century with a tower added in 1799. Furnishings include a Baroque pulpit-altar and a superb late-Gothic winged altarpiece with carved wooden statues of Saints Anne, Mary, and Nicholas.

Pankow

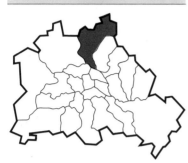

Pankow and its neighbor to the west, Reinickendorf, are the northernmost districts of Berlin. Until 1989 they were separated by the Wall. Pankow's name derives from the Panke, a small tributary of the Spree River that flows through the district. The original village of Pankow, first mentioned in 1370 but probably founded earlier, in the thirteenth century, of which the church and green are still extant, forms the center of the district. In the nineteenth century Pankow became a popular site for elegant patrician houses. They were framed by expansive parks, such as the Bürgerpark, laid out in 1854, or the romantic Brose-Park on Dietzgenstrasse, which was built for the banker Wilhelm Brose, a friend of Schinkel. The construction of Schloss Niederschönhausen and the extension of Schönhauser Allee forged a more direct link between Pankow and the royal court in the center of Berlin after 1704. In 1920 the town merged with the neighboring rural communities of Niederschönhausen, Rosenthal, Blankenfelde, Heinersdorf, Buchholz, Blankenburg, Buch, and Karow to form an administrative district of Greater Berlin. The district was part of East Berlin after World War II. Today, 8,880 acres of Pankow's 24 square miles are devoted to agriculture, and the current population is 108,000.

156 Schloss Niederschönhausen

Niederschönhausen Palace
Ossietzkystrasse 65

Along with Köpenick and Friedrichsfelde, one of a trio of important Baroque palaces in the eastern part of the city.

Between 1949 and 1959 the palace was the seat of the first and only President of the German Democratic Republic, Wilhelm Pieck; after that it served as a guest house for the GDR government; its last visitor was Soviet President Mikhail Gorbachev, who was housed here in 1989 during his visit on the occasion of the fortieth anniversary of the GDR.

The **palace** was built for Prince Elector Frederick III, the later King Frederick I, between 1691 and 1693 by Johann Arnold Nering on the foundations of a 1664 patrician mansion and enlarged in 1704 by Johann Friedrich Eosander von Göthe. In 1740 Frederick the Great gave the palace to his wife, Elisabeth Christine, as her residence. Ransacked by Russian troops in 1760, it was remodelled once again four years later by Johann Boumann the Elder. The **interior** is decorated mainly in the Rococo style popular under Frederick the Great. Highlights are an artful stairwell, a ballroom on the upper floor, the Zederne Galerie (Cypress Gallery) in the south wing, and the Marmorierte Galerie (Marbled Gallery) above it. The lavishly decorated rooms constitute a stylistic history of aristocratic living in the second half of the eighteenth century.

The **park**, originally a Rococo pleasure garden in the French style, was transformed into an English-style landscape

Schloss Niederschönhausen

garden between 1828 and 1831 by Peter Joseph Lenné. The park and palace are temporarily closed to the public at the time of this writing.

Across from the palace gardens, west of Ossietzkystrasse, is a street called **Majakowskiring**, former address of numerous well-known GDR politicians. Wilhelm Pieck lived at No. 29, Otto Grotewohl at No. 48.

157 Carl-von-Ossietzky-Oberschule

Carl von Ossietzky Secondary School

Görschstrasse 42-44

The most imposing school building from the beginning of this century in the Berlin region.

Built in 1909-10 under the direction of Carl Fenten with architects Rudolf Klante and Eilert Franzen as well as the sculptors Hans Schmidt and Franz Pristel, the four-story structure is organized around several courtyards. The ornate facades, richly appointed with portals, bay windows, towers, gables, and decorative facade gables known as *Zwerchhäuser*, seem to deliberately recall German Renaissance style and thereby express the sixteenth-century ideal that humanism is central to education.

158 Sowjetisches Ehrenmal

Soviet War Memorial

Volkspark Schönholzer Heide

A tomb and memorial built from 1947 to 1949 for the 13,200 Soviet soldiers who died in 1945 in the Battle of Berlin.

The complex was designed by Soviet architects and sculptors in the heroic-patriotic style of the 1940s and 1950s. Decorative elements include columns marking the entrance to the elongated grounds and a sculpture of a mother weeping over her dead son. This larger-than-life-size bronze group is situated in front of a 110-foot-high obelisk that houses a Hall of Honor in its pedestal.

The Roman Catholic **Maria-Magdalenen-Kirche** (Mary Magdalene Church), a late-Expressionist brick structure built in 1929-30 to plans by Felix Sturm, is located on Platanenstrasse about a mile to the east. The design, particularly of the tower and the basilica-like interior, represents an effective departure from tradition.

Carl-von-Ossietzky-Oberschule

159 Städtisches Klinikum Berlin-Buch

Berlin-Buch Municipal Clinic

Wiltbergstrasse 50

Exemplary hospital architecture by Ludwig Hoffmann, a former Berlin city planner.

The former village of Buch in the northeasternmost corner of Berlin borders on the rural county of Bernau. It is the site of perhaps the most impressive Baroque parish **church** (Alt-Buch) in the Mark Brandenburg region, a centrally planned structure built between 1731 and 1736 by Friedrich Wilhelm Diterichs. The tower was destroyed in 1943 and has yet to be reconstructed. The town is best known outside the region, however, for the **hospitals, nursing, and social-service facilities** that were built here by the city of Berlin, mainly between 1899 and 1915, to plans by Ludwig Hoffmann. Notwithstanding alterations to the interiors of the buildings, the facility has remained a noteworthy architectural ensemble. Hoffmann organized the immense complex around an exemplary system of pavilions, and he incorporated elements of Dutch and northern German Baroque architecture to create a homey atmosphere. The clinic served as a model for hospital and sanatorium architecture for many years.

Weissensee

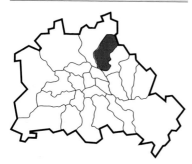

This district evolved from a village on the Weissensee (White Lake), founded in 1230 and situated on the medieval trade route connecting Berlin to Bernau and the Niederbarnim region to the northeast. In the nineteenth century the area developed into a suburb of Berlin, and by 1895 the community already had a population of 25,000. In 1920 Weissensee was incorporated into the city of Berlin as a district encompassing several adjacent villages and farming communities. It was part of East Berlin after World War II. At an area of 11½ square miles, the district has 52,000 inhabitants.

Several residential housing developments are of interest: the Gemeindeforum am Kreuzpfuhl on Tassostrasse and Woelckpromenade, built between 1908 and 1912 by Carl James Bühring using Art Nouveau elements, Bruno Taut's 1926 to 1928 houses on Trierer Strasse, and his 1928 to 1930 developments on Buschallee and Gartenstrasse.

Of particular significance from the perspective of cultural history are the two Jewish cemeteries in Weissensee, both laid out in 1880. The larger of the two is described at right. The smaller, built for the Orthodox Adass Jisroel congregation, is located on Wittlicher Strasse.

160 Karow Village Church
Alt-Karow

One of Berlin's oldest ecclesiastical structures.

The village of Karow, stretched along both sides of a main road, has retained much of its rural character. The earliest mention of the settlement dates from 1244, and its Romanesque fieldstone church was built around that time. The plan of the church is similar to those in Mariendorf and Marienfelde [Nos. 128, 132]: a rectangular nave abutting a narrower choir with semicircular apse. The **interior** is largely original, save an 1830 flat barrel vault, which replaced the earlier timber ceiling. Among the fine furnishings are a late-Renaissance pulpit, baptismal font, choir stalls, and a

gallery, most dating from around 1622. The Romanesque-style tower was added from 1845 to 1847.

161 Jüdischer Friedhof
Jewish Cemetery
Herbert-Baum-Strasse 45

The largest Jewish cemetery in Western Europe.

The gate and buildings near the entrance were designed by Hugo Licht in Italian early-Renaissance style in 1880, the year the cemetery opened. Paths flank elaborate tombs of various historical styles as well as modern designs, among them ones

The Jewish Cemetery in Weissensee

by such distinguished artists and architects as Fritz Klimsch, Walter Gropius, Ludwig Hoffmann, Hugo Lederer, and Bruno Schmitz. Buried here are many prominent Berliners: the publishers Rudolf Mosse and Samuel Fischer, the artist Lesser Ury, the cigarette manufacturer Garbaty, the hotelier Kempinski, and the founders of the two largest German department store groups, Adolf Jandorf (KaDeWe) and Hermann Tietz (Hertie). By 1980, approximately 115,000 burials had taken place on the hundred-acre site.

Located in the southern section of the grounds is one of the most attractively designed military cemeteries in Berlin, a resting place for Jewish soldiers who died in World War I. Since 1945 the cemetery has also served as a memorial to the victims of the Holocaust, the millions of Jews who died in the concentration camps of the Third Reich.

Hohenschönhausen, Marzahn, Hellersdorf

These three newest districts of former East Berlin were created in the late 1970s and 1980s on the outskirts of neighboring Lichtenberg and Weissensee districts. A 1976 law required all municipal building collectives throughout the German Democratic Republic to participate in a campaign to provide new housing for about 500,000 people on the northeastern and eastern periphery of Berlin. The result was an enormous concentration of industrial-style, concrete-slab mass housing—in Hohenschönhausen alone, housing for 100,000 has been built since 1984—an extreme example of urban planning as dictated by the construction crane. The centers of the former villages of Marzahn, Hellersdorf, Biesdorf, Kaulsdorf, Mahlsdorf, and Hohenschönhausen, all of which date back to the Middle Ages, have remained essentially intact. With their parish churches and former farms, they strike a note of rural idyll in the midst of the highly impersonal satellite cities. Population statistics: Hohenschönhausen, 118,000 on 10 square miles; Marzahn, 167,000 on 12 square miles; and Hellersdorf, 121,000 on 11 square miles.

162 Hohenschönhausen Village Church

Hauptstrasse

One of the smallest of Berlin's village churches.

Apart from a rectangular fieldstone choir that probably goes back to the thirteenth century, the loveliest feature of the church is its late-medieval vaulting on four spans supported by a square central pillar.

A tower once rose above the west end of the nave, but it was severely damaged in a 1945 air-raid and later demolished. The **furnishings**, mostly seventeenth century in origin, include a number of high-quality pieces: two carved figures dating from about 1430, a medieval wooden chest, and a sixteenth-century lectern adorned with low-relief carvings.

163 Pfarrkirche St. Martin in Kaulsdorf
St. Martin's Parish Church, Kaulsdorf
Giesestrasse

A Neue-Sachlichkeit-style masonry structure with a striking tower.

First mentioned in 1285, the old village of Kaulsdorf has survived largely intact, with a green, a church, and several farmhouses marking the former center. From a population of about 750 in 1895, it had grown to 4000 by the year 1920. The rapidly expanding Catholic congregation built a community center in 1929-30 that included this exceptionally modern **church** in the *Neue Sachlichkeit* (New Objectivity) style, designed by Josef Bachem. The massive, smooth-sided tower with its sharply incised window openings and the protruding cylindrical chapels flanking the main structure is particularly striking. The church is conceived as a basilica with a nave and two side aisles. Located in the baptismal chapel is a 1930 cycle of large-format glass paintings depicting scenes from the life of St. Martin. The superb **furnishings**, most of them gifts to the church, include an Italian Renaissance tabernacle, a large wooden Crucifix dating from the fourteenth century, a carved altarpiece with the Virgin and crescent moon (c. 1480), and a carved Pietà (c. 1420).

The Roman Catholic St. Martin Pfarrkirche

Lichtenberg

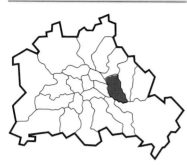

First mentioned in 1288, the village of Lichtenberg was acquired by the city of Berlin in 1391. In 1907 it achieved autonomous town status, only to be reintegrated into Berlin as a district in 1920. Having yielded its rural eastern rim to newly founded Marzahn in 1979, Lichtenberg now comprises around the same area, 10¼ square miles, as it did before its incorporation into Greater Berlin. Its current population is 167,000.

Lichtenberg's chief attractions are Schloss Friedrichsfelde (Friedrichsfelde Palace) and the Tierpark zoo in the palace grounds. Removed somewhat from the city center, the district is also the site of two important municipal facilities. The first is Berlin's central municipal cemetery on Gudrunstrasse, laid out in 1881. A resting place of numerous leaders of the political left, in 1951 the East Berlin government built a Gedenkstätte der Sozialisten (Socialist Memorial) here, consisting of a round, thirteen-foot-tall porphyry monolith surrounded by a wall. Located more or less in the center of the elongated grounds are the graves of artists Käthe Kollwitz (1867-1945) and Otto Nagel (1894-1967). Rosa Luxemburg and Karl Liebknecht are also buried here.

The second major public facility in Lichtenberg is the Grosskraftwerk Klingenberg of 1924 to 1926, a high-capacity power station located on a site adjoining the Spree River. Named after its builder, Walter Klingenberg, the plant is one of the most important examples of industrial architecture of the 1920s.

Central municipal cemetery on Gudrunstrasse: tomb (1928) by Käthe Kollwitz for the Schmidt-Kollwitz family

164 Knorr-Bremse-Werk
Knorr Brake Factory
Hirschberger Strasse 4

Fine specimen of 1920s industrial architecture.

The Knorr Company (est. 1890), a manufacturer of airbrakes, particularly for railroad rolling stock, built this factory, one of the major industrial projects of the 1920s in Berlin, from 1922 to 1927. Alfred Grenander was the architect, and he subsequently made a name for himself as the designer of Berlin's U-Bahn stations. He superbly integrated the multiple-wing, rectangular plant with the two intersecting railroad lines on the site. Its compact volume lends the factory building an almost fortified appearance. The truncated towers rising from the corner projections of the wings are overtopped by the plant's massive western tower, which is skirted at close quarters by a branch of the S-Bahn.

165 Schloss Friedrichsfelde and Tierpark Berlin
Friedrichsfelde Palace and Berlin Zoo
Am Tierpark 125

A country manor in the Dutch style surrounded by a lovely park with zoo.

The original, smaller **palace**, made up of only the central section below the portico, was designed by Johann Arnold Nering for the General Director of the Navy, Benjamin Raule, and built from 1694 to 1695. In 1719 it was enlarged to its present size by Martin Böhme. The mansard roof is an early-nineteenth-century addition. After years of restoration and reconstruction work, the sixteen historical rooms, the elaborate entry hall, and the early neoclassical banquet room of 1785 on the upper floor were reopened to the public in 1981. Some of the rooms on the ground floor are

Schloss Friedrichsfelde, designed by Johann Arnold Nering

decorated with hand-painted eighteenth-century wallpapers taken from other country estates and castles in the Mark Brandenburg region.

The Baroque park was redesigned in 1821 by Peter Joseph Lenné. A zoo was part of the park from its inception. The present design and layout go back to plans of 1954 to 1964 by Graffunder, Bendig, and Köster. Opened in 1955, the **Tierpark Berlin** is one of the largest zoos in the world, with an area of nearly 400 acres, and is certainly one of the most beautiful. At present it houses about 5,300 animals of 900 species in over 150 animal houses, open-air enclosures, and watercourses.

An avenue leads from the palace to the Terrassencafé and thence to the polar bear enclosure, whose bluish-black stone stems largely from the ruins of the former Reichsbank. To the east lies a **Childrens' Zoo** with café and pony rides. Passing the childrens' circus one arrives at the **Alfred Brehm House**, built from 1956 to 1963 as a warm-climate house for big cats, small mammals, birds, and reptiles.

Dotted all around the park are **animal sculptures**, mostly contemporary in origin. The two larger-than-life lion pairs are older, created by August Kraus and August Gaul for Reinhold Begas's 1892 to 1897 monument to Kaiser Wilhelm I, a huge and pompous ensemble then located in front of Berlin City Palace, a "Wilhelm in the Lions' Den," as Berliners quipped [photo, pp. 22-23].

The **Gedenkstätte Karlshorst**, a memorial museum south of the Tierpark on Fritz-Schmenkel-Strasse in the Karlshorst section of the district, commemorates the end of World War II. In the Great Hall of this former barracks the unconditional capitulation of the German Wehrmacht was signed on May 8, 1945. On display in the fourteen rooms of the museum are over 15,000 documents, photographs, uniforms, and battle plans relating to the war, with an emphasis on the campaigns of the Red Army.

Tierpark Berlin: Berlin's heraldic animal in a white version

Köpenick

At 49 square miles, this is Berlin's largest district. In addition to the formerly independent town of Köpenick with its charming medieval center, the district encompasses the communities of Oberschöneweide, Friedrichshagen, Rahnsdorf, Müggelheim, Grünau, and Schmöckwitz. It boasts the greatest proportion of woods and lakes, and it is the least densely populated area, with 124,000 inhabitants.

Earliest references to Köpenick are from the twelfth century, when a water-bound Slavic castle was located on the site where the Dahme River flows into the Spree (a certain Jaxa de Copnic played an important role in the settling of the Brandenburg March as an adversary of Albert the Bear). Town status was probably conferred in the thirteenth century. In the eighteenth and nineteenth centuries Köpenick prospered, as Bohemian and Silesian textile weavers set up shops here. The district is still the most heavily industrialized area of former East Berlin, and it is the site of several masterpieces of industrial architecture created by Peter Behrens and others. The historical core of the district is the Altstadt (Old Town), with its crowded, intricate plan dictated by the narrow channel of the island on which it stands. The Rathaus (City Hall [No. 166]) and Schloss (Palace [No. 167]) are located on an adjacent island separated from the town by a moat. Northeast of the Altstadt, in Wuhlheide, a wooded area typical of the region, is a 296-acre athletics and recreational center for children and young people, built in 1951 as Pionierpark Ernst Thälmann.

Two of eastern Berlin's most popular waterside recreation areas are the Grosser Müggelsee [No. 168], and the Langer See, south of the Müggelberge hills between Schmöckwitz and Grünau. Both offer beaches for sunbathers, and the Langer See has a race course for rowing regattas. The local rowing club was founded in 1881, and international boat races are held here.

166 Rathaus Köpenick

Köpenick City Hall
Alt-Köpenick 21

A historical revival structure in the style of northern German brick Gothic, famous among Germans for its role in a popular tale.

The Rathaus was built between 1901 and 1904 by Hans Schütte. The building was the scene of a 1906 holdup that became the basis of a popular play, Carl Zuckmayer's tragicomic *Der Hauptmann von Köpenick*

(The Captain of Köpenick). It tells the story of the cobbler Wilhelm Voigt and how he unmasked the authoritarian bureaucracy of the time, whose rigid regulations prevented his reintegrating into society after a stay in prison. He disguised himself as a military captain, got twelve infantrymen under his command, and stormed the city hall. There Voigt arrested the mayor of Köpenick and seized the city treasury. These events are reenacted annually during the Köpenick summer festival.

Kunstgewerbemuseum in Schloss Köpenick: Ottonian piece of jewelry, c. 1020

167 Schloss Köpenick and Kunstgewerbemuseum

Köpenick Palace and Museum of Decorative Arts
Lange Brücke

A palace preserved almost entirely intact with original High Baroque interior decoration and a fine applied arts museum.

As early as the ninth century the palace island was the site of a fortress, the seat of the Slavic prince Jaxa de Copnic. The existing **palace** was built between 1677 and 1683 by Rutger van Langervelt, replacing a sixteenth-century hunting lodge used by the Swedish King Gustav Adolf as his

Schloss Köpenick

headquarters during the Thirty Years' War. Built in the Dutch Baroque style, the present palace is one of the most important seventeenth-century secular buildings in the Brandenburg region. The sumptuous **Wappensaal** (Coat of Arms Hall) was the setting of the court martial in 1730 of young Crown Prince Frederick (the later Frederick the Great) and his friend Lieutenant von Katte. They had tried to flee country and responsibility, for which Katte was beheaded. The **Schlosskapelle** (Palace Chapel), a particularly beautiful example of Baroque design, was built from 1682 to 1684 to plans by Johann Arnold

Nering. Nering also designed the 1688 gallery wing facing the city and the 1682 portal at the entrance to the island.

The **Kunstgewerbemuseum**, a branch of the institution in Tiergarten [No. 58], moved into the palace in 1963. Its furniture collection is unparalleled in Germany, containing masterpieces from the Middle Ages to the nineteenth century. Other precious holdings include a treasure vault, the jewelry of the Empress Gisela (c. 1000), a desk by the famous cabinetmaker David Roentgen, and a panelled room of 1548 worked in inlay. A token reminder of the splendid furnishings of the Berlin City

Schloss Köpenick, the Wappensaal

Müggelsee, a water sports paradise

Palace is the large silver service of 1695 to 1698 by the Augsburg silversmiths Johann Ludwig and Albrecht Biller. At the present time the museum is undergoing renovation, and parts or all of it may be closed.

168 Müggelsee and Müggelturm
Müggel Lake and Müggel Tower

The largest lake within the city limits and one of the most beautiful and popular weekend destinations of Berliners.

The Waterworks in Friedrichshagen

The recreation area surrounding the 1,840-acre lake comprises playgrounds, athletics fields, wooded hiking trails, lodges, and restaurants. Steamboats criss-cross the lake and some take passengers all the way to Treptower Park. Situated on the northern shore is the large Strandbad Müggelsee bathing facility built in 1930 by Martin Wagner and Paul Rudolf Henning, and an open-air theater. The southern shore is the site of the Rübezahl and Müggelseeperle restaurants. Further south, surrounding tiny **Teufelssee** (Devil's Lake), are a few small, wooded hills, the Großer (Large, 380 feet) and Kleiner (Small, 300 feet) Müggelberg. **Müggelturm**, a 100-foot tower-restaurant on the smaller hill, offers a panoramic view of the woods and lakes of eastern Berlin.

169 Wasserwerk Friedrichshagen
Friedrichshagen Waterworks
Müggelseedamm 301-308

A utilities building in the Gothic Revival style.

Located on an eighty-six acre lot on the shore of the Müggelsee, this waterworks was erected by Gill and Schultze from 1889 to 1893. Along with the waterworks in Tegel (1877) and the Charlottenburg pump station this plant once supplied the entire city with water. The facility comprises a number of buildings in the northern German brick Gothic style, of which the Water Engine Houses B and C, equipped with the original machinery, are accessible as a museum.

Treptow

This district in former East Berlin comprises the communities of Treptow, Baumschulenweg, Niederschönweide, Johannisthal, Adlershof, Alt-Glienicke, and Bohnsdorf. Most of the district was not settled until the late nineteenth century. Industry and worker housing then shaped its appearance. A vacant tract in Johannisthal is all that remains of the airfield, built in 1909, that played an important role in World War I as a center for aircraft construction and pilot training. The flight pioneer Otto Lilienthal conducted experiments here.

Treptow has the second-largest concentration of industry in eastern Berlin. Worker housing, therefore, has long been a subject of concern to district planners. Among the well-known architects who built here were Hermann Muthesius and Bruno Taut. Taut's 1913 to 1915 Siedlung Falkenberg on Akazienhof near S-Bahn station Grünau, known as the "Tuschkasten-Siedlung" (Paint-Box Colony), is an interesting example of early modern housing design. The Spree riverscape, Treptower Park, and Königsheide (King's Heath) Park provide Treptow with a distinctively idyllic setting. The district has an area of 15½ square miles and 102,000 inhabitants.

170 Treptower Park

An English-style landscape garden popular as a recreation spot for surrounding districts.

The 131-acre Treptower Park was laid out between 1876 and 1882 by Gustav Meyer. An 1890 marble bust of Meyer on a red granite pedestal stands on the lawn to the east of Treptower Park S-Bahn station. Pushkinallee, a wide, plane-tree-lined avenue, bisects most of the park. North of it is a ferry boat landing. Just to the east is a rose garden with over 5,000 bushes. A path running southwest from the avenue leads to the **Sowjetisches Ehrenmal** (Soviet War Memorial, 1946–49) built from rubble of the destroyed Reichskanzlei. Buried in the large Ehrenhain (Memorial Grove) are Soviet soldiers who died in

and around Berlin at the end of World War II.

On a hill at one end of the grove is the cylindrical **mausoleum**, a domed structure with a monumental sculpture of a Soviet soldier holding a child and shattering a swastika with his sword. A statue of a mourning *Mutter Heimat* (Mother Homeland) stands in the courtyard at the entrance to the complex.

The **Archenhold-Sternwarte** (Archenhold Observatory), east of the memorial, was built for the Berlin Industrial Fair of 1896. Restored between 1977 and 1983, today it serves as a research institute for the history of astronomy and houses a planetarium. Its main attraction is a sixty-nine-foot-long telescope.

Soviet War Memorial in Treptower Park

At the end of Pushkinallee is **Restaurant Zenner**. The original 1822 building by Carl Ferdinand Langhans was destroyed in World War II and replaced by a simplified reconstruction in 1955-56. An open-air theater and a large beach are located on the nearby Insel der Jugend, a small island in the Spree.

East of Treptower Park, between the Spree and Neue Krugallee, is more open space, the 270-acre **Plänterwald Park**. Its northern tip is a 30-acre amusement park named **Kulturpark**, featuring a ferris wheel, roller coaster, and other attractions.

Berlin
Practical Tips

General Information

Telephone: country code for Germany: 49
city code, calling from abroad: 30
city code, calling within Germany: 030

Information Bureaus

Verkehrsamt Berlin, Martin-Luther-Strasse 105, W-1000 Berlin 62, Tel. 2 12 34, Fax 21 23 25 20.

The Verkehrsamt Berlin offers many brochures, which they will send on request, including the current schedule of events, *Berlin Turns On*, an annual schedule of exhibitions, congresses, trade fairs, theater performances, concerts, sports events, and other occasions. A listing of hotels is also available, and the Verkehrsamt can make room reservations. Brochures and information are also available at the German National Tourist Office, which has branches in most countries.

The Verkehrsamt Berlin has several offices in central locations in the city:

Berlin Tourist Information

City center west: Europa-Center (entrance on Budapester Strasse), W-1000 Berlin 30, Tel. 26 26 031. Mon. to Sat. 8 a.m.-10:30 p.m., Sun. 9 a.m.-9 p.m.
City center east: Fernsehturm (on Alexanderplatz), Tel. 2 42 46 75 and 2 42 45 12. Open daily 8 a.m.-8 p.m.
Airport: Flughafen Tegel (Main Hall), Tel. 41 01 31 45. Mon. to Sun. 8 a.m.-11 p.m.
Train Station: Bahnhof Zoologischer Garten (Main Hall), Tel. 3 13 90 63. Mon. to Sat. 8 a.m.-11 p.m.

Prices are listed in the following sections as a general guide only, and they may change.
Note: The German character ß is pronounced like a double s. In the text of this book it has been converted to ss, but it appears on the maps and on many street signs.

Accommodations

Berlin's 400 hotels, hotel-pensions, and pensions offer a total of more than 37,000 beds, but the city could use many more. Make reservations as early as possible. There are more places to stay in the western districts than in former East Berlin, though new hotels are opening in the eastern districts almost daily. Below are a few recommendations in each price range. The reservations service of the tourist office, the Verkehrsamt, has many more listings and will help arrange room reservations in all price ranges.

Verkehrsamt Berlin, Tel. 21 23-23 93 or 27 97, Fax 21 23 25 20.

First Hotel Reservierung Berlin, Tel. 88 11 15, Fax 88 26 6 44. Open Mon. to Fri. 9 a.m.-5 p.m. Arranges reservations in luxury and first-class hotels.

To stay in a youth hostel, contact: Deutsches Jugendherbergswerk, Landesverband Berlin e.V., Tempelhofer Ufer 32, W-1000 Berlin 61, Tel. 26 23 0 24. IYHF membership necessary, but can be purchased from the organization.

Luxury Hotels

Bristol Hotel Kempinski Berlin, Kurfürstendamm 27 (Charlottenburg), Tel. 88 43 40. Single DM 420-470, double DM 460-510, breakfast DM 27. Luxuriously appointed rooms with marble baths. No dogs permitted.
Grand Hotel, Friedrichstrasse 158-164 (Mitte), Tel. 2 32 70. Single DM 370, double DM 440, breakfast DM 25. Elegant modern hotel, built by a Japanese consortium in the mid-80s. 100-foot-high atrium lobby with large, sweeping staircase.
Grand Hotel Esplanade, Lützowufer 15 (Tiergarten), Tel. 26 10 11. Single DM 380, double DM 430, breakfast DM 25. Modern, designer interiors.
Hotel Metropol, Friedrichstrasse 150-153 (Mitte), Tel. 2 38 75. Single DM 300-350,

The Grand Hotel on Friedrichstrasse

double DM 360-410, breakfast DM 25. Swedish-designed interiors with natural-wood comfort.
Palasthotel, Karl-Liebknecht-Strasse 5 (Mitte), Tel. 2 38 28, Fax 23 82 75 90. Single DM 270-340, double DM 340-420, breakfast DM 25. Modern, thousand-bed palace right next to the Dom.

First-class Hotels

Art Hotel Sorat, Joachimstaler Strasse 28/29 (Charlottenburg), Tel. 88 44 70. Single DM 215-235, double DM 255-275, breakfast DM 22. New hotel with avant-garde designer interiors, small, but very pleasant rooms.
Berlin Hilton, Mohrenstrasse 30 (Mitte), Tel. 2 38 20. Single DM 345-475, double DM 395-520, breakfast DM 29. The restaurant on the top floor, La Coupole, is one of the finest in Mitte district. Opened in 1990 as Dom-Hotel; located right on Gendarmenmarkt. Lobby with greenery and waterfall.
Boulevard, Kurfürstendamm 12 (Charlottenburg), Tel. 88 42 50. Single DM 250, double DM 350, breakfast DM 25. Right next to the Kaiser-Wilhelm-Gedächtniskirche in the center of western Berlin.
Hotel Seehof Berlin, Lietzensee-Ufer 11 (Charlottenburg), Tel. 32 00 20. Single DM 110-325, double DM 320-390, breakfast DM 22. Idyllically situated on a lake.
Mondial, Kurfürstendamm 47 (Charlottenburg), Tel. 88 41 10. Single DM 220-350, double DM 260-480, breakfast included. Pleasant hotel and wheelchair accessible.

Moderate Hotels

Frauenhotel Artemisia, Brandenburgische Strasse 18 (Wilmersdorf), Tel. 87 89 05 or

87 63 73, Fax 86 18 65 3. Single DM 99-200, double DM 159-240, breakfast included. 8 rooms in a renovated prewar building. For women only.
Residenz, Meinekestrasse 9 (Charlottenburg), Tel. 88 44 30. Single DM 195, double DM 260, breakfast DM 20. Nice old building with large rooms in a relatively quiet side street of Ku'damm.
Riehmers Hofgarten, Yorckstrasse 83 (Kreuzberg), Tel. 78 10 11. Single DM 196-216, double DM 236-256, breakfast included. Part of a beautiful, turn-of-the-century residential complex [No. 123].

Less Expensive Hotels

Hotel am Anhalter Bahnhof, Stresemannstrasse 36 (Kreuzberg), Tel. 2 51 03 42. Single DM 80-110, double DM 110-150, triple DM 135-185, breakfast included. Simple and inexpensive.
Bialas, Carmerstrasse 16 (Charlottenburg), Tel. 3 12 50 25. Single DM 55-75, double DM 90-120, breakfast included. Medium-size hotel.
Crystal, Kantstrasse 144 (Charlottenburg), Tel. 3 12 90 47. Single DM 80-120, double DM 110-140, breakfast included. Convenient location, right on Savignyplatz.
Heidelberg, Knesebeckstrasse 15 (Charlottenburg), Tel. 31 01 03, Fax 3 13 58 70. Single DM 75-130, double DM 130-170, breakfast included. Medium size, friendly staff, and convenient location.

Lobby of the Art Hotel Sorat

Hotel-Pensions, Pensions

Hotel-Pension am Lehniner Platz, Damaschkestrasse 4 (Charlottenburg), Tel. 3 23 42 82. Single DM 75, double DM 118-130, breakfast included. Large, simple rooms, suitable for families. Quiet, despite proximity to Ku'damm.
Hotel-Pension Tauentzien, Nürnberger Strasse 14 (Tiergarten), Tel. 2 18 59 35. Single DM 130, double DM 160, breakfast included. A pleasant place.
Pension Haus Hannelore, Platanenallee 10 (Charlottenburg), Tel. 3 02 28 29. Single DM 75, double DM 105-115, breakfast included. Convenient location.
Pension Zimmer des Westens, Tauentzienstrasse 5 (Tiergarten), Tel. 2 14 11 30. Single DM 60, double DM 85, breakfast included. Casual, friendly atmosphere.
Seeblick, Neue Kantstrasse 14 (Charlottenburg), Tel. 3 21 30 72. Single DM 107-154, double DM 144-154, breakfast DM 13. Relatively expensive for a pension, but a good value.

Camping

Sites are inexpensive and well-equipped, but far from the center.
Central information: Deutscher Camping-Club e.V., Geisbergstrasse 11, W-1000 Berlin 30, Tel. 2 18 60-71 or 72. Mon 10:30 a.m.-6 p.m., Wed. 8 a.m.-4 p.m., Fri. 8 a.m.-1 p.m.

Dreilinden, Albrechts Teerofen (Wannsee), Tel. 8 05 12 01. Open from April to mid-October. Tents only.
Haselhorst, Pulvermühlenweg (Spandau), Tel. 3 34 59 55. Open year-round. Tents and camper vehicles.
Internationales Jugendcamp, Ziekowstrasse 161 (Reinickendorf), Tel. 4 33 86 40.
Kladow, Krampnitzer Weg 111-17 (Spandau), Tel. 3 65 27 97. Open year-round. Tents and camper vehicles. Facilities equipped for handicapped access.

Private Accommodations, Apartment Shares, Short-term Rentals

Mitwohnzentrales are agencies that will arrange, for a fee, any type of private accommodation—a room in a shared apartment to a whole flat—usually with a minimum stay of one week. Fees vary according to price of room and length of stay.

Mitwohnzentrale Charlottenburg, Sybelstrasse 53, Tel. 3 24 30 31. Mon. to Fri. 9 a.m.-8 p.m., Sat. 10 a.m.-6 p.m.

Mitwohnzentrale Ku'damm-Eck, Kurfürstendamm 227 (Charlottenburg), Tel. 88 30 51. Mon. to Fri. 10 a.m.-7 p.m., Sat. 11 a.m.-3 p.m.
Mitwohnagentur Streicher, Immanuelkirchstrasse 8 (Prenzlauer Berg), Tel. 4 27 41 72. Mon. to Fri. noon-7 p.m., Sat. noon-4 p.m. By women for women only.

Arrival

By Air

Berlin has three airports: **Flughafen Berlin-Tegel** "Otto Lilienthal" (5 miles from the center of town), **Flughafen Tempelhof** (3 miles from the center), and **Flughafen Berlin-Schönefeld** (2½ miles beyond the city line to the south). Most flights arrive at Tegel.

Ground transportation from Tegel: to get to the center of former West Berlin, take Bus 109, direction Charlottenburg—Zoo–Budapester Strasse. To get to Reinickendorf, Wedding, and Pankow, take Bus 128, direction Kurt-Schumacher-Platz—Wilhelmsruh, Fontanestrasse. There are also buses to Potsdam. A taxi to the center will cost about DM 30-35.
From Tempelhof: U-Bahn 6 stops here, or you can take Bus 119, which runs right through the center of western Berlin. A taxi to the center will cost about DM 30-35.
From Schönefeld: The airport has an S-Bahn station. S9 runs through the center of Berlin; S10 will take you to Ostkreuz, where you can transfer to S-Bahns bound for the center of town. Bus 171 will take you to U-Bahn station Rudow, from where you can take U-Bahn 7 diagonally through western Berlin. A taxi to the center will cost about DM 45.

By Train

Train connections to and from other German cities are good. Berlin has several major train stations: **Bahnhof Zoologischer Garten** (Bahnhof Zoo, for short) is the central station for long-distance trains in the western part of the city; **Hauptbahnhof** and Bahnhof Lichtenberg service former East Berlin. All three stations are well-connected by U- and S-Bahn to other districts in the city. If your destination is in the southwest of Berlin you may want to get off at **Potsdam-Stadtbahnhof** or **Berlin-Wannsee.** Trains from Hamburg also stop at **Spandau,** convenient for those whose destination is in the west or north-west of the city. **Auto-rail** service is available as well. Cars are loaded at Berlin-Wannsee station.

Information on schedules and fares is available at all ticket counters and agencies of Deutsche Reichsbahn/Deutsche Bundesbahn, at DER-Reisebüros in German cities, and at many other travel agencies. In Berlin the national railroad company has an office, **DB-Reisezentrum**, Hardenbergstrasse 20, W-1000 Berlin 12.

Train Schedule Information by Phone in Berlin: Tel. 27800 or 19419.

Reservations by Phone in Berlin: 3110 21 15.

By Bus

Daily coach service is available to and from most large cities in Germany. There are connections to some 200 towns, most served daily. The cost is usually less than that of second-class rail travel. Information on routes, fares, schedules, discounts for weekend travel or short stays, as well as discounts for those under 27 or over 60 is available at travel agencies.

The terminal for scheduled bus services in western Berlin is at **Zentral-Omnibusbahnhof** on Masurenallee 4-6, corner of Messedamm, across from the International Congress Centrum. City Bus 149 and the U-Bahn at Kaiserdamm run to the center from there. Taxis are also available. There are several bus terminals in former East Berlin, all close to S-Bahn stations.

For information, call Tel. 3018028.

By car

All *Autobahns* to Berlin end on the "Berliner Ring," the highway that circles the city. Visitors who prefer to drive on local roads for the scenery along the way should be prepared to run into construction. It will take a number of years before the roads have been rebuilt to western standards. Traffic is heavy on the *Autobahns* and on local roads close to Berlin. In former East Germany and East Berlin the alcohol limit for drivers is 0.0.

Sharing a Ride (*Mitfahrzentrales*)

Offices that arrange shared rides for a fee have sprung up in all larger German cities. Share-a-ride transportation is much less expensive than travelling by train or plane or in your own car. You can arrange a ride, or, if you are driving between Berlin and another German city in your own car, you can offer rides via the local *Mitfahr-zentrale*. The office will charge the passenger a fee for its services and the passenger will pay the driver a share of the expenses (check with the *Mitfahrzentrale* how much the driver is allowed to charge). It is usually easy to get a ride or passengers from Berlin to other cities at any time of the day or night, as there are several large *Mitfahrzentrales* in various parts of the city. A selection of those with convenient locations:

City-Netz Mitfahrzentrale, Kurfürstendamm 227, Tel. 19444. A network of six offices in Berlin, all reachable under the same number, and branches in other German cities.

Mitfahrzentrale in U-Bahnhof Zoo, Tel. 310331. Mon. to Sat. 8 a.m.-9 p.m.

Mitfahrzentrale in U-Bahnhof Alexanderplatz, Tel. 2463151. Mon. to Fri. 9 a.m.-7 p.m., Sat 9 a.m.-3 p.m., Sun. and holidays 11 a.m.-3 p.m.

Mitfahrzentrale Ku'damm Eck, Husemann & Klaus, Tel. 8827604. Open daily 8 a.m.-9 p.m.

There is also a **Mitflugzentrale**, to share a ride on a private plane. Departures are from Flughafen Tempelhof: City-Flug, Tel. 3053162.

Banks, Post Offices, Telephones

Banks and Exchange Offices

Travellers' checks or cash can be exchanged at all banks, post offices, and at some large department stores. The exchange counters at Tegel airport and Bahnhof Zoo are open outside regular banking hours:

Deutsche Verkehrs-Bank at Bahnhof Zoo, Tel. 8817117. Mon. to Sat. 7.30 a.m.-10 p.m., Sun. and holidays 8 a.m.-7 p.m.

Flughafen Tegel, open daily 8 a.m.-10 p.m.

American Express has an office at Kurfürstendamm 11, Tel. 8827575. Mon. to Fri. 9 a.m.-5:30 p.m., Sat. 9 a.m.-noon.

Credit cards are used less frequently in Germany than elsewhere. Large hotels, restaurants, and upscale shops catering to an international clientele will accept them, but many smaller places will not.

Currency: The **Deutsche Mark (DM)** comes in notes of DM 5, DM 10, DM 20, DM 50, DM 100, DM 500, and DM 1,000; and coins of 1, 2, 5, 10, and 50 Pfennigs, and 1, 2, and 5 marks. New bills have recently been issued, but both the old and new design bills are in circulation. The current exchange rate is around DM 1.50 to 1.60 to the US dollar, DM 2.80 to 3.00 to the pound sterling. The rates fluctuate and can be checked in newspapers.

Post Offices

Opening hours of most post offices in Berlin are Mon. to Fri. 8 a.m.-6 p.m. and Sat. 8 a.m.-noon. A few post offices located in shopping districts have extended hours on Thursdays, until 8:30 p.m. The following post offices have longer hours:
Postamt Berlin 17 (near Hauptbahnhof), Strasse der Pariser Kommune 8-10, O-1017 Berlin (Friedrichshain), Tel. 5895773. Mon.-Fri. 7 a.m.-9 p.m., Sat., Sun. 8 a.m.-8 p.m.
Postamt in Flughafen Tegel, open daily 6:30 a.m.-9 p.m.
Postamt in Bahnhof Zoo, Tel. 3139799. Open 24 hours. Mail addressed "hauptpostlagernd" can be picked up here.

Telephones

Country code for Germany: 49
City code: 030 (drop the first 0 if you are calling from abroad)
Directory information in Germany: 01188
International directory information: 00118
International calls can be made from most public phones located around the city and at post offices.

To use those labelled "münzfrei telefonieren," you need to purchase a phone card at a post office.

Minimum charge for a local call is DM 0.30. This amount is often higher in restaurants or hotels. The rates on long-distance calls within Germany are discounted Mon. to Fri. from 6 p.m. to 8 a.m. and all day Saturday and Sunday. There is no discount period for most overseas calls.

Telephone service to and from former East Germany and East Berlin is improving rapidly, but integration of the two phone systems is not yet completed.

Climate

A mixture of continental weather and sea winds—cold in winter, hot in summer, and unpredictable year-round. May and June are probably the most pleasant months, but the weather stays good until about October, and anyway, Berlin has plenty to offer in all seasons.

Weather Averages

	Daytime Temperature		Hours of Sun per Day	Rainy Days
	°F	°C		
January	30	−1	1.4	11
February	32	0	2.3	9
March	40	4	4.1	8
April	48	9	5.0	9
May	53	12	6.4	9
June	60	16	8.5	9
July	64	18	7.1	11
August	62	17	6.3	9
September	56	13	5.7	8
October	49	9	3.5	9
November	40	4	1.6	10
December	34	1	1.1	9

Consulates

Britain, Uhlandstrasse 7-8 (Charlottenburg), Tel. 3095292.
Canada, Friedrichstrasse 95 (Mitte), Tel. 26111-61 or 62.
Ireland, Ernst-Reuter-Platz 10 (Charlottenburg), Tel. 34800822.
Japan, Wachtelstrasse 8 (Zehlendorf), Tel. 8327026.
United States of America, Clayallee 170 (Zehlendorf), Tel. 8324087.

Other countries can be found in the telephone book under *Konsulate*.

Dining

Some people say real, traditional Berlin food can be found only in eastern Berlin: *Boulette* (a sort of meatball) with potato salad (homemade, just like mother used to), or on a *Schrippe* (hard roll), *Matjes* hering with potatoes, a Berlin bratwurst and the beloved *Bockwurst* (aficionados claim it tastes just right only on the Spree), and the famous *Berliner Weisse mit Schuss* (a light beer with a shot of raspberry or woodruff sirup).

But you can find just about any cuisine you like in Berlin: African, Indonesian, Arabic, Czech, Austrian, Indian, Israeli, Russian, Chinese, Yugoslav, Italian, Thai, Turkish, and even North American ... all quite authentic. For those in a hurry, there are corner stand-up places and plenty of fast-food joints as well.

Berlin is open around the clock. There are no official closing hours, so some places open relatively late and close only at dawn or not at all.

The Berlin Tourist Information Office publishes a free, biannual guide to restaurants, bars, bistros, cafés, typical Berlin pubs, scene-joints, wine bars, in-places, discos, etc., helpful in finding just the right place.

Dining recommendations are difficult to make—there are so many places to choose from. Below is a small selection to help you make a choice, the finest, the most typical, and a few for good, simple fare.

Nouvelle Cuisine

Not so long ago, Berlin was a culinary hinterland. New cooking was met with indifference. The situation has improved somewhat; there are now several places, both with and without Michelin stars, where fine cooking can be enjoyed. The stars among Berlin's chefs are Siegfried Rockendorf and Peter Frühsammer.

Alt Luxemburg, Windscheidstrasse 31 (Charlottenburg), Tel. 3238730. Dinner only. Closed Sun. and Mon. Prix fixe about DM 98, entrees around DM 38. Chef Karl Wannemacher has long been touted as one of Berlin's best.

Bamberger Reiter, Regensburger Strasse 7/Bamberger Strasse (Schöneberg), Tel. 2184282. Dinner only. Closed Sun. and Mon. Prix fixe DM 115 and DM 155, entrees about DM 48. Chef Franz Raneburger's **Bistro** right next door offers good Austrian cuisine at moderate prices.

Fioretto bei Carmers, Carmerstrasse 2 (Charlottenburg), Tel. 3123115. Lunch and dinner. Closed Sat. lunchtime and Sun. Prix fixe at lunch about DM 60, at dinner DM 80, entrees around DM 28. Chef Doris Burneleit moved here from Köpenick, and her Italian cuisine and wine list are still superb.

Frühsammer's "An der Rehwiese," Matterhornstrasse 101 (Nikolassee, Zehlendorf district), Tel. 8032720. Dinner only. Closed Sun. Prix fixe DM 120-145, entrees around DM 55. No menus, daily specials presented at the table. Chef Peter Frühsammer is hard on Siegfried Rockendorf's heels for "Berlin's best" honors.

Le Grand Restaurant Silhouette, in the Grand Hotel, Friedrichstrasse 158-164 (Mitte), Tel. 2092400. Dinner only. Closed Sun. Prix fixe DM 80-140, entrees around DM 35. Live music in the background.

Märkisches Restaurant, in the Palasthotel, Karl-Liebknecht-Strasse 5 (Mitte), Tel. 2382 7626. Prix fixe at lunch about DM 30, at dinner DM 50, entrees around DM 25.

Maxwell, Helmstedter Strasse 9 (Wilmersdorf), Tel. 8544737. Dinner only. Closed Mon. and Tues. Prix fixe around DM 70, entrees DM 33.

November, Schöneberger Ufer 65 (Tiergarten), Tel. 2613882. Dinner only. Closed Mon. and Tues. Prix fixe DM 75 and DM 98, entrees about DM 42. Near the Philharmonie and Neue Nationalgalerie.

Ponte Vecchio, Spielhagenstrasse 3 (Charlottenburg), Tel. 3421999. Dinner only. Closed Tues. Prix fixe about DM 80, entrees DM 35. Italian cooking at its finest.

Rockendorf's Restaurant, Düsterhauptstrasse 1 (Waidmannslust, Reinickendorf district), Tel. 4023099. Closed Sun. and Mon. Prix fixe at lunch DM 95-115, at dinner DM 160-200. No question, the best restaurant in the city. The long ride to the north of Berlin is worth it.

Trio, Klausener Strasse 14 (Charlottenburg), Tel. 3217782. Dinner only. Closed Wed. and Thurs. Prix fixe DM 45 and DM 84, entrees around DM 32.

Local Favorites with Berlin Atmosphere, Specialty Restaurants, and *Kneipes* (Pubs)

Anselmo, Damaschkestrasse 17 (Wilmersdorf), Tel. 3233094. Tues. to Sun. noon-midnight. Highly rated Italian cuisine served in stylish designer surroundings.

Blockhaus Nikolskoe, Nikolskoer Weg (Wannsee, Zehlendorf district), Tel. 8052914. Fri. to Wed. 10 a.m.-10 p.m., in winter until 7 p.m. The building was a gift of King Friedrich Wilhelm III to Czar Nicholas and his wife [see No. 147]. Beautiful view of the surroundings, in summer a pleasant outdoor "coffee garden," but service can be slow.

Anselmo—Italian cuisine in a stylish setting

Café Tiago, Knesebeckstrasse 15 (Charlottenburg), Tel. 3129042. Mon. to Sat. 8 a.m.-2 a.m., Sun. 10 a.m.-2 a.m. Vegetarian fare.

Ermeler Haus, Am Märkischen Ufer (Mitte), Tel. 2793617. Open daily noon-midnight. From cellar (Raabe-Diele) to attic, Berlin flair with a French touch. In the Baroque rooms one flight up, a French menu is served. Dancing after 7 p.m.

Grossbeerenkeller, Grossbeerenstrasse 90 (Kreuzberg), Tel. 2513064. Mon. to Fri. 4 p.m.-2 a.m, Sat. from 6 p.m. Old Berlin with a Kreuzberg flair. Beer and home-fried potatoes and Silesian dishes are the specialty.

Hardtke, Meinekestrasse 27 (Charlottenburg), Tel. 8819827. Open daily 11 a.m.-1 a.m. The waiters alone are worth a trip—their charm is as robust as the food. Hearty fare from its own butchery.

Hollyfood, Zossener Strasse 12 (Kreuzberg), Tel. 6928672. Open daily noon-2 a.m. Creative vegetarian cooking.

Jüdisches Gemeindehaus, Fasanenstrasse 79-80 (Wilmersdorf), Tel. 8842 0339. Restaurant and café serving kosher dishes.

Kartoon, Französische Strasse 24 (Mitte), Tel. 2299305. Cabaret-Kneipe where the actors wait tables (and the waiters act).

Kellerrestaurant Brechthaus, Chausseestrasse 125 (Mitte), Tel. 2823843. Mon. to Sat. from 7 p.m. Viennese cooking à la Helene Weigel, Brecht's actress-wife.

Konopkes Imbiss, Schönhauser Allee, under the elevated tracks at Eberswalder Strasse (Prenzlauer Berg). Mon. to Fri. 5 a.m.-7 p.m., Sat. 6 a.m.-6 p.m. A favorite local snack bar serving the longest and tastiest *Bockwurst* in Berlin and other traditional fare.

Müggelseeklause, Müggelseedamm 233 (Köpenick), Tel. 6455422. Mon. to Fri. 4 p.m.-midnight, Sat., Sun. 11 a.m.-midnight.

Offenbach-Stuben, Stubbenkammerstrasse 8 (Prenzlauer Berg), Tel. 4484106. Open daily from 7 p.m. Beautiful restaurant in a typical Prenzlauer Berg neighborhood. Rooms decorated with props from the Komische Oper and Metropol-Theater.

Opernpalais, Unter den Linden 5 (Mitte), Tel. 2002269. Four separate establishments in the elegant surroundings of the former Princesses Palace: **Operncafé,** open daily 8:30 a.m.-midnight; **Schinkelklause** (hearty Berlin fare), Tues. to Sat. noon-2 p.m., 6 p.m.-midnight, Sun. 11 a.m.-2 p.m.; **Operntreff** (mediterranean buffet, cocktail bar), open daily 5 p.m.-1 a.m.; **Restaurant Königin Louise**

Elegant dining room in the Ermeler Haus—the Fechhelm Hall

(German nouvelle cuisine), Tues. to Sat. 6 p.m.-midnight.

Paris-Bar, Kantstrasse 152 (Charlottenburg), Tel. 3138052. Mon. to Sat. noon-1 a.m. A favorite of "in" people.

Paris-Moskau, Alt-Moabit 141 (Tiergarten), Tel. 3942081. Open daily 6 p.m.-midnight. Fine timbered building in otherwise plain area. Ambitious cuisine, French-inspired.

Rosalinde, Knesebeckstrasse 16 (Charlottenburg), Tel. 3135996. Open daily 9 a.m.-2 a.m. Southwest-German cooking—a favorite haunt of theater people, students, and journalists.

Tadshikische Teestube, Palais am Festungsgraben, Am Festungsgraben 1-2 (Mitte), Tel. 2080843. Open daily 5 p.m.-1 a.m. Superb Russian food served in an authentic divan atmosphere; tea from a samovar.

Tomasa, Motzstrasse 60 (Schöneberg), Tel. 2132345. Open daily 9 a.m.-3 a.m. Café, bar, and restaurant with a pleasant atmosphere.

Zillemarkt, Bleibtreustrasse 48a (Charlottenburg), Tel. 8817040. Open daily 9 a.m.-1 a.m. Imaginative *Kneipe* in a former garage; serves breakfast, lunch, and dinner, on nice days in its courtyard.

Zur letzten Instanz, Waisenstrasse 14-16 (Mitte), Tel. 2425528. Mon. 4 p.m.-midnight, Tues. to Thurs. 11 a.m.-midnight, Sat., Sun. 11 a.m.-1 a.m. Berlin's oldest inn.

Zwiwwel, Bruchsaler Strasse 6 (Wilmersdorf), Tel. 8532578. Open daily 6 p.m.-

Outdoor café on Kurfürstendamm

2 a.m. A cozy, nostalgic wine bar; serves fresh onion tarts late into the night.

Cafés

Blisse 14, Blissestrasse 14 (Wilmersdorf), Tel. 8 21 20 79. Mon. to Fr. 8 a.m.-midnight, Sun. 10 a.m.-6 p.m. Very friendly atmosphere. Wheelchair access.

Café Ecke Schönhauser, Kastanienallee 2/Schönhauser Allee (Prenzlauer Berg), Tel. 4 49 43 56 or 4 48 33 31. Mon. to Fri. 8 a.m.-3 a.m. Sat., Sun. 3 p.m.-3 a.m. Huge selection of cakes, tortes, ice cream, and ten different kinds of coffee.

Café Kranzler, Kurfürstendamm 18-19 (Charlottenburg), Tel. 88 26 9 11 or 88 57 7 20. Open daily 8 a.m.-midnight. World-famous, though it has lost some of its prewar flair.

Café Möhring, Kurfürstendamm 234 (Charlottenburg), Tel. 88 23 8 44. Open daily 8 a.m.-midnight. Most beautiful 1870s café. Has several branches, including one on Gendarmenmarkt in Mitte district.

Schwarzes Café, Kantstrasse 148 (Charlottenburg), Tel. 3 13 80 38. Open 24 hours, closed Mon. 3 a.m. to Tues. 6 p.m. Caters mostly to young people, sometimes funky, sometimes not.

Schalander, Olivaer Platz 4 (Wilmersdorf), Tel. 88 36 1 25. Open daily 9 a.m.-1 a.m., Fri., Sat. until 2 a.m. Breakfast served until 3 p.m.—good basic fare.

Café New York, Olivaer Platz 15 (Wilmersdorf), Tel. 88 36 2 58. Sun. to Thurs. 10 a.m.-4 a.m., Fri., Sat. until 6 a.m. Breakfast served from 2 a.m. Crowded and lively, even in the small hours.

Musik-Café, Lietzenburger Strasse 2 (Schöneberg), Tel. 2 11 17 80. Breakfast served from 3 a.m.

Emergencies, Safety

Phone Numbers

Police 1 10
Fire Department 1 12
Ambulance 1 12
Medical emergency services 1 15
Dental emergency services 11 41
Doctors on call off-hours 31 00 31
Pharmacy emergency services 11 41
Poison information center 30 23 0 22
Women's crisis center 85 11 0 18
Emergency counseling hotline 1 11 01
Drug abuse emergency services 2 18 70 33
AIDS crisis center, emergency services 1 94 11

Doctors and Hospitals

In an emergency the ambulance (Tel. 1 12) will take you to the hospital best suited to handle your case. Most doctors in Berlin speak English. To be certain, the US and British consulates as well as the tourist information center in Europa-Center have lists of English-speaking doctors.

Pharmacies

Prescriptions are filled at *Apothekes*. A few are always open after hours and on weekends; they are posted on each *Apotheke* door, or you can call the number above for the location of the nearest one.

Lost-and-Found

Zentrales Fundbüro, Platz der Luftbrücke 6 (Tempelhof), Tel. 69 93 64 - 44, 46 or 48. Berlin Public Transport (BVG), Potsdamer

Strasse 184 (Tiergarten), Tel. 216 14 13.
S-Bahn (DR), S-Bahn station Hackescher
Markt (Mitte), Tel. 2972 1671.

Safety

In general, Berlin is a safe place at all
hours. Still, it is best to take the normal
precautions you would in any large city:
keep your valuables in a hotel safe, watch
your personal belongings, and be aware of
your surroundings.

Festivals and Fairs

Berliners like to celebrate, and they prove
it at their numerous festivals and neighborhood fairs. The Verkehrsamt, Tel. 21234
[see p. 159], has listings of current events.

January to March

There is always something going on in Berlin, around the clock and year-round. The
winter months are a little quieter. The
highlight of society life in January is the
Presseball in the ICC, a benefit ball with
many of local and national celebrities in
attendance (Tel. 8826688). February is
the month of the **International Film Festival,** the Berlinale (Tel. 254890). Viewings
and events are held in theaters throughout
the city, and special interest festivals ac-
company the main affair. At the end of
March many people flock to the Domäne
Dahlem for their **Schlachtefest,** celebrat-
ing local meat products (Tel. 8315900).

April to June

The beginning of spring rings in the district
fairs, neighborhood parties held in all
parts of the city. For those with a knowledge of German and a love of the theater,
May has lots to offer. The **Theatertreffen
Berlin** holds performances of jury-selected
plays staged by companies from all over
Germany, followed by the **Theatertreffen
der Jugend**, organized by student theaters
and independent groups (Tel. 254890 for
information on both).

District Fairs:
Frühlingsfest Luna-Park, Lützowplatz
(Schöneberg), Tel. 7838888. End of
March to mid-April.

Britzer Baumblütenfest, Parchimer Allee
(Neukölln). Mid- to late April.
Neuköllner Maientage, Jahn-Park
(Neukölln). End of April to late May.
**Kinder- und Volksfest in der Gartenstadt
Staaken,** Ungewitterweg (Spandau),
Tel. 3661586. Early to mid-May.
Marzahner Frühling, Am Akaziengrund
(Marzahn). Mid-May.
Steglitzer Woche, Bäke-Park (Steglitz),
Tel. 7904 3813. End of May to early June.
Frühkonzerte im Freien. Live music, tradi-
tional brass bands as well as rock and pop,
performed in outdoor restaurants through-
out the city and in the Zoo. At Whitsun.
Treptow in Flammen, Treptower Park.
Mid-June.
Sonnwendfest in Britzer Garten
(Neukölln), Tel.7009060. Summer sol-
stice celebration with fireworks and music.
First Saturday after June 21.

July to September

Fests, fests everywhere: Volksfests and
many summer concerts.

German-French Volksfest, Kurt-
Schumacher-Damm at Tegel Airport
(Reinickendorf). One of the biggest fairs
in Berlin, each year dedicated to a differ-
ent region or city of France. End of June
to mid-July.
Internationales Drehorgelfest (Hand Organ
Festival), held every other year around
Kaiser-Wilhelm-Gedächtniskirche (Char-
lottenburg), Tel. 2162126. June/July.
Köpenicker Sommer, Altstadt Köpenick.
Festival with a large parade in historical
costume. Early July.
Berliner Rocksommer, Insel der Jugend
(Treptow). A rock music festival. Mid- to
late July.
Jazz in July, Quasimodo, Kantstrasse 12a
(Charlottenburg), Tel. 3128086. Interna-
tional performers.
Berliner Sommernachtstraum (Midsummer
Night's Dream), Tel. 21234. A spectacle
with music and laser show. July/August.
German-American Volksfest, Hüttenweg
(Dahlem, Zehlendorf district),
Tel.8196842. End of July to mid-August.
Kreuzberger Festliche Tage. Volksfest in
Victoriapark around the Kreuzberg, Tel.
2588 3300. End of August to early Sep-
tember.
Berliner Tierparkfest (Friedrichsfelde).
End of August.
Turmstrassenfest. Volksfest in Moabit
(Tiergarten). Early September.

A brass band in Spandau Altstadt

Weissenseer Blumenfest (Flower Celebration) in the park on Weisser See (Weissensee). With performances in the outdoor theater. Early September.

Schollenfest, Waidmannsluster Damm (Tegel, Reinickendorf district). Early September.

Fest an der Panke, Johannes-R.-Becher-Strasse (Pankow). Mid-September.

Berliner Festwochen. Tel. 254890. Concerts and theater performances in many locations. Most of September.

Berliner Oktoberfest, on the square in front of Eissporthalle, Jaffestrasse (Charlottenburg), Tel. 2133290. Mid-September to mid-October.

October to December

Music is top of the entertainment charts in these months: the **Berliner Jazztreff** is held for three days in September or October in the Musikinstrumenten-Museum; in mid-November the **Junge Musik-Szene** celebrates new music; and a highlight at the end of the month is the **JazzFest Berlin**. German authors hold readings and discussions at the **Treffen Junger Autoren** at the end of November, of interest for those with a command of the language. The Domäne Dahlem farm museum puts on an international **textile crafts market** in November (Tel. 8325000). In December circus acts and acrobats perform at **Menschen, Tiere, Sensationen** in the Deutschlandhalle arena and then it gets Christmassy around the city: **Weihnachtsmärkte (Christmas Markets)** set up at the Kaiser-Wilhelm-Gedächtniskirche in Charlottenburg, on Alexanderplatz/Marx-Engels-Platz in Mitte, at Domäne Dahlem farm museum, Königin-Luise-Strasse (Zehlendorf), Rixhardplatz in Neukölln, and in other districts. One of the prettiest is in the Old Town of Spandau.

Museums, Commemorative Sites, Galleries, Libraries, Archives

Listings include the nearest U- or S-Bahn station and the buses that pass nearby.

Museums and Commemorative Sites

There are four museum centers in the city: the Museumsinsel in Mitte district, Schloss Charlottenburg and environs, the museums in Dahlem, and the Kulturforum at the edge of Tiergarten park. Berlin's state collections were split into East and West branches during the years of the Wall. Administratively they were reunited in 1992, so the branches now carry the same names in East and West. Since this separation and duplication was practical only as long as the Wall existed, the state collections (called **Staatliche Museen zu Berlin—Preussischer Kulturbesitz; SMBPK,** for short, Tel. 2666) will be reorganized and reunited in the course of this decade. In a few years' time, some collections may therefore not be found at the addresses listed below. Call beforehand or check with the tourist information offices.

On **Museumsinsel**, situated on the island between the Spree and Kupfergraben, you will find treasures from antiquity to the present day exhibited in four buildings: The **Alte Nationalgalerie, Altes Museum, Bode Museum**, and the **Pergamon Museum**. They house the eastern branches of the state museums. Two of the buildings house more than one collection: The Bode Museum contains Egyptian, papyrus, painting, sculpture, and numismatic collections as well as a museum of pre- and early history; the Pergamon Museum houses antiquities, the Near Eastern, Islamic, East Asian, and late antique and Byzantine collections. All Museumsinsel galleries are open Wed. to Sun. 10 a.m.-5 p.m. (Tel. 203550).

In **Schloss Charlottenburg** one can visit the former summer residence of the Prussian kings (Spandauer Damm, Tel. 320911. Tues. to Fri. 9 a.m.-5 p.m., Sat., Sun. 10 a.m.-5 p.m.)

The palace also houses the Museum für Vor- und Frühgeschichte (Pre- and Early History) and the Galerie der Romantik. Across the street from the palace are the Ägyptisches (Egyptian) Museum and the Antikensammlung (Antiquities Collection).

The **Museum Dahlem** complex between Arnimallee and Lanssstrasse in Zehlendorf district contains nine museums: the western branches of the state painting, sculpture, print, East Asian, Islamic, Indian, late antique and Byzantine art collections as well as the ethnological and folklore museums (the folklore museum is located two blocks to the north). Open Tues. to Fri. 9 a.m.-5 p.m., Sat., Sun. 10 a.m.-5 p.m. About a mile to the northwest, at the edge of Grunewald forest, is the Brücke-Museum.

Development of the **Kulturforum** complex on the Tiergarten began in the 1960s. The Mies van der Rohe-designed Neue Nationalgalerie, the Philharmonie, museums of decorative arts and musical instruments, as well as the state library have been completed. More museum buildings are planned, such as a new home for the reunited prints and drawings collection—the Kupferstichkabinett—which is scheduled for completion in 1993, and a new Gemäldegalerie, scheduled to open in 1996, which will house the reunited painting collection now split between Dahlem and Museumsinsel.

The culture and art of Berlin through the centuries is the focus of the collections in the Berlinische Galerie in the Martin-Gropius-Bau and the Berlin Museum (both in Kreuzberg), the Domäne Dahlem farm museum, and the Märkisches Museum with its eight branches.

Each district has its own **Heimatmuseum**, a museum of local history and culture.

Ägyptisches Museum und Papyrussammlung (Egyptian Museum and Papyrus Collection), SMBPK

> **Charlottenburg:** Schlossstrasse 70, Tel. 320911. Bus 109, 145, 204. Mon. to Thurs. 9 a.m.-5 p.m., Sat., Sun. 10 a.m.-5 p.m.

> **Museumsinsel** (Mitte): in Bode Museum, Monbijoubrücke, Tel. 203550. U- and S-Bahn station Friedrichstrasse; S-Bahn station Hackescher Markt. Wed. to Sun. 10 a.m.-6 p.m.

Altes Museum, SMBPK, Lustgarten (Mitte), Tel. 203550. U- and S-Bahn station Friedrichstrasse; S-Bahn station Hackescher Markt. Wed. to Sun. 10 a.m.-6 p.m. Berlin's oldest museum. Contains Neue Berliner Galerie with twentieth-century paintings, and the Kupferstichkabinett collection of prints and drawings.

Antikensammlung (Antiquities Collection), SMBPK

> **Charlottenburg:** Schlossstrasse 1, Tel. 320911. Bus 109, 145, 204. Mon. to Thurs. 9 a.m.-5 p.m., Sat., Sun. 10 a.m.-5 p.m.

> **Museumsinsel** (Mitte): in Pergamon Museum, Am Kupfergraben, Tel. 203550. U- und S-Bahn station Friedrichstrasse, S-Bahn station Hackescher Markt. Wed. to Sun. 10 a.m.-6 p.m. Mon. and Tues. only the architecture galleries are open; same hours.

Bauhaus-Archiv, Museum für Gestaltung (Design Museum), Klingelhöferstrasse 14 (Tiergarten), Tel. 2540020. Bus 100, 106, 109, 129, 341. Wed. to Mon. 10 a.m.-5 p.m. History of the Bauhaus design school in Weimar, Dessau, and Berlin (1919-33); special exhibitions, library.

Berliner Handwerksmuseum (Trades Museum), Mühlendamm 5 (Mitte), Tel. 24313325. U2 Klosterstrasse. Tues. to Fri. 9 a.m.-5 p.m., Sat. 9 a.m.-6 p.m., Sun. 10 a.m.-5 p.m.

Berlin Museum, Lindenstrasse 14 (Kreuzberg), Tel. 25862839. U1, U6 Hallesches Tor; Bus 141. Tues. to Sun. 10 a.m.-8 p.m. History of art and culture in Berlin from the sixteenth century to today, with an emphasis on the nineteenth and twentieth centuries.

Berlinische Galerie in Martin-Gropius-Bau, Stresemannstrasse 110 (Kreuzberg), Tel. 254860. S1, S2 Anhalter Bahnhof; Bus

129, 341. Tues. to Sun. 10 a.m.-8 p.m. Museum of Berlin's contribution to twentieth-century art, architecture, and photography.

Bode Museum, SMBPK, Monbijoubrücke (Mitte), Tel. 203550. U- and S-Bahn station Friedrichstrasse; S-Bahn station Hackescher Markt. Wed. to Sun. 10 a.m.-6 p.m. Contains numerous collections listed separately in this section: Egyptian, papyrus, painting, sculpture, and numismatic collections and the museum of pre- and early history.

Botanisches Museum, Königin-Luise-Strasse 6-8 (Zehlendorf, on the district line with Steglitz), Tel. 830060. U2 Dahlem Dorf; S1 Botanischer Garten; Bus 101, 148, 180. Tues. to Sun. 10 a.m.-5 p.m.

Brecht-Haus, Chausseestrasse 125 (Mitte), Tel. 2829916. U6 Zinnowitzer Strasse; Tram 22, 46; Bus 157. Tues. to Fri. 10-11:30 a.m., Thurs. 5-6:30 p.m., Sat. 9:30-11:30 a.m. and 12:30-1:30 p.m.

Bröhan-Museum, Schlossstrasse 1a (Charlottenburg), Tel. 3214029. Bus 109, 145, 204. Tues. to Sun. 10 a.m.-6 p.m., Thurs. until 8 p.m. Art Nouveau and Art Deco.

Brücke-Museum, Bussardsteig 9 (Zehlendorf), Tel. 8312029. Bus 115. Wed. to Mon. 11 a.m.-5 p.m. Works of the Expressionist artists' group *Brücke*.

Deutsches Historisches Museum (Museum of German History), Unter den Linden 2 (Mitte), Tel. 203180, 215020. S-Bahn station Hackescher Markt; Bus 100. Thurs. to Tues. 10 a.m.-6 p.m. In the former Zeughaus (Arsenal).

Deutsches Rundfunkmuseum (German Broadcasting Museum), Hammarskjöldplatz 1 (Charlottenburg), Tel. 3028186. U1 Theodor-Heuss-Platz or Kaiserdamm; Bus 104, 105, 110, 149, 219. Wed. to Mon. 10 a.m.-5 p.m. A documentation of the development of radio (1923-45) and television (until 1967).

Domäne Dahlem, Königin-Luise-Strasse 49 (Zehlendorf), Tel. 8325000. U2 Dahlem Dorf. Wed. to Mon. 10 a.m.-6 p.m. A farm museum with animal husbandry and crafts; sale of farm products.

Ephraim Palais, Poststrasse 16 (Mitte), Tel. 24313302. U- and S-Bahn station Alexanderplatz; U2 Klosterstrasse. Tues. to Fri. 9 a.m.-5 p.m., Sat. 9 a.m.-6 p.m., Sun. 10 a.m.-5 p.m. Views of Berlin from the Baroque to Biedermeier.

Friedrichswerdersche Kirche, Schinkel-Museum, Werderstrasse (Mitte), Tel. 2081323. U2 Hausvogteiplatz. Wed. to Sun. 10 a.m.-6 p.m.

Friseurmuseum (Hairdressing Museum),

Husemannstrasse 8 (Prenzlauer Berg), Tel. 4495380. U2 Eberswalder Strasse. Mon. 10 a.m.-6 p.m., Tues. to Thurs. 10 a.m.-5 p.m., Sat. 10 a.m.-6 p.m., Sun. 10 a.m.-4 p.m.

Galerie der Romantik, Schloss Charlottenburg, East Wing (Charlottenburg), Tel. 32091207. Bus 109, 145, 204. Tues. to Fri. 9 a.m.-5 p.m., Sat., Sun. 10 a.m.-5 p.m. Early nineteenth-century painting, the Romantics, Biedermeier. The collection is a department of the National-galerie, SMBPK.

Gedenkstätte Deutscher Widerstand (Commemorative to German Resistance), Stauffenbergstrasse 13-14 (Tiergarten), Tel. 26042202. Bus 129, 148, 248, 341. Mon. to Fri. 9 a.m.-6 p.m., Sat., Sun. 9 a.m.-1 p.m.

Gedenkstätte Haus der Wannsee-Konferenz, Am Grossen Wannsee 56-58 (Zehlendorf), Tel. 80500125. S1, S3, S5 to Wannsee, then Bus 114. Tues. to Fri. 10 a.m.-6 p.m., Sat., Sun 2-6 p.m. Holocaust memorial in the building where the notorious Wannsee conference was held.

Gedenkstätte Karlshorst, Fritz-Schmenckel-Strasse (Lichtenberg), Tel. 5084839. S3 Karlshorst. Tues. to Fri. 9 a.m.-1 p.m. and 3-6 p.m., Sat. 9 a.m.-4 p.m., Sun. 9 a.m.-2 p.m. World War II museum in the rooms where the capitulation was signed on May 8, 1945. Emphasis on the Red Army.

Gedenkstätte Plötzensee, Hüttigpfad (Charlottenburg), Tel. 3443226. Bus 105, 123, 126. Open daily 8:30 a.m.-4 p.m. in winter, 8 a.m.-6 p.m. in summer. Memorial to victims of the Nazis.

Gemäldegalerie (Picture Gallery), SMBPK
  Dahlem (Zehlendorf): Arnimallee 23-27, Tel. 83011. U2 Dahlem Dorf. Tues. to Fri. 9 a.m.-5 p.m., Sat., Sun 10 a.m.-5 p.m.
  Museumsinsel (Mitte): in Bode Museum, Monbijoubrücke, Tel. 203550. U- and S-Bahn station Friedrichstrasse; S-Bahn station Hackescher Markt. Wed. to Sun. 10 a.m.-6 p.m.

Georg-Kolbe-Museum, Sensburger Allee 25 (Charlottenburg), Tel. 3042144. Bus 149. Tues. to Sun. 10 a.m.-5 p.m.

Haus am Checkpoint Charlie, Friedrichstrasse 44 (Kreuzberg), Tel. 2511031. U6 Kochstrasse; U2 Stadtmitte; Bus 121. Open daily 9 a.m.-10 p.m. Museum of the history of the Wall, including some of the more spectacular contraptions used to escape from the East.

History Exhibition in the Reichstag Building, Platz der Republik (Tiergarten),

Tel. 39770. S1, S2 Unter den Linden; Bus
100, 248. Tues. to Sun. 10 a.m.-5 p.m. On
national holidays also open Mon.

Hugenottenmuseum in the Französischer
Dom, Gendarmenmarkt (Mitte), Tel.
2291760. U2 Hausvogteiplatz or Französische Strasse; Bus 142, 147, 257. Tues.,
Wed., Thurs., Sat. noon-5 p.m., Sun. 1-5
p.m.

Hundemuseum (Dog Museum), Alt-Blan-
kenburg 33 (Weissensee), Tel. 4813931.
Bus 158, 258. Tues., Thurs., Sat. 3-6 p.m.,
Sun. 11 a.m.-5 p.m.

Jagdschloss Grunewald (Grunewald Hunting Lodge), on Grunewaldsee (Zehlendorf), Tel. 8133597. Bus 110, 115, 180 to
Königin-Luise-Strasse/Clayallee, then a
20 min. walk. Tues. to Sun. 10 a.m.-
4 p.m. Nov. to Feb., until 5 p.m. Mar. to
Oct. Fifteenth- to nineteenth-century German and Netherlandish paintings.

Käthe-Kollwitz-Museum Berlin, Fasanen-
strasse 24 (Charlottenburg),
Tel. 8825210. U3 Uhlandstrasse. Wed. to
Mon. 11 a.m.-6 p.m.

Knoblauchhaus, Poststrasse 23 (Mitte),
Tel. 24313392. U2 Klosterstrasse; Bus
147. Tues. to Fri. 9 a.m.-5 p.m., Sat.
9 a.m.-6 p.m., Sun. 10 a.m.-5 p.m. History of the Knoblauch family and of Berlin
in the nineteenth century.

Kupferstichkabinett (Collection of Prints
and Drawings), SMBPK. Both branches
will move to Kulturforum (Tiergarten) in
1993.

  Dahlem (Zehlendorf): Arnimallee 23-
27, Tel. 83011. U2 Dahlem Dorf. Partly closed. Tues. to Fri. 9 a.m.-4 p.m.

  Museumsinsel (Mitte): in Altes Museum,
Lustgarten, Tel. 203550. U- and S-
Bahn station Friedrichstrasse; S-Bahn
station Hackescher Markt. Mon.,
Wed., Fri. 9 a.m.-noon and 1-4 p.m.

Kunstgewerbemuseum (Museum of Decorative Arts), SMBPK

  Kulturforum (Tiergarten): Tiergartenstrasse 6, Tel. 2666. Bus 129, 148, 248.
Tues. to Fri. 9 a.m.-5 p.m., Sat., Sun.
10 a.m.-5 p.m.

  Schloss Köpenick (Köpenick): Schlossinsel, Tel. 6572651. S85 Spindlersfeld;
Tram 83, 84, 86; Bus 168, 169. Partly
closed for renovation. Wed. to Sun.
10 a.m.-6 p.m.

Jüdisches Museum (Jewish Museum), a department of Berlin Museum, in Martin-
Gropius-Bau, Stresemannstrasse 110
(Kreuzberg), Tel. 25862839. S1, S2 Anhalter Bahnhof; Bus 129, 341. Tues. to
Sun. 10 a.m.-8 p.m., special exhibitions
until 10 p.m.

Märkisches Museum, Am Köllnischen Park
5 (Mitte), Tel. 2700514. U2 Märkisches
Museum. Wed. to Sun. 10 a.m.-6 p.m.
Fine and applied arts of the seventeenth to
the twentieth century from the Berlin region; city history; Berlin theater history of
the eighteenth to the twentieth century.

Martin-Gropius-Bau, Stresemannstrasse
110 (Kreuzberg), Tel. 254860. S1, S2 Anhalter Bahnhof; Bus 129, 341. Tues. to
Sun. 10 a.m.-8 p.m., special exhibitions
until 10 p.m. Home of the Berlinische
Galerie, Jüdisches Museum, and Werkbund-Archiv. Venue for special exhibitions.

Münzkabinett (Numismatic Collection),
SMBPK, in Bode Museum, Monbijoubrücke, Tel. 203550. U- and S-Bahn station Friedrichstrasse; S-Bahn station
Hackescher Markt. Wed., Thurs. 9 a.m.-
5 p.m., Fri. 10 a.m.-5 p.m.

Museum Berliner Arbeiterleben,
Husemannstrasse 12 (Prenzlauer Berg),
Tel. 4485675. U2 Eberswalder Strasse.
Tues. to Thurs. and Sat. 10 a.m.-6 p.m.,
Fri. 10 a.m.-3 p.m. Exhibition on the life
of the Berlin proletariat around 1900.

Museum der Verbotenen Kunst (Museum of
Forbidden Art), Puschkinallee /
Schlesische Strasse (Treptow),
Tel. 8529203. U1 Schlesisches Tor;
S-Bahn station Treptower Park. Sat., Sun.
3-6 p.m. Housed in Berlin's last watch-
tower. Arranges tours of the sites of the
1989 revolution. Call for information and
reservations.

Museum für Indische Kunst (Indian Art),
SMBPK, Lansstrasse 8 (Zehlendorf),
Tel. 83011. U2 Dahlem Dorf, Tues. to
Fri. 9 a.m.-5 p.m., Sat., Sun. 10 a.m.-
5 p.m.

Museum für Islamische Kunst (Islamic Art),
SMBPK

  Dahlem (Zehlendorf): Lansstrasse 8,
Tel. 83011. U2 Dahlem Dorf. Tues. to
Fri. 9 a.m.-5 p.m., Sat., Sun. 10 a.m.-
5 p.m.

  Museumsinsel (Mitte): in Pergamon
Museum, Am Kupfergraben, Tel.
203550. U- and S-Bahn station
Friedrichstrasse; S-Bahn station Hackescher Markt. Wed. to Sun. 10 a.m.-
6 p.m.

Museum für Naturkunde (Natural History),
Invalidenstrasse 43 (Mitte), Tel.
28972540. S1, S2 Nordbahnhof. Tues. to
Sun. 9:30 a.m.-5 p.m.

Museum für Ostasiatische Kunst (East Asian
Art), SMBPK

  Dahlem (Zehlendorf): Lansstrasse 8,
Tel. 83011. U2 Dahlem Dorf. Tues. to

Fri. 9 a.m.-5 p.m., Sat., Sun. 10 a.m.-5 p.m.

Museumsinsel (Mitte): in Pergamon Museum, Am Kupfergraben, Tel. 2035 50. U- and S-Bahn Friedrichstrasse. S-Bahn station Hackescher Markt. Wed. to Sun. 10 a.m.-6 p.m.

Museum für Spätantike und Byzantinische Kunst (Late Antique and Byzantine Art), SMBPK

Dahlem (Zehlendorf): Arnimallee 23-27, Tel. 83011. U 2 Dahlem Dorf. Tues. to Fri. 9 a.m.-5 p.m., Sat., Sun. 10 a.m.-5 p.m.

Museumsinsel (Mitte): in Pergamon Museum, Am Kupfergraben, Tel. 2035 50, U- and S-Bahn Friedrichstrasse; S-Bahn station Hackescher Markt. Wed. to Sun. 10 a.m.-6 p.m.

Museum für Völkerkunde (Ethnology), SMBPK, Lansstrasse 8 (Zehlendorf), Tel. 83011. U 2 Dahlem-Dorf. Tues. to Fri. 9 a.m.-5 p.m., Sat., Sun. 10 a.m.-5 p.m.

Museum für Volkskunde (Folklore), SMBPK

Dahlem (Zehlendorf): Im Winkel 6-8, Tel. 8390101. U 2 Dahlem Dorf. Tues. to Fri. 9 a.m.-5 p.m., Sat., Sun. 10 a.m.-5 p.m.

Museumsinsel (Mitte): in Pergamon Museum, Am Kupfergraben, Tel. 2035 50. U- and S-Bahn Friedrichstrasse; S-Bahn station Hackescher Markt. Wed. to Sun. 10 a.m.-6 p.m. Will move to Dahlem in the future.

Museum für Verkehr und Technik (Transportation and Technology), Trebbiner Strasse 9 (Kreuzberg), Tel. 254840. U 1 Gleisdreieck; Bus 129. Tues. to Fri. 9 a.m.-5:30 p.m., Sat., Sun. 10 a.m.-6 p.m.

Museum für Vor- und Frühgeschichte (Pre- and Early History), SMBPK

Charlottenburg: Schloss Charlottenburg, West Wing, Tel. 32091 1. Bus 109, 145, 204. Mon. to Thurs. 9 a.m.-5 p.m., Sat., Sun. 10 a.m.-5 p.m.

Museumsinsel (Mitte): in Bode Museum, Monbijoubrücke, Tel. 2035 50. U- and S-Bahn station Friedrichstrasse; S-Bahn station Hackescher Markt. Wed. to Sun. 10 a.m.-6 p.m.

Museumsdorf Düppel, Clauertstrasse 11 (Zehlendorf), Tel. 8026671. Bus 115, 211. Sun. 10 a.m.-5 p.m., Thurs. 3-7 p.m. Guided tours by appointment only. Reconstruction of a medieval village.

Musikinstrumenten-Museum (Musical Instruments), Tiergartenstrasse 1 (Tiergarten), Tel. 254810. Bus 129, 148, 248.

Tues. to Fri. 9 a.m.-5 p.m., Sat., Sun. 10 a.m.-5 p.m.

Nationalgalerie, SMBPK

Alte Nationalgalerie, Museumsinsel (Mitte): Lustgarten, Tel. 2035 50. U- and S-Bahn station Friedrichstrasse; S-Bahn station Hackescher Markt. Wed. to Sun. 10 a.m.-6 p.m.

Neue Nationalgalerie, Kulturforum (Tiergarten): Potsdamer Strasse 50, Tel. 2666. Bus 129, 148, 248. Tues. to Fri. 9 a.m.-5 p.m., Sat., Sun. 10 a.m.-5 p.m.

Nikolaikirche, Nikolaikirchplatz (Mitte), Tel. 24313146. U- and S-Bahn station Alexanderplatz; U 2 Klosterstrasse. Tues. to Fri. 9 a.m.-5 p.m., Sat. 9 a.m.-6 p.m., Sun. 10 a.m.-5 p.m.

Otto-Nagel-Haus, Märkisches Ufer 16-18 (Mitte), Tel. 2791402. U- and S-Bahn station Jannowitzbrücke; U 2 Märkisches Museum; Bus 142, 147. Sun. to Thurs. 10 a.m.-6 p.m. The Nationalgalerie's collection of revolutionary and antifascist art.

Pergamon Museum, SMBPK, Am Kupfergraben (Mitte), Tel. 2035 50. U- and S-Bahn station Friedrichstrasse; S-Bahn station Hackescher Markt. Wed. to Sun. 10 a.m.-6 p.m., architecture galleries open daily. Contains numerous collections listed separately in this section: antiquities, Near Eastern, Islamic, East Asian, late antique and Byzantine art collections and a folklore department.

Postmuseum Berlin, An der Urania 15 (Schöneberg), Tel. 21711701. U 1, U 2, U 3 Wittenbergplatz; Bus 109, 119, 129, 146, 185, 219. Mon. to Thurs. 9 a.m.-5 p.m., Sat., Sun. 10 a.m.-5 p.m.

Postmuseum, Leipziger-/Mauerstrasse (Mitte), Tel. 2285 47 10. U 2 Mohrenstrasse. Bus 142. Tues. to Sat. 10 a.m.-6 p.m.

Schloss Friedrichsfelde, Am Tierpark (Lichtenberg), Tel. 5 1001 11. U 5 Tierpark. Guided tours Tues. to Sun. 11, 1, and 3 p.m. or by special arrangement. Palace life in the eighteenth and nineteenth centuries.

Schloss Köpenick, Schlossinsel (Köpenick), Tel. 6571504, 6572651. S 85 Spindlersfeld; Tram 83, 84, 86; Bus 168, 169. Wed. to Sun. 10 a.m.-6 p.m. Partly closed for renovation.

Skulpturensammlung (Sculpture Collection), SMBPK

Dahlem (Zehlendorf): Arnimallee 23-27, Tel. 83011. U 2 Dahlem Dorf. Tues. to Fri. 9 a.m.-5 p.m., Sat., Sun. 10 a.m.-5 p.m.

Museumsinsel (Mitte): in Bode Museum, Monbijoubrücke, Tel.

20 35 50. U- and S-Bahn station Friedrichstrasse; S-Bahn station Hackescher Markt. Wed. to Sun. 10 a.m.-6 p.m.

Staatliche Kunsthalle Berlin, Budapester Strasse 42 (Charlottenburg), Tel. 26 17 0 68. U- and S-Bahn station Zoologischer Garten. Tues. to Sun. 10 a.m.-6 p.m., Wed. until 10 p.m. Changing exhibitions of twentieth-century and contemporary art.

Topographie des Terrors, Exhibition hall next to Martin-Gropius-Bau, Stresemannstrasse 110 (Kreuzberg), Tel. 25 48 67 03. S 1, S 2 Anhalter Bahnhof; Bus 129, 341. Tues. to Sun. 10 a.m.-6 p.m. Permanent exhibition on the site of Gestapo, SS, and Reich Security headquarters.

Vorderasiatisches Museum (Near Eastern Art), SMBPK, in Pergamon Museum, Am Kupfergraben (Mitte), Tel. 20 35 50. U- and S-Bahn station Friedrichstrasse; S-Bahn station Hackescher Markt. Open daily 10 a.m.-6 p.m. Mon. and Tues. only the architecture galleries are open.

Werkbund-Archiv, Martin-Gropius-Bau, Stresemannstrasse 110 (Kreuzberg), Tel. 25 48 69 00. S 1, S 2 Anhalter Bahnhof; Bus 129, 341. Tues. to Sun. 10 a.m.-8 p.m., special exhibitions until 10 p.m. Museum of twentieth-century design for everyday living.

Zitadelle Spandau, Am Juliusturm (Spandau), Tel. 33 91 2 97. U 7 Zitadelle; Bus 133. Tues. to Fri. 9 a.m.-5 p.m., Sat., Sun. 10 a.m.-5 p.m.

Galerie GKB, Kurfürstenstrasse, corner of Budapester Strasse

Galleries

Berlin has an active art scene and many galleries to support it—large and established ones as well as small, experimental venues. Art can be found in unexpected places: Tegel Airport has an exhibition space and so do some banks, hotels, and department stores. Art can be enjoyed while having a drink or a meal, too, at the numerous gallery-cafés and gallery-*Kneipes*. Listed below is a selection of better-known galleries as a start to an exploration on your own. There are many others, and in former East Berlin numerous new galleries are joining the scene. The best place to find out what is showing is the comprehensive listings of gallery exhibitions published in the quarterly *Berliner Kunstblatt*, the monthly *Berliner Kunstkalender*, and in the city magazines *tip*, *zitty*, and *Prinz*. A concentration of established galleries is near Kurfürstendamm, on Fasanenstrasse and the streets nearby, such as Uhlandstrasse, Knesebeckstrasse, and Mommsenstrasse. **Auction houses** are represented in Berlin as well: **Leo Spik KG**, the oldest in the city (Kurfürstendamm 66, Charlottenburg, Tel. 88 36 1 70); **Villa Grisebach**, which holds biannual auctions of nineteenth- and twentieth-century art (Fasanenstrasse 25, Charlottenburg, Tel. 88 59 1 50); **Galerie Gerda Bassenge**, which specializes in illuminated manuscripts and prints (Erdener Strasse 5 a, Wilmersdorf, Tel. 89 29 0 13); and the international auctioneers **Sotheby's** (Palais am Festungsgraben, Unter den Linden, Mitte, Tel. 39 43 0 60) and **Christie's** (Fasanenstrasse 72, Charlottenburg, Tel. 88 27 7 78).

Elefanten Press Galerie, Oranienstrasse 25 (Kreuzberg), Tel. 61 50 51 25, Mon. to Sat. 10 a.m.-6:30 p.m., Sun. 1-6 p.m. Photo documentaries, collages, a varied program.

Galerie Brusberg Berlin, Kurfürstendamm 213 (Charlottenburg), Tel. 88 27 6 82. Tues. to Fri. 10 a.m.-6:30 p.m., Sat. 10 a.m.-2 p.m., Mon. by appointment. Modern art with an emphasis on Surrealism and Dada.

Galerie am Chamissoplatz, Chamissoplatz 6 (Kreuzberg), Tel. 6 92 53 81. Tues. to Sun. 1-6.30 p.m. Painting, satire, caricature, photography, and cabaret.

Galerie Anselm Dreher, Pfalzburger Strasse 80 (Wilmersdorf), Tel. 88 35 2 49. Tues. to Fri. 2-6:30 p.m., Sat. 11 a.m.-2 p.m. Minimalist and conceptual art.

Galerie Fahnemann, Fasanenstrasse 61 (Wilmersdorf), Tel. 88 39 8 97. Tues.

Bücherbogen book store on Savignyplatz

to Fri. 11 a.m.-6:30 p.m., Sat. 11 a.m.-
2 p.m. Contemporary art.
Galerie Lietzow, Knesebeckstrasse 32
(Charlottenburg), Tel. 881 2895. Mon.
to Fri. 11 a.m.-6:30 p.m., Sat. 10 a.m.-
2 p.m. Contemporary figurative art.
Galerie Eva Poll, Lützowplatz 7 (Tiergar-
ten), Tel. 261 7091. Mon. 10 a.m.-1 p.m.,
Tues. to Fri. 11 a.m.-1 p.m. and 4-7 p.m.,
Sat. 11 a.m.-3 p.m. Contemporary Euro-
pean figurative art.
Galerie Pels-Leusden, Fasanenstrasse 25
(Charlottenburg), Tel. 88591 50. Mon. to
Fri. 10 a.m.-6:30 p.m., Sat. 10 a.m.-
2 p.m. Nineteenth- and twentieth-century
painting, sculpture, prints, and drawings.
Galerie Nikolaus Sonne, Kantstrasse 138
(Charlottenburg), Tel. 312 2355. Tues. to
Fri. 11 a.m.-1 p.m. and 3-6:30 p.m., Sat.
11 a.m.-2 p.m. Contemporary art.
Galerie Springer, Fasanenstrasse 13 (Char-
lottenburg), Tel. 317063. Mon. to Fri.
10 a.m.-7 p.m., Sat. 11 a.m.-2 p.m. Con-
temporary painting and sculpture.
Raab Galerie, Potsdamer Strasse 58 (Tiergarten), Tel. 261 92 17. Mon. to Fri.
10 a.m.-6:30 p.m., Sat. 10 a.m.-2 p.m.
Contemporary painting and sculpture; first
promoter of the Neo-Expressionist artists.
Wewerka & Weiss Galerie, Pariser Strasse
63 (Wilmersdorf), Tel. 882 6739. Tues. to
Fri. 3-6:30 p.m., Sat. 11 a.m.-2 p.m. Contemporary art.
Zwinger Galerie, Dresdener Strasse 125
(Kreuzberg), Tel. 615 4605. Tues. to Fri.
2-7 p.m., Sat. 11 a.m.-2 p.m. Contemporary art.

Libraries and Archives

Amerika-Gedenkbibliothek (America
Memorial Library), Blücherplatz 1
(Kreuzberg), Tel. 6905o. U1 Hallesches
Tor, U6 Mehringdamm; Bus 141, 241,

341. Mon. 3-7 p.m., Tues. to Sat.
11 a.m.-7 p.m. Berlin's main public
library.
Bauhaus-Archiv (listed under Museums)
Bibliothek der Akademie der Künste
(Library of the Academy of Arts),
Hanseatenweg 10 (Tiergarten),
Tel. 39000760. U9 Hansaplatz; S3 Bel-
levue; Bus 106, 123. Tues., Wed. 9 a.m.-
3 p.m., Thurs. noon-6 p.m., Fri. 9 a.m.-
2 p.m., by appointment. Art, architec-
ture, theater, music, film, and writings.
Bibliothek der Akademie der Wissenschaften
(Library of the Academy of Sciences), Un-
ter den Linden 8 (Mitte), Tel. 20370487.
U- and S-Bahn station Friedrichstrasse;
Bus 100, 157. Mon. to Fri. 9 a.m.-5 p.m.
Scientific research and history of science.
Geheimes Staatsarchiv (Secret State Ar-
chive), Archivstrasse 12-14 (Zehlendorf),
Tel. 83901 00. U2 Podbielskiallee or Dah-
lem Dorf. Mon. to Fri. 8 a.m.-3:45 p.m.,
Tues. 8 a.m.-7:30 p.m. Important collec-
tion of official documents, maps, registers.
Access must be requested in advance,
naming the subject to be researched.
Holds the archives of Mark Brandenburg
and the former Prussian State Archive in
Königsberg.
Kunstbibliothek, SMBPK
Moving to a new building in Kulturforum
in 1993.
**Staatsbibliothek zu Berlin—Preussischer
Kulturbesitz** (State Library)
House 1: Unter den Linden 8 (Mitte),
Tel. 20 37 80. U- and S-Bahn station
Friedrichstrasse; Bus 100, 157. Mon. to
Fri. 9 a.m.-9 p.m., Sat. 9 a.m.-5 p.m.
House 2: Potsdamer Strasse 33 (Tiergar-
ten), Tel. 2661. U1 Kurfürstenstrasse;
Bus 129, 148, 248, 341. Mon. to Fri.
9 a.m.-9 p.m., Sat. 9 a.m.-5 p.m.
Werkbund-Archiv (listed under Museums)

Nightlife

There are hundreds of *Kneipes* with live music, discos, jazz clubs, and other fun places to while away the night—all night, if desired. Comprehensive listings of the goings-on are published in the city magazines *tip, zitty,* and *Prinz,* and it's a good idea to check there as the scene changes frequently, and the "in" places come and go. A few suggestions:

Discos

Big Eden, Kurfürstendamm 202 (Charlottenburg), Tel. 882 61 20. Large discotheque catering to a younger crowd.
Dschungel, Nürnberger Strasse 53 (Schöneberg), Tel. 246698. Closed Tues. Disco with music from the 50s to the 90s. Has been around for a while and a bit expensive, but continues to attract crowds. Doorman is selective.
Joe Hasenheide, Hasenheide 13 (Kreuzberg), Tel. 885 90 10. Tues. to Sat. Disco.
Metropol, Nollendorfplatz 5 (Schöneberg), Tel. 216 41 22. Berlin's largest discotheque. Live music venue during the week.
Quartier, Potsdamer Strasse 96 (Tiergarten), Tel. 262 55 31. Disco with the most stylish dance floor.
Sophienclub, Sophienstrasse 6 (Lichtenberg), Tel. 282 45 52. Weekend disco.

Ballrooms, Bars, Nightclubs

Altdeutsches Ballhaus, Ackerstrasse 144 (Mitte), Tel. 282 68 19. Phone for reservations, Thurs. to Mon. from 6 p.m.
Ballhaus Berlin, Chausseestrasse 102 (Mitte), Tel. 282 75 75. Closed Sun. and Mon. Telephones on each table.
Bar am Lützowplatz, Lützowplatz 7 (Tiergarten), Tel. 262 68 07. Supposedly the longest bar in town. Thirty-five brands of malt whisky.
Café VIS-a-VIS, Friedrichstrasse 127 (Mitte), Tel. 282 31 16.
Chez Nous, Marburger Strasse 14 (Charlottenburg), Tel. 2 13 18 10. Cabaret and transvestite show with elaborate costumes, catering to a more mature audience.
Clärchens Ballhaus, Auguststrasse 24-25 (Mitte), Tel. 282 92 95. Evergreens, live, in Old Berlin atmosphere.
Franz-Club, Schönhauser Allee 36-39 (Prenzlauer Berg), Tel. 448 55 67. Blues is the specialty here. Dancing nightly after 7 p.m. Garden café open from May to September.

Hafenbar, Chausseestrasse 20 (Mitte), Tel. 282 85 93. Closed Sun.
La vie en rose, Europa-Center, Breitscheidplatz (Charlottenburg), Tel. 323 60 06. Revue shows.
Lolott, Schönhauser Allee 56 (Prenzlauer Berg), Tel. 448 44 15.
Nachtbar im Operncafé, Unter den Linden 5 (Mitte), Tel. 200 02 56.
Quasimodo, Kantstrasse 12 a (Charlottenburg), Tel. 312 80 86. Berlin's best jazz club; shows start after 10 p.m.
Spielbank Berlin, Europa-Center, Breitscheidplatz (entrance on Budapester Strasse; Charlottenburg), Tel. 250 08 90. Gambling casino. Shirt and tie required.

Public Holidays

New Year's Day, Good Friday, Easter Sunday and Monday, Labor Day (May 1), Ascension Day, Whitsunday and Whitmonday, German Unity Day (October 3), Day of Prayer and Repentance (third Wednesday in November), Christmas Day and the day after.

Shopping

Berlin has shops to suit everyone, in all price ranges and catering to all tastes. Its most famous department store is KaDeWe, one of some 15,000 stores in the western part of the city alone. In eastern Berlin new shops are opening daily.

The largest shopping center and that offering the greatest variety is the "glamour mile" of **Kurfürstendamm**. Since Berlin was officially made the German capital again, rents here have skyrocketed. This drove out some of the traditional merchants, and many of the spaces have been rented by cafés and fast-food restaurants. Some of the more interesting shops are located on side streets: in **Fasanenstrasse** (exclusive boutiques, art galleries, antique stores), **Uhlandstrasse** (a colorful mix of shops), and the area around **Savignyplatz** (book stores specializing in art and design or politics, record and video stores, and an oriental department store). The largest indoor mall, with over 100 shops, is the **Europa-Center** on Breitscheidplatz.

Each district has its own downtown with a concentration of shops and department stores, Schlossstrasse in **Steglitz**, for instance, or Wilmersdorfer Strasse and Kantstrasse in **Charlottenburg**, Bölschestrasse in **Friedrichshagen**, Berliner Allee in **Weissensee**, and the Old Town of **Spandau**.

Those looking for the unusual may just find it at one of the numerous flea markets and second-hand shops, or at one of the avant-garde designers' shops. A mecca for unusual shops—and not just for the very young—is **Kreuzberg** district (Bergmannstrasse, Oranienstrasse). Others are located in **Schöneberg** (Winterfeldtplatz, Goltzstrasse, Hauptstrasse), **Charlottenburg** (Bleibtreustrasse), and **Prenzlauer Berg** (Schönhauser Allee and the side streets of Breitscheidstrasse).

Store hours are Mon. to Fri. 9 a.m.-6 p.m., Sat. 9 a.m.-1 p.m. Department stores and shops in the center are open until 6:30 p.m. weekdays and 2 p.m. Sat. On Thursdays many stores have extended hours to 8:30 p.m., and on the first Saturday of each month large stores stay open until 4 p.m. (in summer) or 6 p.m. (in winter).

VAT: If you live outside of the EC countries and you make purchases of over DM 60 in any one store, you can request a *Mehrwertsteuer* (Value-Added Tax) refund receipt. If you present the receipts and the goods to the customs office at the airport (you must go before checking your luggage) to have them stamped, you will receive a refund of 8 to 11 percent of the purchase price. Refunds are given at a designated counter at most German airports.

Second-hand store on Fasanenstrasse

Department Stores

Everything from delicatessens to lingerie and electronics can be purchased here. Like large stores everywhere, good, solid selections but no particular bargains to be had. The biggest ones in the center are listed below. Several have branches in other districts.

Hertie, Wilmersdorferstrasse 118 (Charlottenburg), Tel. 8500070, and Blücherplatz 3 (Kreuzberg), Tel. 2510761.

KaDeWe, Wittenbergplatz (Schöneberg), Tel. 21210. The largest store on the continent, with a fabulous food department.

Karstadt, Wilmersdorferstrasse 109 (Charlottenburg), Tel. 31890, and Hermannplatz (Neukölln), Tel. 69081.

Wertheim, Kurfürstendamm 231 (Charlottenburg), Tel. 882061.

After-hours Shopping

German law prohibits stores from staying open after hours or opening on Sundays. The only exceptions are stores in or near the train stations:

Grocery stores

Metro, U-Bahn station Kurfürstendamm (Charlottenburg), open daily 11 a.m.-11 p.m., Sat. until midnight.

Bioladen, Leibnizstrasse 51 (Charlottenburg), Mon. to Fri. 7 a.m.-8 p.m., Sat until 6 p.m.

Edeka, U-Bahn station Schlossstrasse (Steglitz), entrance Zimmermann-/Deitmerstrasse, Mon. to Fri. 3-10 p.m., Sat. 1-10 p.m., Sun. 10 a.m.-8 p.m.

Metro, U-Bahn station Fehrbelliner Platz (Wilmersdorf), open daily 11 a.m.-10:30 p.m.

Books, Newspapers

Kiosk, Bahnhof Zoo, open daily 5:30 a.m.-11:30 p.m.

Heinrich Heine Book Store, S-Bahnhof Zoo, Mon. to Sat. 10 a.m.-8 p.m., Sun. 2-8 p.m.

Internationale Presse, Joachimstaler Strasse 1 (at Bahnhof Zoo), open daily 7 a.m.-midnight (sells gifts, souvenirs, and goods for the traveller as well).

Outdoor and Indoor Markets

Arminius-Markthalle, Arminiusstrasse 2 (Tiergarten), Mon. to Fri. 8 a.m.-6 p.m., Sat. 8 a.m.-1 p.m. Indoor market selling fresh vegetables, flowers, and many other things.

Künstlermarkt am Zeughaus, near Schlossbrücke (Mitte), Thurs. to Sat. 10 a.m.-

4 p.m. Berlin artists—many from former East Berlin—sell their work here. For some it's the only source of income.

Market in front of Berlin Rathaus, near Alexanderplatz (Mitte), Tues. 8 a.m.-5 p.m., Sat. 8 a.m.-2 p.m. Produce and other groceries, many from the Brandenburg region.

Türkenmarkt on Maybachufer (Neukölln), Tues. to Fri. noon-6:30 p.m. Oriental bazaar atmosphere—everyone, from the Anatolian family to the fashionable businesswoman and the punks, likes to shop here.

Winterfeldtmarkt on Winterfeldtplatz (Schöneberg), Wed. and Sat. 8 a.m.-2 p.m. One of the most popular.

Flea Markets

Flohmarkt on Arkonaplatz (Mitte), Sat. and Sun. 9 a.m.-4 p.m. Has something of the comfortable Old Berlin atmosphere.

Trödelmarkt with Berlin Kunstmarkt, Strasse des 17. Juni, near S-Bahn station Tiergarten (Tiergarten), Sat. and Sun. 10 a.m.-5 p.m. Old treasures and potpourri, Berlin's largest flea market.

Trödelmarkt in Ku'damm-Karree, Kurfürstendamm 206-208 (Charlottenburg), daily (except Tues.) 3-10 p.m., Sat., Sun. noon-10 p.m. A bit touristy, and high prices to match.

Clothing

Berlin prides itself on being a fashion center. Most of Berlin's designers have their shops outside the center, on the edge of Charlottenburg and in Schöneberg and Kreuzberg districts. A few pioneers have settled in Prenzlauer Berg and Mitte districts as well.

Many shops of the international designers are clustered around Fasanenstrasse and Kurfürstendamm in Charlottenburg. The newest trends can be admired in Mini-City at the Europa-Center. A hot tip for younger fashions are the shops on Bleibtreustrasse (between Kurfürstendamm and Kantstrasse) and on Ludwigkirchstrasse (between Uhlandstrasse and Olivaer Platz) in Charlottenburg.

Blue Moon, Wilmersdorfer Strasse 80 (Charlottenburg), Tel. 3237088. The complete outfitter for punks, Teds, "Grufties," and Madonna-wanna-bes.

Evento, Grolmanstrasse 53-54 (Charlottenburg), Tel. 3133217. Elegant classics.

Fantazzi, Urbanstrasse 65 (Kreuzberg), Tel. 6919412. Exclusive and beautiful.

G. B. Boutique, Veteranenstrasse 25 (Mitte), Tel. 2822692.

Hennes & Mauritz, Kurfürstendamm 20 (Charlottenburg), Tel. 8825124. Up-to-the-minute designs, often at affordable prices.

Hot Couture, Winterfeldtstrasse 48 (Schöneberg), Tel. 2156634. High fashion with pretty designs at affordable prices.

Kamikaze, Kollwitz-/Sredzkistrasse (Prenzlauer Berg). Rather untypical of the district—exclusive designer fashion.

Kostümhaus, Veteranenstrasse 22 (Mitte), Tel. 2815224. Pretty and wearable fashions by young Berlin designers.

Molotow, Gneisenaustrasse 112 (Kreuzberg), Tel. 6930818. Berlin fashions by Berlin designers.

Larger Sizes

Extraweit, Nürnberger Strasse 1 (Charlottenburg), Tel. 244292. Fashions in sizes 42 to 60.

Men's Fashions

Männersache, Winterfeldtstrasse 45 (Schöneberg), Tel. 2151071. Exclusive haute couture.

Manfred Klinke, Kurfürstendamm 188 (Charlottenburg), Tel. 8834730. A complete outfitter for the businessman, Italian designers.

Marc & Bengels, Grunewaldstrasse 92, (Schöneberg), Tel. 7848464. Elegant underwear.

norberts, Bleibtreustrasse 24 (Charlottenburg), Tel. 8831874, 8811148. High fashion, outfitter of celebrities.

Vincente, Wilmersdorfer Strasse 107a (Charlottenburg), Tel. 3245135. Avant-garde and elegant men's clothes.

Books

Many of Berlin's larger bookstores have English-language sections. The largest concentration of bookstores is found around Knesebeckstrasse in Charlottenburg.

Autorenbuchhandlung, Carmerstrasse 10 (Charlottenburg), Tel. 310151. Some English-language books.

Buchhandlung Assmus, Kaiser-Friedrich-Strasse 1 (Charlottenburg), Tel. 3421137. A general bookstore.

Bücherbogen am Savignyplatz, S-Bahnbogen 593 (Charlottenburg), Tel. 3121932. Huge selection of books on art, architecture, photography, design, theater, and film. Right next door is the **Architektur-Galerie Aedes** and **Café Aedes**, a popular meeting place not just among architects.

Bücherbogen am Tattersall, S-Bahnbogen 585 (Charlottenburg), Tel. 3 13 25 15. Specializes in books on film, theater, dance, and textiles.

Herder Buchhandlung, Kurfürstendamm 69 (Charlottenburg), Tel. 2 12 44 01. Large general bookstore.

Kiepert, Hardenbergstrasse 4-5 (Charlottenburg), Tel. 3 11 00 90. Berlin's largest bookstore. Some English-language books and a very good travel book department.

Kunstbuchhandlung Galerie 2000, Knesebeckstrasse 56-58 (Charlottenburg), Tel. 88 38 467. Art, architecture, film, photography, and design books. Many exhibition catalogues.

Marga Schoeller, Knesebeckstrasse 33-34 (Charlottenburg), Tel. 881 11 12. Some English-language books.

Wasmuth, Hardenbergstrasse 9a (Charlottenburg), Tel. 31 69 20. Art, architecture, design, archaeology, and anthropology books, some second hand.

Sightseeing

Bus Tours

Sightseeing tours of Berlin as well as day trips to Dresden and Potsdam:

BBS Berliner Bären Stadtrundfahrt GmbH, Rankestrasse 35 (Charlottenburg), Tel. 2 13 40 77. Departures from: Breitscheidplatz, Ku'damm, corner of Rankestrasse; Alexanderplatz in front of Hotel Stadt Berlin; and Internationales Handelszentrum at Friedrichstrasse station.

Berolina Stadtrundfahrten, Kurfürstendamm 220 (Charlottenburg), Tel. 882 20 91. Departures from: Ku'damm, corner of Meinekestrasse, and Palasthotel, Karl-Liebknecht-Strasse (Mitte).

BVB Stadtrundfahrten, Kurfürstendamm 225 (Charlottenburg), Tel. 885 98 80. Departures from: Joachimstaler Strasse, corner of Ku'damm, and Unter den Linden, corner Friedrichstrasse.

Severin & Kühn—Berliner Stadtrundfahrten, Kurfürstendamm 216 (Charlottenburg), Tel. 883 10 15. Departures from: Ku'damm, corner of Fasanenstrasse.

Special-Interest Tours and Guided Walks

Not all may offer tours in English, but they will arrange one for groups.

Berliner Geschichtswerkstatt, Goltzstrasse 49 (Schöneberg), Tel. 2 15 44 50.

Kultur Büro Berlin, Kirchstrasse 16 (Tiergarten), Tel. 3 92 37 47. Walks with a focus on architecture.

Kultur-Kontor, Savignyplatz 9-10 (Charlottenburg), Tel. 31 08 88. Bus tours and walks with cultural and historical themes.

Boat Tours

Berlin has 113 miles of navigable waterways. Tour boats leave from Wannsee, Treptower Park, Greenwichpromenade in Tegel, and Kongresshalle in Tiergarten district. For information on scheduled tours call the **Reederverband** (shipping association) at Tel. 8 33 95 53, or one of the tour companies:

Stern- und Kreisschiffahrt GmbH, Sachtlebenstrasse 60 (Zehlendorf), Tel. 8 10 00 40. This company runs the Weisse Flotte boats in former East Berlin, too.

Reederei Heinz Riedel, Planufer 78 (Kreuzberg), Tel. 6 91 37 82 or 6 93 46 46. Interesting tours of the canals, to Pfaueninsel, and to points beyond the city line.

Kultur-Kontor, address above. Theme tours.

Berliner Geschichtswerkstatt, address above. Theme tours.

Parks, Public Gardens

Botanischer Garten, entrances at Unter den Eichen 5-10 (Steglitz) and Königin-Luise-Strasse 6-8 (Zehlendorf), Tel. 83 00 60. S 1 Botanischer Garten. Open daily 9 a.m. to 4 p.m. from Nov. to Feb., until 5 p.m. in March and Oct., until 7 p.m. in April and Sept., and until 8 p.m. from May to Aug.

Britzer Garten, south of Mohriner Allee (Neukölln). Bus 144, 181.

Freizeitpark Tegel (Reinickendorf). U6 Tegel. Tennis, volleyball, bicycle and boat rentals, etc.

Humboldthain (Wedding), S 1, S 2 Humboldthain. Highest elevation in the north of Berlin, rose garden.

Insulaner (Schöneberg). Fine view of south Berlin from an artificial hill, outdoor pool, sledding hill, observatory.

Kulturpark Berlin (Plänterwald), Kiehnwerderallee (Treptow), Tel. 6 32 99 31. Bus 166, 167, 265. Open daily March to October. Amusement park with rides.

Pfaueninsel (Zehlendorf), Tel. 8 05 30 42. S1, S3 Wannsee, then Bus 216, 316 to ferry. Open daily 10 a.m.-4 p.m., longer in summer months. Beautiful park with palace.

Schlosspark Charlottenburg, Tel. 32 09 11. Bus 109, 121, 145, 204. Schinkel Pavillon and Belvedere open Tues. to Fri. 9 a.m.-5 p.m., Sat., Sun. 10 a.m.-5 p.m. Mausoleum closed in winter.

Boat excursion on the Spree River. The Palasthotel is in the background

Tiergarten, S-Bahn station Tiergarten. Large park in the center of the city, boat rentals on Neuer See.

Treptower Park, S-Bahn station Treptower Park. Excursion boat dock, rose garden, Soviet War Memorial.

Volkspark Friedrichshain, U 5 Friedrichshain. Fairy-tale fountain.

Volkspark Hasenheide (Neukölln). U 7, U 8 Hermannsplatz.

Volkspark Jungfernheide (Charlottenburg), U 7 Halemweg. Outdoor pool, boat rentals, playing fields.

Volkspark Rehberge (Wedding), U 6 Rehberge. Outdoor pool, boat rentals.

Wuhlheide (Köpenick), Tel. 63 88 70. S 3 Wuhlheide. Mon. to Fri. 9 a.m.-9 p.m., Sat. 1-5 p.m., Sun. and during school vacations 10 a.m.-5 p.m. Nature preserve with recreation center. Indoor pool open daily except Mon. Tel. 635 18 33.

Zoos

Tierpark Berlin, Am Tierpark 125 (Lichtenberg), Tel. 5 100 1 11. U 5 Tierpark. Open daily 9 a.m. to dusk.

Zoologischer Garten and Aquarium, Hardenbergplatz 8 (Tiergarten), Tel. 25 40 10. U- and S-Bahn station Zoologischer Garten. Open daily 9 a.m. to dusk, 6:30 p.m. at latest, in winter until 5 p.m.

Observatories

Archenhold-Sternwarte in Treptower Park, Tel. 272 88 71. S-Bahn station Treptower Park. Wed. to Sun. 2-4:30 p.m. Telescope viewings Wed. at 6 p.m., Sat., Sun. at 4 p.m.

Zeiss-Grossplanetarium, Prenzlauer Allee 80 (Prenzlauer Berg), Tel. 42 28 40. S 8, S 10 Prenzlauer Allee. Wed. to Sun. 1-8 p.m.

Zeiss-Planetarium and **Wilhelm-Foerster-Sternwarte** (Schöneberg), Tel. 79 00 930. S 2 Priesterweg; Bus 170, 174, 176, 187. Planetarium demonstrations Tues., Thurs. to Sun. 8 p.m., Mon., Tues., Thurs. also during the day. Observatory demonstrations Tues. and Thurs. to Sun. 9 p.m. Additional demonstrations on Sat. and Sun.

Excursions

If you have time, there are many wonderful places near Berlin that are worth a visit. A day trip to **Potsdam** (about 15 miles to the southwest, last stop on the S 3) with its Sanssouci and Cecilienhof palaces and their splendid parks is a must. The sightseeing companies listed above all offer tours of Potsdam.

For material on the city and its sights, contact Potsdam-Information, Friedrich-Ebert-Strasse 5, O-1561 Potsdam, Tel. (03 31) 2 11 00. To join a tour of Sanssouci Palace and gardens, it is advisable to reserve in advance: Besucherbetreuung, Am Grünen Gitter 2, O-1560 Potsdam, Tel. (03 31) 23 8 19.

Architecture buffs will want to see the famous Einstein Tower by Erich Mendelsohn, located on Telegrafenberg off Luckenwalder Strasse.

Southeast of Berlin is a lovely area called **Spreewald,** a rural district criss-crossed by countless brooks, streams, and canals, all branches of the Spree River. The best way to see the Spreewald is to take a one-hour train ride to Lübbenau and board one of the boats there that leave every few minutes for cruises on the waterways, some for trips of up to ten hours.

By boat is the best way to see the beautiful **Havel lakes**, too. Contact the tour boat organizations listed above for schedules. They also offer trips on the **Dahme River** to the Teupitzer lakes and on the Scharmützelsee southeast of the city. A lovely excursion can be made by boat to the northeast, to **Werbelinsee**, stopping at the charming town of **Bernau** with its intact town wall, the Cistercian monastery in **Chorin**, and at **Niederfinow** with its technical marvel, a 1930s lock that lifts boats almost 120 feet between the Havel and Oder rivers.

Sports and Recreation

Sports fans won't be bored in Berlin, neither those preferring spectator events, nor those who like to work up a sweat themselves. One of the largest marathons in the world is held here every October, there is a race track, and Berlin has national-league teams in many sports. The German national soccer championship final is held in the Olympia Stadion every May. The city magazines *tip*, *zitty*, *Prince*, and the official *Berlin-Programm* have complete listings of these events.

Information about public sports facilities can be requested from: Landessportbund, Jesse-Owens-Allee 2, W-1000 Berlin 19, Tel. 300020 (Mon. to Thurs. 9 a.m.-3 p.m., Fri. 9 a.m.-2 p.m.). They publish a free annual calendar.

Bicycling

Berlin's lakes and forests are perfect bicycling territory. You needn't even bike all the way there—bicycles can be taken on the U- and S-Bahns. Within the city there are plenty of marked bicycle paths as well.

Bicycle Rentals

Fahrradausleihe Siwy, Riebekeweg 18 (Köpenick), between Müggelheimer Damm and Wendenschlossstrasse, a great starting point for tours around the Müggelsee. Sat. 8 a.m.-7 p.m. No telephone yet.
Fahrradbüro Berlin, Hauptstrasse (Schöneberg), at U-Bahn station Kleistpark, Tel. 7845562. Minimum rental 24 hours.

Fahrrad-Krause, Mariendorfer Damm 34 (Tempelhof), at U-Bahn station Ullsteinstrasse, Tel. 7063312.
Freizeitpark Tegel, Campestrasse 11 (Tegel), at U-Bahn station Tegel, Tel. 4346666.
Kultur Kontakt Dannehl, Prenzlauer Allee 10 (Prenzlauer Berg), Tel. 4390373.
Räderwerk, Körtestrasse 14 (Kreuzberg), at U-Bahn station Südstern, Tel. 6918590.

Golf

Golfplatz am Stölpchenweg (Zehlendorf), Tel. 8055075. Reservations Tues. to Sun. 9 a.m.-6 p.m. Open to visiting players on weekdays only.

Horseback Riding

Preussenhof, Staaker Strasse 64 (Spandau), Tel. 3317945.
Reiterhof Lübars, Alt-Lübars 5 (Lübars, Reinickendorf district), Tel. 4025684.
Reitsportschule Onkel Toms Hütte, Onkel-Tom-Strasse 172 (Zehlendorf), Tel. 8132081.
Reit- und Springschule am Poloplatz (Frohnau, Reinickendorf district), Tel. 4015835.

Recreation Centers

Erlebnispark Lübars, entrance on Quickborner Strasse (Reinickendorf). Open daily noon-7 p.m.
Freizeitpark Tegel, Campestrasse 11 (Reinickendorf), Tel. 4346666. Tennis, minigolf, etc.
Sport- und Erholungszentrum, Landsberger Allee 77 (Friedrichshain), Tel. 3428330. Indoor and outdoor swimming and diving pools, wave machine, water slide, sauna, bowling, ice and roller skating, fitness center.

Sailing and Rowing

Boots-Charter Lüders, Strandbad Wannsee, (Zehlendorf), Tel. 8034590. Sail, row, and pedal boats, kayaks, sail boards.
Marina Lanke-Werft, Scharfe Lanke 109-131 (Spandau), Tel. 3615066. Largest sailboat marina.
Segel-Schule Berlin, Friederikestrasse 24 (Tegel, Reinickendorf district), Tel. 4311171. Sailing school and boat rental.
Stiebeler, Schildhorn 1, at Havelchaussee (Wilmersdorf), Tel. 3040304. Motor, sail, and row boats.

Skating

Eisstadion Wilmersdorf, Fritz-Wildung-Strasse 9 (Wilmersdorf), Tel. 8 24 10 12. On ice in winter, on rollers in summer.
Roller Skating Center, Hasenheide 108 (Kreuzberg), Tel. 6 21 10 29.

Swimming Pools, Lake Beaches, and

Saunas

Beware, the outdoor sites tend to be very crowded on sunny days. Bathing and saunas are usually mixed and often European in style—sans suit.

blub Badeparadies, Buschkrugallee 64 (Neukölln), Tel. 6 06 60 60. Indoors and outdoors. Wave pool, water slide, wildwater canal, waterfalls, whirlpools, grottoes, saunas, fitness center.
Schöneberger Thermen, Kaiser-Wilhelm-Platz 1-2 (Schöneberg), Tel. 7 84 36 58. Indoor bio-sauna, Finnish sauna, steam sauna, and pool, above the roofs of the city.
Seebad Friedrichshagen, Müggelseedamm 216 (Köpenick), Tel. 6 45 57 56. Lake beach.
Solf-Sauna, Bundesallee 187 (Wilmersdorf), Tel. 8 54 50 14. Indoor pool, whirlpool, saunas, massages, fitness center, bar, restaurant.
Stadtbad Charlottenburg, Krumme Strasse 10 (Charlottenburg), Tel. 34 30 32 14. Oldest indoor pool in the city, opened in 1898. Beautiful tiles.
Stadtbad Neukölln, Ganghoferstrasse 3-5 (Neukölln), Tel. 68 09 26 53. The most beautiful indoor pool in Berlin. Upon its opening in 1914 it was declared the most beautiful in all Europe.
Strandbad Wannsee, Wannseebadweg (Zehlendorf), Tel. 80 35 450. Lake beach.

Tennis

Tennis-Center Tegel, Flohrstrasse 11-21 (Reinickendorf), Tel. 4 32 64 17.
Tennishalle in der City, Franklinstrasse 9/10 (Charlottenburg), Tel. 39 19 074.
Tennis + Squash City, Brandenburgische Strasse 53 (Charlottenburg), Tel. 8 79 09 97.

Theater and Concerts

Cultural events have always been something special in Berlin—and at the same time a totally normal part of life in the city. Culture is in the air here. The offerings range from "close-to-the-people" events in each neighborhood to subsidized high art of international renown, worthy of a capital. Nearly 1 billion marks (about $600 million) were spent by the government on cultural institutions in Berlin in 1992 (2.35% of the city budget). About half that amount was spent on the theaters. Berlin's official theaters, with over fifty stages, make for a lively scene, but there are many more: some 500 independent ensembles perform everything from the classical to the avant-garde. The city boasts over 100 cinemas, a flourishing literary scene, museums, exhibitions, and concert halls for every musical taste.

The what, where, and when is listed in the daily papers, in the bi-weekly city magazines *tip*, *zitty*, and *Prinz*, and in the official *Berlin-Programm* of the Verkehrsamt.

Tickets

Reservations can be made at the theater itself, or tickets can be purchased for a small fee at one of the central ticket agencies (a selection):

City-Center, Kurfürstendamm 16 (Charlottenburg), Tel. 8 82 65 63.
Kulturelle Betreuung Otfried Laur, Hardenbergstrasse 6 (Charlottenburg), Tel. 3 13 70 07.
Theaterkasse in KaDeWe department store, Tauentzienstrasse 21 (Schöneberg), Tel. 2 18 10 28.
Theaterkasse Wertheim, Kurfürstendamm 231 (Charlottenburg), Tel. 8 82 52 54.
Berliner Theaterkassen und Konzertkassen GmbH—At Palasthotel, Spandauer Strasse (Mitte), Tel. 2 42 71 82.
Theaterkasse in Hertie department store, Am Hauptbahnhof, 3rd floor (Friedrichshain), Tel. 4 35 35 54.
Theaterkasse in Kaufhof department store, Am Alexanderplatz, 2nd floor (Mitte), Tel. 2 46 47 69.
Ticket Hotline, Postfach 3 48, W-1000 Berlin 37, Tel. 8 02 24 24, Fax 8 02 90 91. Theater and concert tickets by phone.
Last-minute service: Half-price tickets for same-day performances are sold daily from 4 to 8 p.m. at the "lila Kiosk" on Alexanderplatz (Mitte), Tel. 6 11 81 16. Theater, cabaret, and musicals only.

Opera, Operetta, Ballet, Musicals

Addresses include the nearest U- and S-Bahn stop and the bus lines that pass nearby.

Deutsche Oper Berlin, Bismarckstrasse 35 (Charlottenburg), Tel. 3410249. U1 Deutsche Oper; U7 Bismarckstrasse; Bus 101 Bismarckstrasse.

Deutsche Staatsoper, Unter den Linden 7 (Mitte), Tel. 2004762. U- and S-Bahn station Friedrichstrasse; Bus 100, 157.

Komische Oper Berlin, Behrenstrasse 55-57 (Mitte), Tel. 2292555. U6 Französische Strasse; S1, S2 Unter den Linden; Bus 100.

Metropol-Theater, Friedrichstrasse 101/102 (Mitte), Tel. 2082715. U- and S-Bahn station Friedrichstrasse; Bus 147, 157.

Neuköllner Oper, Karl-Marx-Strasse 131-133 (Neukölln), Tel. 6876061. U7 Karl-Marx-Strasse; Bus 104.

Tanzfabrik, Möckernstrasse 68 (Kreuzberg), Tel. 7865861. U6, U7 Mehringdamm; S1, S2 Yorckstrasse; Bus 119, 247.

Theater des Westens, Kantstrasse 12 (Charlottenburg), Tel. 3190319 3. U- and S-Bahn station Zoologischer Garten.

Renaissance-Theater

Theaters

A selection of the largest stages. The official *Berlin-Programm* has listings for many others. Naturally, performances are in German.

Addresses include the nearest U- and S-Bahn stop and the bus lines that pass nearby.

Berliner Ensemble, Am Bertolt-Brecht-Platz (Mitte), Tel. 2888155. U- and S-Bahn station Friedrichstrasse; Bus 147, 247.

Berliner Kammerspiele, Alt-Moabit 99 (Tiergarten), Tel. 3915543. U9 Turmstrasse; Bus 106, 245. Youth theater and musicals.

Deutsches Theater/Kammerspiele, Schumannstrasse 13a (Mitte), Tel. 2871225, U- and S-Bahn station Friedrichstrasse; Bus 147.

Freie Volksbühne, Schaperstrasse 24 (Wilmersdorf), Tel. 8842080. U2, U9 Spichernstrasse; Bus 219.

Grips Theater, Altonaer Strasse 22 (Tiergarten), Tel. 3914004. U9 Hansaplatz; Bus 106, 123. Award-winning children's and youth theater.

Hansa-Theater, Alt-Moabit 48 (Tiergarten), Tel. 3914460. U9 Turmstrasse; Bus 101, 123, 245.

Hebbel-Theater, Stresemannstrasse 29 (Kreuzberg), Tel. 2510144. U1, U6 Hallesches Tor; S1, S2 Anhalter Bahnhof.

Komödie, Kurfürstendamm 206 (Charlottenburg), Tel. 8827893. U3 Uhlandstrasse; Bus 119, 129, 249.

Maxim Gorki Theater, Am Festungsgraben 1 (Mitte), Tel. 2082783 or 48. U- and S-Bahn station Friedrichstrasse; Bus 100, 157; Tram 22, 46, 70, 71.

Renaissance-Theater, Hardenbergstrasse 6 (Charlottenburg), Tel. 3124202. U1 Ernst-Reuter-Platz; Bus 145, 245.

Schaubühne am Lehniner Platz, Kurfürstendamm 153 (Wilmersdorf), Tel. 890023. U- and S-Bahn station Adenauerplatz; Bus 119, 129, 219.

Schiller-Theater/Werkstatt, Bismarckstrasse 110 (Charlottenburg), Tel. 3126505. U1 Ernst-Reuter-Platz; Bus 101, 145, 245.

Schlosspark Theater, Schlossstrasse 48 (Steglitz), Tel. 7931515. U- and S-Bahn station Rathaus Steglitz; Bus 117, 130, 148.

Theater am Kurfürstendamm, Kurfürstendamm 206 (Charlottenburg), Tel. 8823789. U3 Uhlandstrasse; Bus 119, 129.

Tribüne, Otto-Suhr-Allee 18 (Charlottenburg), Tel. 3412600. U1 Ernst-Reuter-Platz; Bus 101, 145, 245.

Volksbühne, Rosa-Luxemburg-Platz (Mitte), Tel. 2823394. U2 Rosa-Luxemburg-Platz; Bus 140, 240; Tram 20, 24, 28, 63, 71.

Revue

Friedrichstadtpalast, Friedrichstrasse 107 (Mitte), Tel. 2836474.

Cabaret, Variety Shows

BKA (Berliner-Kabarett-Anstalt), Mehringdamm 32-34 (Kreuzberg), Tel. 2 51 01 12. U6, U7 Mehringdamm. In summer, performances held in a tent at the Philharmonie.
Die Distel, Friedrichstrasse 101 (Mitte), Tel. 2 00 47 04. U- and S-Bahn station Friedrichstrasse; Bus 147, 157.
Kartoon, Französische Strasse 24 (Mitte), Tel. 2 29 93 05. U6 Französische Strasse.
Stachelschweine, Europa-Center, Breitscheidplatz (Charlottenburg), Tel. 2 61 47 95. U- and S-Bahn station Zoologischer Garten; U3 Kurfürstendamm; Bus 119, 129, 145, 146, 149, 219, 249.
Varieté Chamäleon, Rosenthaler Strasse 40-41 (Mitte), Tel. 2 82 71 18. U8 Weinmeisterstrasse; Tram 15, 20, 24. A hot tip for variety shows.
Wühlmäuse, Nürnberger Strasse 33 (Wilmersdorf), Tel. 2 13 70 47. U2 Augsburger Strasse.

Music

Berlin has several orchestras: the Berlin Philharmonic, the Radio-Symphonie-Orchester, Staatskapelle Berlin, Symphonisches Orchester Berlin, and Berliner Sinfonie-Orchester im Schauspielhaus Berlin (the most beautiful concert hall in the city), to name only the most prominent. Concerts are performed in the Philharmonie and the Schauspielhaus, as well as in Jagdschloss Grunewald (especially in summer), in Schloss Charlottenburg and in Schloss Friedrichsfelde (chamber music is played in the Tierpark year-round), in the Deutsche Staatsoper Berlin, the Deutsche Oper Berlin, and in many of the city's churches.

A special attraction are the two large **carillons,** one in Tiergarten (for information call 25 90 04 46) and the other in the tower of the Französischer Dom (information 2 29 20 42). Carillon concerts are held regularly—a special musical treat.

Concert Halls

Philharmonie/Kammermusiksaal, Matthäikirchstrasse 1 (Tiergarten), Tel. 2 54 88-0. Bus 129, 148, 248, 341.
Schauspielhaus, Gendarmenmarkt (Mitte), Tel. 2 09 00. U2 Hausvogteiplatz; U2, U6 Stadtmitte.

Large Multi-Purpose Halls

Deutschlandhalle, Messedamm 26 (Charlottenburg), Tel. 30 38-1. U1 Kaiserdamm, Theodor-Heuss-Platz.

Werner-Seelenbinder-Halle, Fritz-Riedel-Strasse (Prenzlauer Berg), Tel. 4 20 20. S8, S10 Landsberger Allee.
Waldbühne, Am Glockenturm (Charlottenburg), near Olympia Stadion, Tel. 3 04 06 76. U1 Olympia Stadion; Bus 94. Large, outdoor amphitheater.

Cinemas

Berliners love the movies. They have the programs of over 100 cinemas to choose from, featuring the latest from Hollywood, revivals of old favorites, as well as films by independent filmmakers. Wednesday is "cinema day" at most Berlin movie theaters, with ticket prices reduced to around 8 marks.

Regular showings cost 10 to 15 marks. Many theaters hold weekend film nights with all-night showings. Movie listings are found in the daily papers and in the city magazines like *tip, zitty,* and *Prinz,* and they are posted on the *Litfassäulen,* the advertising pillars around town. Several theaters show films in their original language. On movie schedules those films are listed as OF (*Original Fassung*) or OMU (*Original mit Untertitel*), if they have German subtitles.

February is the month of the international film festival, the **Berlinale,** the second most important such event on the Continent after Cannes.

Trade Fairs and Exhibitions

For information contact Ausstellungs-Messe-Kongress GmbH (AMK) Berlin, Messedamm 22, W-1000 Berlin 19, Tel. 3 03 80.

January/February
International Green Week

March
International Tourism Exchange
ModaBerlin
Gründertage Berlin

April/May
Freie Berliner Kunstausstellung (arts)

May/June
Medical Congress and Pharmaceutical Exhibition

June
Import Fair

August/September
International Consumer Electronics Fair (every other year, next in 1993)

September
ModaBerlin

October
Automobile Show (AAA; every other year, next in 1992)

November
belektro (electronics)

November/December
Antiqua, sales exhibition of art and antiques

Transportation

Berlin has an efficient public transportation network of trains (the U- and S-Bahns), buses (including double-deckers), and trams, all run by the Berliner Verkehrsbetriebe (BVG). Visitors can reach practically any sight in the city by public transport and see lots along the way. A map of the U- and S-Bahn lines as well as a list of the information booths can be found on the inside back cover. Trains and buses run every 5 to 10 minutes during the day, and there are night buses every 30 minutes from about 1 to 4 a.m.

Fares: A normal ticket is valid for two hours of travel on any of the trains, trams, or buses, on some ferries in Berlin, and on public transportation in Potsdam, too. Within that time unlimited transfers and even round trips are permitted.

Tickets can be purchased from vending machines at all stops, from ticket counters in some stations, and from the drivers of buses. Available are single tickets (*Einzelfahrscheine*) at normal, short-distance (*Kurzstrecken*, 3 stops by train or 6 stops by bus), or child fares (ages 6 to 14); and multiple tickets (*Sammelkarte*) with 5 fares. The multiple tickets must be stamped before each use in the red boxes in buses or at the station booths. There are several special tickets: the *Ku'damm-Ticket*, a cheap fare without transfers for trips up and down that avenue; the *Berlin-Ticket* for 24 hours of unlimited travel; a 6-day or one-month *Umweltkarte*; and special family tickets.

Berlin is currently integrating the transportation lines of the East and West parts of the city. As routes and station names may change, it is best to pick up the current map and information brochures on your arrival from the Verkehrsamt (tourist office) or the BVG information booths listed on page 192.

Taxis

Taxis can be hired at taxi stands (found all over the city) or by telephone:
City-Funk 240202
Funktaxi 3644 or 3366
Taxi-Funk 6902
Taxi-Ruf 261026
Würfelfunk 210101
All taxis are equipped with meters. There is a small surcharge for luggage. It is customary to give a small tip.

Car Rentals

The larger rental companies all have counters at Tegel Airport, a few at Schönefeld Airport, too. City bureaus of rental companies:
AVIS, Budapester Strasse 43 (Tiergarten), Tel. 2611881.
InterRent Europcar, Kurfürstendamm 178-179 (Charlottenburg), Tel. 8818093; and Karl-Liebknecht-Strasse 19-21 (Mitte), Tel. 243632-09 or 10.
Sixt Budget, Budapester Strasse 18 (Tiergarten), Tel. 2611357.

Car with Chauffeur

Allround Autovermietung, Tel. 2611456
Oldtimer-Taxi Berlin, Tel. 8338867
Reisedienst Brocke, Tel. 4362727

Airports

Tegel, Tel. 41011
Tempelhof, Tel. 69091
Schönefeld, Tel. 67870

Long-Distance Train Information

In person: Reisezentrum der Bundesbahn at Bahnhof Zoo, Hardenbergstrasse 20 (Charlottenburg).
By phone: Tel. 27800 or 19419.

Visas

Citizens of the United States, Canada, Australia, and New Zealand need only a valid passport for stays in Germany of up to three months. Citizens of the United Kingdom or any other EC country need only an identity card. All others should check with a German consulate.

Vocabulary

It is not difficult to learn a bit of German, and, although English is understood by many people, knowing a few words and phrases is helpful. The effort will be appreciated.

German pronunciation is much less tricky than it looks. Every word is pronounced as written, and vowels are pronounced according to the following general rules: a as in f**a**ther, e as in g**e**t or f**ai**r, ei as in **i**, i as in b**e**, o as in c**o**tton, u as in r**oo**t. Umlauts, the vowels with two dots over them are pronounced as if an e had been added to the letter: ä as in p**a**nts, ö as in t**ur**n, ü as in the French r**ue**.

A few essential phrases

Yes, No	*Ja, Nein*
Please, You're welcome	*Bitte*
Thank you	*Danke*
Good morning	*Guten Morgen*
Good evening	*Guten Abend*
Good day, hello	*Guten Tag*
Goodbye	*Auf Wiedersehen*
Excuse me	*Entschuldigen Sie*
Sorry	*Verzeihung*
Mr., Mrs.	*Herr, Frau*
Do you speak English?	*Sprechen Sie Englisch?*
I (don't) understand	*Ich verstehe (nicht)*
Where is ...?	*Wo ist ...?*
the station	*der Bahnhof*
a hotel	*ein Hotel*
a restaurant	*ein Restaurant*
the rest room	*die Toilette*
a doctor	*ein Arzt*
right, left	*rechts, links*
straight ahead	*geradeaus*
What time is it?	*Wie spät ist es?*
Can you help me?	*Können Sie mir helfen?*
How much does it cost?	*Wieviel kostet es?*
too expensive	*zu teuer*
I would like ...	*Ich möchte ...*
a room	*ein Zimmer*
to eat	*essen*
Breakfast	*Frühstück*
Lunch	*Mittagessen*
Dinner	*Abendessen*
Do you have ...?	*Haben Sie ...?*
The check, please	*Die Rechnung, bitte*
Help!	*Hilfe!*
Hospital	*Krankenhaus*
open	*geöffnet*

closed	*geschlossen*
today, tomorrow	*heute, morgen*
yesterday	*gestern*
Monday	*Montag*
Tuesday	*Dienstag*
Wednesday	*Mittwoch*
Thursday	*Donnerstag*
Friday	*Freitag*
Saturday	*Samstag*
Sunday	*Sonntag*
Street	*Strasse*
Square	*Platz*
Church, Cathedral	*Kirche, Dom*
Palace, Castle	*Schloss, Burg*
Cinema	*Kino*
Station	*Bahnhof*
Airport	*Flughafen*

Numbers

0	*null*
1	*eins*
2	*zwei*
3	*drei*
4	*vier*
5	*fünf*
6	*sechs*
7	*sieben*
8	*acht*
9	*neun*
10	*zehn*
11	*elf*
20	*zwanzig*
30	*dreissig*
40	*vierzig*
50	*fünfzig*
60	*sechzig*
70	*siebzig*
80	*achtzig*
90	*neunzig*
100	*hundert*
200	*zweihundert*
300	*dreihundert*
400	*vierhundert*
500	*fünfhundert*
1000	*tausend*

Index

Index

Photograph Credits

AEG 64 – Jörg P. Anders 93 bottom, 134 bottom – Klaus Anger 86 top – Art Hotel Sorat (photo: O. T. W.) 160 bottom – Hans-Joachim Bartsch 97 top – Berlin Museum 120 bottom – Berliner Wasser-Betriebe (photo: Mechthild Wilhelmi, Berlin) 156 bottom – Constantin Beyer, Weimar 113 top, 114 top, 115, 148, 151 – Klaus Beyer, Weimar 32, 50 top – Jan Cordes, Berlin 12 bottom – Deutsches Rundfunk-Museum, Berlin 101 bottom – Deutsches Theater Berlin 58/59 – Joachim Fait, Berlin 152 – Freies Deutsches Hochstift, Frankfurter Goethe Museum 21 top – Ralf Freyer, Freiburg/Breisgau front cover – Georg-Kolbe-Museum, Berlin 102 bottom – Ingrid Geske 97 bottom – Pressedienst Paul Glaser, Berlin 40 – Hans Christian Glave, Berlin 14 bottom, 15 top, 16 left, 17 bottom, 27, 28/29, 35 (2), 36 top, 45 bottom, 48 bottom, 50 bottom, 52, 54, 63, 64 top, 67, 75, 76 bottom, 81 bottom, 82/83, 86 bottom, 91, 98, 102 top, 103, 106, 109 (2), 110, 111 top, 112, 113 bottom, 116, 118, 121 bottom, 122 bottom, 123 top right, 126 top, 127, 128, 130 bottom, 138, 144, 160 top, 166 – Jürgen Henkelmann, Berlin 12 top, 13, 14 top, 16 right, 17 center, 33 (2), 37, 39, 49 top, 57 top, 60, 61, 70, 74 top, 87 top, 104 bottom, 117, 123 bottom, 130 top, 153 bottom, 164, 165, 173, 174, 176 – Landesbildstelle Berlin 22/23 top, 25 top – Klaus Lehnartz, Berlin 65, 69, 77, 79, 88, 120 top, 122 top, 125, 133, 153 top – Fritz Mader, Hamburg-Barsbüttel front inside cover, 25 bottom, 30, 31, 42/43 top, 46/47, 51, 53, 55, 68, 72 top, 78, 89, 90, 100/101 top, 107, 119 top, 141, 142, 143, 145, 146, 147, 157, 168, 179, back cover – Metropol Theater, Berlin (photo: Gueffroy) 57 bottom – Museum für Verkehr und Technik, Berlin 119 bottom – Werner Neumeister, München 34, 45 top, 48 top, 62, 155 top – Papadopoulos 136 – Uwe Rau, Berlin 24 bottom, 44 top and bottom, 123 top left, 124, 158, 182 – Gordon H. Roberton, London 137 – Johann Scheibner, Berlin 5, 15 bottom, 17 top, 36 bottom, 41 bottom, 49 bottom, 51 bottom, 84, 95, 104 top, 108, 126 bottom, 131, 150 – Schiller-Theater, Berlin (photo: Christian Brachwitz, Hamburg) 87 bottom – Atelier Schneider, Berlin 66 – Günter Schneider, Berlin 105, 111 bottom, 121 top and center – Achim Sperber, Hamburg 85, 132, 191 – Staatliche Museen zu Berlin – Preußischer Kulturbesitz: *Ägyptisches Museum* 43 bottom right, 96 – *Gemäldegalerie* 44 center, 134 top – *Kunstbibliothek* 21 bottom – *Kunstgewerbemuseum* 72 bottom, 154, 155 bottom – *Münzkabinett* 41 top – *Museum für Islamische Kunst* 43 bottom left, 135 top – *Museum für Völkerkunde* 135 bottom – *Nationalgalerie* 42 bottom, 73, 74 bottom, 92 – Städtische Galerie im Lenbachhaus, München 22 bottom (2) – Ullstein, Hampel, Berlin 94 – Verwaltung der Staatlichen Schlösser und Gärten, Berlin 93 top, 139 – Zeiss-Großplanetarium Berlin 114 bottom

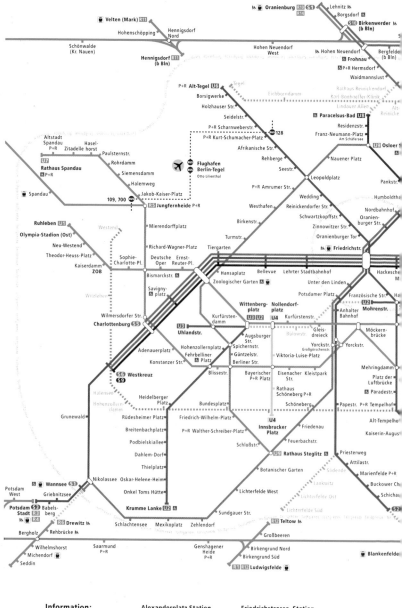

Information:

Customer Information
Potsdamer Str. 188
1000 Berlin 30
☎ 216 50 88

Pavillon Zoo
Hardenbergplatz
☎ 256 24 62

Information Spandau
Münsingerstr. 4
☎ 333 98 33

Alexanderplatz Station
☎ BVG 24 36 22 77
☎ S-Bahn 29 72 24 89

Hauptbahnhof Station
☎ BVG 279 13 13
☎ S-Bahn 29 72 72 21 21

Lichtenberg Station
☎ BVG 525 37 00
☎ S-Bahn 29 74 25 05

**Flughafen Station
Berlin-Schönefeld**
☎ BVG 67 87 33 82
☎ S-Bahn 29 74 75 80

Friedrichstrasse Station
☎ S-Bahn 29 72 18 95

Schöneweide Station
☎ S-Bahn 29 77 24 44

BVG Lost and Found
Potsdamer Str. 184
☎ 216 14 13

S-Bahn (DR) Lost and Found:
Station Hackescher Markt
☎ 29 72 16 71

**Potsdam Transport
Information:**
Potsdam, Bassinplatz
☎ 037 33-229 66